ENRICO ACERBI

THE FIRST ARMY OF MARIA THERESA

THE AUSTRIAN ARMY FROM 1740 TO 1748

SOLDIERS&WEAPONS 047

SOLDIERSHOP PUBLISHING

THE AUTHOR

Enrico Acerbi was born in Valdagno (Vicenza) 8/13/1952; medical graduate, expert in toxicology, worked in local hospital, now retired. Partner of the Rovereto War Museum, member of the Napoleonic Association of Italy and historiographer of the Great War. Enrico Acerbi has developed a passion for historical research since the 1990s. For five years he collaborated with the Center for Great War Studies in Asiago. He has also collaborated with the Arsiero Mountain Community as a teacher at the People's University (historical training courses on World War I) and with the Agno-Chiampo Mountain Community (reconstruction of fortifications made during the Great War). Partner of the Rovereto War Museum and founding member of the Great War Historical Research Group of Valdagno, currently engaged in the study of Napoleonic history in Veneto and Italy. Graphic illustrator of articles on Napoleonic history. He has to his credit several historical publications for various publishing houses and several titles also for Soldiershop!

NOTE EDITORIALI

Tutto il contenuto dei nostri libri, in qualsiasi forma prodotti (cartacei, elettronici o altro) quando non diversamente specificato è copyright soldiershop.com. I diritti di traduzione, riproduzione, memorizzazione con qualsiasi mezzo, digitale, fotografico, fotocopie ecc. Sono riservati per tutti i Paesi. Nessuna delle immagini presenti nei nostri libri può essere riprodotta senza il permesso scritto di soldiershop.com. L'Editore rimane a disposizione degli eventuali aventi diritto per tutte le fonti iconografiche dubbie o non identificate. I marchi Soldiershop Publishing, Bookmoon, Museum s e relative collane sono di proprietà di soldiershop.com o Luca Cristini Editore; di conseguenza qualsiasi uso esterno non è consentito.

PUBLISHING'S NOTES

None of unpublished images or text of our book may be reproduced in any format without the expressed written permission of Soldiershop.com when not indicate as marked with license creative commons 3.0 or 4.0. Soldiershop Publishing has made every reasonable effort to locate, contact and acknowledge rights holders and to correctly apply terms and conditions to Content. In the event that any Content infringes your rights or the rights of any third parties, or Content is not properly identified or acknowledged we would like to hear from you so we may make any necessary alterations. In this event contact: info@soldiershop.com. Our trademark: Soldiershop Publishing ©, The names of our series & brand: Museum book, Bookmoon, Soldiers&Weapons, Battlefield, War in colour, Historical Biographies, Darwin's view, Fabula, Altrastoria, Italia Storica Ebook, Witness To History, Soldiers, Weapons & Uniforms, Storia etc. are herein © by Soldiershop.com.

LICENSES COMMONS

This book may utilize part of material marked with license creative commons 3.0 or 4.0 (CC BY 4.0), (CC BY-ND 4.0), (CC BY-SA 4.0) or (CC0 1.0). Or derived from publication 70 years old or more and recolored from us. We give appropriate attribution credit and indicate if change were made in the acknowledgements field.
All our books utilize only fonts licensed under the SIL Open Font License or other free use license.

ISBN: 9791255890027   First edition July 2023
THE FIRST ARMY OF MARIA THERESA - Volume 1 (S&W047 EN) by Enrico Acerbi
Editor: Luca Cristini Editore, for the brand: Soldiershop. Cover & Art Design: Luca S. Cristini.

In cover: line infantry (Hungarian) 1741-1743- Collezione Vinkhuijzen courtesy NYPL

THE FIRST ARMY OF MARIA THERESA

INTRODUCTION

Out of the catastrophe of the Thirty Years' War had emerged the triumph of absolutism and the professional soldier. The prince, and his standing army, would characterise the political image of the following century: the '*miles perpetuus*' would be the princely instrument of domestic politics, in the perennial struggle for a strong central state, but abroad it would become the test of sovereignty, in the constant wars of those times. These 'cabinet wars' were, in their tactical forms and effects, very similar to court ballets. They were able to bring about very little structural change in old Europe and, in fact, gave rise to only two timid shifts in the axis of power: English supremacy in Europe and the rise of Prussia in Germany.

A general sense of common purpose, however, emerged from the disasters of the Thirty Years' War - unfortunately on the backs of a tormented civilian population. Perhaps it was precisely in order to exorcise the feeling of their own brutality that the traditions of chivalry, still effective especially among the officer corps of the various armies, were willingly united in war. The common European root of the soldier in the 18th century, as witnessed by the passage of nobles from one potentate to another, as well as in the fluctuation of deserters, also brought out some glimmer of new humanity, against the backdrop of the fulfilment of military duties: care for the wounded and sick, the swift exchange of prisoners, the neutrality of non-combatants, the restriction of campaigns to the summer months and the regular maintenance of supply depots. All this also affected the fate of the civilian population affected by the war.

In this paper, I will essentially only talk about the very first period in which the army was, in the proper sense, '*Teresian*', i.e. from 1740 until the end of the 'Eight Years' War', i.e. 1748. A particularly tragic aspect of that period was that a woman, Maria Theresa, who was originally certainly unaccustomed to anything when it came to the business of warfare, was forced by extraordinary circumstances to treasure her father's inheritance on her own. As time went by, however, she became so attached to her army that, after the death of her husband, when she handed over the military 'keys' to her son, she said: "*This branch of state administration was the only one in which I was really interested.*"

The defence of Austria, in the early years of Maria Theresa's rule, was never given much prominence, as the existing works on the history of the Austrian army usually only touched on this period peripherally, moving succinctly from the glorious period of Prince Eugene of Savoy, to the reform of the army that began in 1748. In the years from 1740 to 1748, however, there was a very important period in the history of the Austrian army, as the latter was freeing itself from a number of problems; not only from the unfortunate wars of the last decade of Charles VI and the unfairness of the state administration, from the lack of concern for the army and the weakness of too many decisive persons placed at the top of its leadership. Internally, a significant step was being taken in the direction of the idea of a national army, born and transmitted thanks to Prince Eugene. The army regained its pride and awareness by fighting in four different theatres of war, often against outnumbered adversaries.

They say that it was at that time, in those enormous difficulties, that the word '*patriotism*' appeared, timidly, first among the people, then in the army, until then only bound to the ruling house by the bond of oath and loyalty to the imperial flag. That word did not yet have that impassioned effect, which it would have later during the Napoleonic wars, yet it became a common part, inadvertently, in citizens and soldiers. "*Whereas the individual corps of the Habsburg hereditary lands once felt that they were always and only part of the army of the Roman-imperial majesty, without comrades or allies ...*" they now had a new ideal, thanks to the recruitment in the crown lands, thanks to the old and new local militias, thanks to the voluntary and strong support, that a common sense of belonging, a new idea of a single nation, was spreading throughout the domain.

1740 was a year of change. In October, the Emperor of the Holy Roman Empire, Charles VI of Habsburg, died in the Neue Favorita in Vienna from poisoning, possibly after eating mushrooms of the species Amanita Phalloides. In 1713 Charles VI had promulgated the Prammatica Sanzione, with which he established that the kingdom could not be divided upon his death and corrected what had been established on 12 September 1703 by Emperor Leopold I with the *Pactum Mutuae Successionis,* also in opposition to the Salic Law,[1] regar-

---

1   The Salic law (Lex Salica, also called Pactus legis Salicae to distinguish it from Carolingian-era drafts) is a code

ding succession in the case of female heirs only (the pact had been kept secret and stated that after the entire male line of inheritance of sons, the government could pass to the eldest of the female daughters). Charles VI had simply guaranteed primogeniture to both males and females when his heir was still Leopold John of Habsburg, who later died in 1716. The 'female' case therefore occurred immediately, when the eldest daughter Maria Theresa, Archduchess of Austria, invoking the Pragmatic Sanction, claimed her right to succession as sovereign of the Habsburg monarchy.[2] If the Edict could be accepted in a national realm (after all, everyone made their own laws as they wished), it could not be accepted when the Habsburg monarchy intersected with a multinational complex such as the Holy Roman Empire. However, it must be emphasised that in the years between 1725 and 1730, Charles VI, thanks to territorial concessions and the help of his advisor, Baron Johann Christof Bartenstein, had obtained the endorsement of most European nations to his Prammatica Sanctio, particularly that of Brandenburg/Prussia (1728) and Great Britain. The endorsement of Russia and Augustus of Saxony cost Austria an unwelcome engagement in the War of Polish Succession (1733 - 1738), where it ended up losing Naples and Sicily, exchanged for the duchies of Parma and Piacenza, and forced intervention alongside Russia against the Turks, causing Austria to lose the Wallachian territories and Servia (today Serbia). The support of France was 'bought' with the cession of Lorraine, a Hapsburg land and Great Britain 'settled' for the cessation of the Ostend Company, a direct maritime commercial competitor of the East India Company.

The Pragmatic Sanction, unlike the *pactum mutuae successionis,* was not only a law of dynastic succession, but was formally incorporated into the legislative apparatus of every state pertaining to the Habsburg Monarchy. The last of these states to approve it was the Diet of the Kingdom of Hungary in 1723.

The political situation changed precisely when Charles VI died. The husbands of Charles VI's granddaughters, Charles Albert of Bavaria and Frederick Augustus of Saxony, reneged on their adherence to Maria Theresa's right of succession[3], and this made the outbreak of a new conflict inevitable: the War of the Austrian Succession (1740 - 1748) - in the context of which the First Silesian War against Prussia (1740 - 1742) took place - which ended with the Peace of Aachen (18 October 1748).

In reality Maria Theresa was never, formally, an empress, although the Austrians liked to call her *Kaiserin*. In 1737, her father had given her in marriage to the Grand Duke of Lorraine, Francis Stephen, as an essential part of the manoeuvre to cede the Grand Duchy to the French, moving Francis to Tuscany and thus giving rise to the Habsburg-Lorraine dynasty. In order to guarantee the independence of Tuscany and not make it a region of the Habsburg state, it was decided to keep the two crowns separate, maintaining the imperial title for the first-born son of the lineage and the grand-ducal one for the second-born. On 13 September 1745, Francis Stephen, male, was elected Emperor of the Holy Roman Empire with the name of Francis I and Maria Theresa became Empress Consort, although hostilities continued.

Maria Theresa had started out as reigning Archduchess of Austria, then as Apostolic Queen of Hungary, reigning Queen of Bohemia (on the death of Charles Albert of Bavaria, who proclaimed himself King of Bohemia during the war) and of Croatia and Slavonia, reigning Duchess of Parma and Piacenza, reigning Duchess of Milan and Mantua and also Grand Duchess Consort of Tuscany; eventually 'Empress Consort' of the Holy Roman Empire.

The so-called War of Austrian Succession was fought between Austria, supported by the maritime powers, on the one hand, and Bavaria, supported directly by the German *Reich* and France, and, very marginally, by Prussia (through the first two Silesian Wars), on the other hand, in the period 1740-1748. The three so-called Silesian Wars, which Prussia waged, because of its hereditary claims on certain Silesian principalities, against Austria, were: the first in 1740-1742, the second between 1744 and 1745, the third during the Seven Years' War.

Apart from Silesia, the War of the Austrian Succession was fought in three other theatres of war, namely in Southern Germany (Bohemia, Upper Austria, Bavaria, the Main and Upper Rhine territories), Northern Italy and the Netherlands. Already before the opening of hostilities in October 1740, Frederick II had entered Silesia with Generals Schwerin and Leopold von Dessau. After the Battle of Mollwitz, between Schwerin and

enacted by Clovis I king of the Franks (481-511) around 503 and related to the population of the Salii Franks. It had various rules, but the most famous was the '*De terra vero nulla* (salica) *in muliere hereditas non pertinebit, sed ad virilem sexum qui fratres fuerint tota terra pertineat.*' i.e. females could not exercise the right of primogeniture.

2   The argument that the Pragmatic Sanction was issued by Charles VI precisely to favour his eldest daughter cannot, however, be considered correct, since Maria Theresa was born in 1717, i.e. four years after the promulgation of the decree (Charles VI had, as mentioned, had a male heir in Leopold John, who died in 1716, seven months after her birth).

3   Frederick II of Brandenburg-Prussia, whose father Frederick Wilhelm I had recognised the Pragmatic Sanction in 1728, also ascended the Prussian throne in the year of the change, contested the Pragmatic Sanction and again made claims on Silesia, which his father had accepted as part of Habsburg territory.

Neipperg, on 10 April 1741, most of the territories of Upper Silesia and Lower Silesia fell into the hands of the Prussians, with the fortresses of Glogau, Breslau, Brieg and Neisse. The year 1741 was also characterised by the advance towards Linz and Bohemia and the conquest of Prague by the Franco-Bavarians. In August 1741, the Franco-Bavarians, at the head of whose vanguard was General Count Moritz von Sachsen[4], came to threaten Vienna, preferring then to head north and occupy Prague together with the forces of Augustus III of Saxony (November 1741), an ally of the Prussians '*obtorto collo*'. The sovereign then turned to the Hungarians. The Magyar ruling class, gathered in Pozsony (Pressburg) at the so-called Coronation Diet, voted its support (11 September 1741) and decreed the start of the *Insurrectio*[5], with the establishment of 6 new infantry and 2 cavalry regiments. "*The conscription permitted by Law No. 63/1741 had an important innovation compared to the past: no difference was made between the call to arms of the orders and the conscription for the imperial army, leading to the formation of a permanent imperial-royal army. The result of the mobilisation was the 21622 infantrymen of the portal militia*[6] *incorporated into the imperial army by filling the ranks of the six new and existing regiments. The Hungarian contribution undoubtedly enabled the young sovereign to hold the field, even if her forces suffered further setbacks.*" [7]

In Frankfurt on 24 January 1742, the Elector of Bavaria Charles Albert crowned himself King of Bohemia. The next step was to be crowned, some twenty days later, Emperor of the Holy Roman Empire with the name Charles VII. Maria Theresa's power was entering a serious crisis. The Habsburg forces, under the command of Field Marshal Count Ludwig Andreas von Khevenhüller, with several Hungarian regiments, marched on Linz, occupied by the Bavarians, and Munich. The offensive forced Charles Albert to ask the Prussians for help again. Frederick II himself led the invasion of Moravia and Bohemia. Khevenhüller was recalled from Munich and the Austrian high command or *Hofkriegsrat* put together the bulk of the remaining forces, entrusting it to the command of the sovereign's brother-in-law, Charles of Lorraine (German: *Lothringen*). In May, the battle was fought at Časlau-Chotusitz, where the Austrians were winning the battle when (it is said) an unforeseen event shifted the balance on the field. The blame was put on the Austrian Hussars and their poor discipline in the field: engaged in looting the Prussian vehicles, they apparently involved the overwhelming Austrian infantry in disorder, unable to cope with the opposing infantry. Maria Theresa had the enemy on her doorstep.

A separate peace with the Saxons and Prussians and British intervention in Hanover meant that in December 1742 Charles of Lorraine's 50,000 men were able to liberate Prague, repelling the Franco-Bavarians of Marshals Maillebois and Belle-Isle. This was the moment when Maria Theresa became aware that she had saved her throne (she would be crowned Queen of Bohemia in 1743). The Peace of Breslau, with which Prussia obtained Silesia, ended the first war. The Second Silesian War took place between Silesia, Bohemia and Saxony in two campaigns, in 1744 and 1745.

The year 1743 was noteworthy for the battles of Simbach and especially Dettingen (on the Main, near Aschaffenburg), where the Austrians flanked the Anglo-Dutch army. The Franco-Bavarians suffered defeats that

---

4   Maurice of Saxony (1696-1750), in French Maurice de Saxe, was the illegitimate son of Augustus II, Grand Elector of Saxony and King of Poland. In 1709 he served in the employ of the Duke of Marlborough and Prince Eugene in Flanders, in 1717 he was with the latter at the siege of Belgrade against the Turks, passing into the service of the King of France in 1720. In the War of the Austrian Succession he excelled in the campaign that culminated in the occupation of Prague on 26 November 1741, but his greatest successes came in the campaigns of 1744-45 and 1746 with the victories of Fontenoy and Roucoux. Appointed maréchal général des camps et armées du roi, he was given command-in-chief in the Netherlands on 16 September 1747. Retiring to private life at the end of the war, he made Chambord Castle, the residence assigned to him by King Louis XV in recognition of his services, a meeting place for poets, scholars and philosophers. He left behind an important work on military theory, *Rêveries ou Mémoires de l'art de la guerre de Maurice comte de Saxe, duc de Curlande et de Sémigalle*, published posthumously in 1756 by Pierre Gosse Jr.

5   In 1715, the king had given the Diet of Nobles a Faculty according to which (ex art. 8) he explained how the Insurgency (Insurrectio) Personalis of their vassals should be proposed and how the Insurgency Banderialis should be."*Quandoquidem Nobiles et omnes illi, quos sub nomenclationem hac, in Ungaria lex complectitur, pro Regni defensione militare, adeoque personaliter insurgere, suaque respectiva Banderia producere et praestare teneantur*". In practice, they were to form Militia and act in the name of the Crown.

6   **Insurrectio Portalis**: poorer vassals (sometimes aided by more important nobles) recruited hussars and foot soldiers according to the law. Porta' is a term meaning house. It was, therefore, a standard unit of taxation, indicating how much money to take from each farm owned by a landowner. In the Hungarian kingdom (it was not the same as the Hungarian crown lands) there were more than 5000 gates. Country soldiers were formally volunteers, but recruitment was not always free of violence. The Portalis and Banderialis Insurrections were often mixed and matched; they did not have different statutes. In reality, except for the Personalis component, nobles and aristocrats recruited as many troops as they wanted; usually more than the number set by the statutes.

7   Maria Terézia hadserége.doc at https://air.uniud.it, p. 6.

forced Marshal de Noailles to retreat across the Rhine and forced the Bavarians to swear allegiance to Maria Theresa, under the supervision of the Hungarian Count, Ban of Croatia, Károly József Bátthyány, as regent. The Habsburg military successes were causing the opposing coalition to gradually crumble.

In the campaign of 1744-45 Sardinia and Saxony came over to Maria Theresa's side[8], despite the fact that her army had been forced to evacuate Bavaria in October 1744, due to the new Prussian threat on Bohemia (the above-mentioned Second Silesian War). The reinstallation of Emperor Charles VII in Munich did not last long: his death in December saw the peace party prevail, with the heir to the throne, Maximilian Joseph III (and his mother, Maria Amalia of Austria) claiming the heir to the Habsburg throne. In April 1745 Field Marshal Count Bátthyány defeated the Franco-Bavarians at Pfaffenhofen. Maximilian Joseph yielded (22nd April - Peace of Füssen), renouncing his rights to the throne. In September of the same year his consort Franz Stephan of Lorraine became Emperor of the Holy Roman Empire with the name Franz I. The war, however, continued on the other fronts. The French had won at Fontenoy (on the right bank of the Scheldt, before Tournai), again led by Marshal De Saxe, against the 'Pragmatic' army under the command of the Duke of Cumberland.

Only France and Spain continued the fight against the 'consort' empress. The electorates, Bavaria, Saxony, Austria and the associated kingdoms of Bohemia and Hungary were firmly in Maria Theresa's hands, also militarily. Marshal De Saxe again defeated the 'Pragmatists' at Huy and Raucourt (Rocourt or Rocoux, on the left bank of the Meuse, near Liège) in 1746. De Saxe almost completed the conquest of the Austrian Netherlands. In the meantime, however, the Austrians were driving the French and Spanish out of northern Italy (Battle of Piacenza).

The year 1747 was characterised by the battle of Lauffeldt or Lawfeld (today Lafelt on the left bank of the Meuse, between Tongeren and Maastricht) and the subsequent conquest of the Maastricht fortress itself. In 1748, the siding of Tsarist Russia in favour of Austria accelerated the conclusion of hostilities until the Peace of Aachen, where Maria Theresa, after passing through moments of serious crisis, obtained the longed-for recognition of her sovereign rights, also by France and Spain.

Emperor Charles VI had intended to ensure the succession to the throne for his eldest daughter Maria Theresa, but had not provided her with a suitable military instrument to defend it. Moreover, it appears that, on the death of Emperor Charles VI, the finances were in shambles and the army in full decline; there was no reforming force in sight that could recall the work of Archduke Eugene thirty years earlier. It was after the peace of 1748 that Maria Theresa devoted herself to the reform of the standing army with a succession of regulatory measures that covered: the technical development of artillery thanks to Prince Liechtenstein, the ordering of the border (*Grenzgebiet* and *Cordon*), the numerical ordering of infantry and cavalry and much more.

The most important phenomena that happened to the Austrian army during the War of Succession were: a greater centralisation of army leadership in the institution of the *Hofkriegsrat* (known as the *Hofkriegsrat* (War Council), which, towards the end of the conflict, seemed to compete with the new power of the General-Kriegs-Commissariat (General War Commissariat) especially in the management of the Military Boundary (*Grenzgebiet*). The army demanded a greater representation of its own people, as opposed to the exuberance of 'foreigners', until then disproportionately present in the Habsburg ranks, and an increasing participation of the local nobility, in the military service, with the impetus for the formation of light troops, which were cheaper, but of growing importance. Charles VI, despite two costly wars that ended badly, had conveyed, in the spirit of Prince Eugene, a new appreciation of the 'craft' of soldiering (which the army began to enjoy at court), and which, after the war, found its fullest expression in the official adoption of a 'uniform' or 'uniform pattern or form' uniform. Until then, the uniform model was established in its general outline, but everything was left to the tastes of the colonel-owners. Only the Hungarian and Croatian populations, and the military border, adopted very different national costumes. For this very special topic, finally, allow me, before moving on to the exposition of the subjects, to personally thank Professor Vladimir Brnardić from Zagreb, for his ever courteous availability and help.

I would also like to emphasise how the different Austrian regiments are presented in this work. I have abandoned the numerical notation of the regiments, as it was totally meaningless before 1769 (nevertheless each unit described has its notation as 'future No. X') and have preferred to group them according to their districts, or rather the locations they had on the eve of the war, describing some peculiarities of the various regions of Austria. As I am wont to say at various meetings, to speak of the Austria of the 16th-17th centuries, the 18th-19th centuries and the beginning of the 20th century is to speak of a continent and not of a single nation.

---

8   The Saxon volte-face was justified by Frederick II's absolute intransigence in ceding to the Saxons a corridor of territory through the invaded Silesia and uniting Saxony with the kingdom of Poland, of which he was the owner.

THE RECRUITMENT IN AUSTRIA

The imperial recruitment system had been renewed in Wallenstein's time and had become a strong and important industry. It was during the Thirty Years' War that new soldiers were referred to as 'recruits'. In fact, we read in a Proclamation of the *Generalissimus* Archduke Leopold (1 May 1645): " ... *new enrollees or recruits.*" Even in earlier years, for example in a presentation of the Moravian territory in 1636, '*recrutirung*' was mentioned. If a person trained in warfare or a military expert offered to form a regiment on horseback or on foot, an imperial patent (a Patente) authorised him to recruit and the *Hofkriegrat* the Court War Council assigned him a place of assembly and training (*Musterplatz*). If the recruitment did not take place in the crown's hereditary lands,

▲ The recruiting Sergeant. John Collet (1725-1780)

but in another territory of the empire (Holy Roman or *Reich*), where, as a rule, no regiments were formed, but simple companies (*Fähnlein*), the Emperor issued instructions to the *Reich* princes concerned to authorise the captain 'such-and-such' to pass through the squares, at the drum roll, to recruit and take with him the people necessary to 'strengthen his *Fähnlein*'. Therefore, with the presentation of the '*Werbpatent*' recruiting licence or a credible piece of writing, one was authorised to enlist people, arrange for them to procure provisions and any other necessities, against payment, guaranteeing freedom of passage.[9] Being designated as a rallying place (*Musterplatz*) was the terror of the villages, in order to be let off the hook one had to pay to stop the threats, people were also stopped in the streets and orders to limit recruitment to eight people (maximum ten) were disregarded. It was not, therefore, as voluntary a type of recruitment as it was said to be. There were also acts of violence, but mainly acts of underhand deception. They said that the recruiting officer, in the square or in the inns, would catch the stupid peasants by sticking a military hat on their heads and saying: "*Now that you have the hat, you are a soldier and can no longer back out.*"

Within the Austrian armed forces, despite repeated calls for reform, almost everything was still unchanged. In particular, the call to arms (*Aufgebot*)[10] completely retained its previous forms, only with the inhibiting right of recruits not to cross the borders of their province. In 1663, due to an imminent invasion by Turkish pirates, the Upper Austrian regions announced that the country had to contribute one man in 13 to its defence, mainly to build field fortifications; shortly afterwards, one man in five was 'called up' in addition to those already summoned. In 1683, the fortified defence structures, to defend against the Turks, were run with greater zeal and Vienna decided that each village should send one worker, for every 20 hearths (houses), to Vienna, every 60 days, to work on the fortifications; these workers received free accommodation and 6 kreuzer per day; landowners, who had less than 20 hearths (houses), had to send one worker per house for three days to work on the fortifications, receiving a subsidy of 30 kreuzer.

At the end of the Thirty Years' War, and especially during the conflicts under Emperor Leopold I, a second type of recruitment model for regiments was introduced. The sorting of recruits was done by the authorities of

---

9   The term '*Werbung*', which today means 'publicity', originated as an 'activity aimed at trying to gain a person's favour' and therefore became 'recruitment' in military parlance. It was done just like an 'advertisement' by banging drums and using planks, in the square, to which people signed the act of consent (the accession of cadets, judged suitable, would also be called *Assentierung*). The actual enlistment in the ranks was done after eligibility (*Musterung*). The location of the muster or enlistment records was called *Musterplatz*, or also training centre: *Lauf- und Musterplatz*.
10   The *Aufgebot* was the 'evocatio ad arma', the moment when a Power (feudal or state) 'compulsorily' invited to enlist.

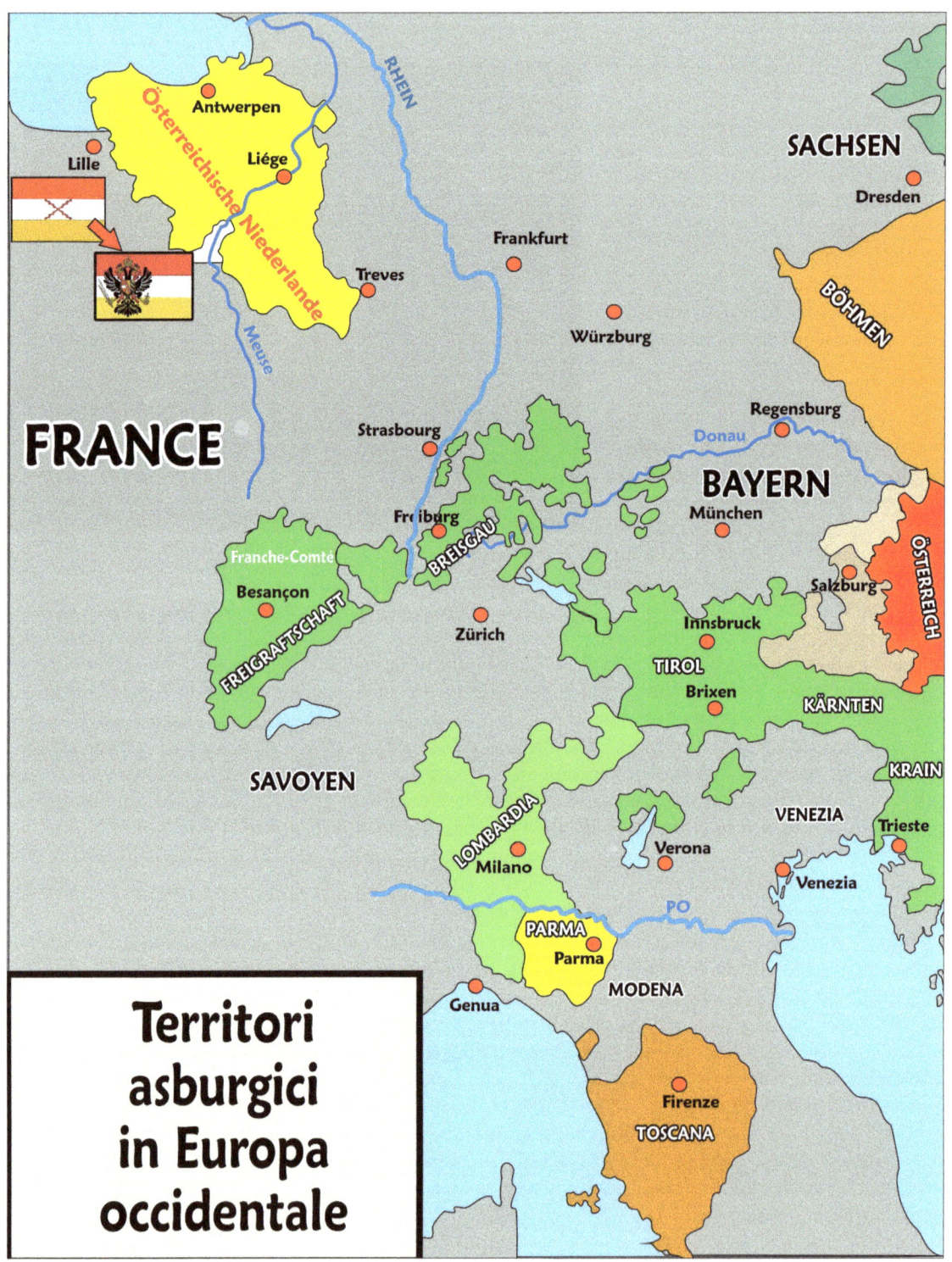

Territori asburgici in Europa occidentale

the imperial hereditary lands. This was a measure imposed by the continuing financial difficulties of the state. Since the sums needed by the regiments at the end of each campaign to replace their losses with recruitment never arrived at the right time, since the contributions (authorisations from the regional *Landtags*) also often arrived months later, '*it was not possible to recruit until the following year*', shortly before the start of operations, thus compromising the effectiveness of the armies. So it was decided to be locally more autonomous in the search for recruits. At the end of the year, the regiments submitted their records of their needs in recruits to the *General* War Commissioner (*General-Kriegs-Commissariat*). This established the criteria for the total number of recruits needed (requirements based on the losses of the last campaign and reinforcements or new numbers needed for operations planned for the coming years), as well as the need for the State funds for recruiting (*Werbegeldern*), and communicated the outcome to both the *Hofkriegsrat* and the *Hofkammer*.

The sums of money or recruits to be taken directly could then be distributed among the individual regions, lordships or municipalities. Troop commands could have recruits from the territory (*Land-Recruten*) assigned to them as replacement troops, who, as such, could be initiated into regiments. Recruitment with funds generally took precedence, although it took many officers out of service for long periods of time, whereas an internal territorial organisation was easier to keep under control.

The limitation of the system was that 'paid' recruits were more prone to desertion than those who had freely signed up to serve the imperial flags; another limitation was the absence of uniform administrations of the regions, which often meant that months passed before new soldiers arrived at their regiments, already engaged in campaigning in faraway war zones (such as Italy or the Rhine). Often the campaign was over before they arrived at the corps. The contribution for uniforms was initially given to the regiment owners, if they had paid for the uniforms out of their own pockets; this is why it was difficult to standardise the so-called 'recruitment fund', as it varied from case to case. Deducted from the fund were the costs of clothing and weapons, as well as payments for the recruits' journeys from the recruiting site to the regiments, and the journeys of the recruiting commander and his aides. In the end, what remained in hand (*Handgeld*) was so little that it had to be confronted with the rules of supply and demand.

During the Hungarian uprisings of 1704, the lands of Lower Austria were ordered by the emperor to make a local, territorial *Landaufgebot* in the regions of March and Leitha to call a regular militia to arms, perhaps even using some elements of the adjacent *Vierteln* (the traditional division of Austria into four regions). Considering the usual futility of the previous systems and the refractory positions of the peasants, the orders were as follows: '*All landowners were to assist the village authorities in gathering troops. All villagers, castle servants, brewers, millers, innkeepers, blacksmiths, schoolmasters, and hitherto excluded persons, with the exception of clergymen, managers, judges and high magistrates, were to report to the camp. Villagers, castle guards and all other unmarried men were to arrive first, especially if they knew how to use a musket. All had to be between 18 and 50 years old*'.

Each village community had to give the men sent two pounds of bread and six kreuzers as pay and, in addition, they had to make sure that each one had muskets, flintlocks, firearms or minor weapons such as short blades, spikes or the like. If they did not have shovels and spikes, they had to at least have ropes with hooks; those who had a rifle had to receive powder, fuses and balls from the community, at least for 20 rounds, perhaps without giving them to the individual men, but handing everything over to their leaders, sergeants (*Führer*).

The judges were to report the troop's offences to the rulers, punish rebels with the confiscation of all land and inheritance, or immediately force them into forced military life, or, if so unworthy, exile them. The same punishments were to be meted out to fugitives and deserters. During the entire period of service in arms, the militiaman was to retain his post, excluding illness or other unavoidable causes. A commissioner of operations was to be appointed in each village of the Military Boundary to receive the flow of troops arriving from the lordships and villages.

During the short rule of Emperor Joseph I and the longer period of Emperor Charles VI, nothing substantial changed in the war constitution in Austria. However, after his ascension to the government, Joseph I took an important step towards the unification of the Supreme War Command and, in June and July 1705, ordered that the *Hofkriegrat of* Inner Austria (Graz), on which the Cordon and the Military Boundary depended, should no longer be a direct extension of the Court Chancellery (*Hofkanzlei*), but should be directly subordinate to the *Hofkriegsrat* in Vienna.

As far as the recruitment process was concerned, there were no established rules by which recruits' pay could be abused or reduced, or poor food or clothing offered, before they were sent to the regiment.

At the beginning of the 18th century, there was a 'German' tradition (for the so-called 'Alemannic' regiments) that recruits had to come from hereditary or imperial lands, i.e.: '*People who were honest, frugal, robust and able to carry and use a rifle, neither too young nor too old: and Hungarians and Croats (not suitable for German regiments) were not to be accepted*'. Prince Eugene of Savoy even introduced the '*verbotene Nationalisten*', i.e. the nations that could not be part of the 'German' regiments: the French, Italians, Swiss, Poles, Hungarians and Croats. The age of recruits had to be between 18 and 46, although later the maximum age was advanced, creating the problem of '50-year-old' soldiers. It should be noted that landowners and peasants' sons, who were needed to cultivate the fields, could not be recruited.

In Hungary, there was an obligation to convene the *Insurrectio*, which will be discussed later, based on a feudal constitution of the country, which obliged the nobility of the great landowners to serve to defend the territory, in return for the rights they enjoyed. To contribute to the completion and sustenance of the '*Hayduck*' regiments, as the Hungarian infantry was called, the authorities of the territory had no obligation, making operations often very difficult. As this feudal militia had always proved inadequate in many past wars, the Magyar authorities, meeting in Parliament in Pressburg in 1715, decided to establish a permanent infantry militia (the '*regulata militia*'), completely unrelated to the insurrectional duty of the nobles.

According to Article VIII of that rule, adopted by the *Landtag*, the King of Hungary had the duty to recruit a certain number of regiments, in the country (or even abroad), by having them maintained by the territory (counties); as for the quantification of the necessary funds, the various *Landtags* had to be authorised on a case-by-case basis. From the state of the infantry in 1715, it can be seen that the rule had only been applied to the *Hayduck* Gyulai regiment (the future 51), which, however, from 1742, following the authorisation of the Pressburg *Landtag* (1741) to form six new regiments, was transferred with its entire organisation to the Transylvanian territory, introducing the new recruitment, different from the *Insurrectio, in* that principality as well.

Recruitments continued to be held at home and abroad. In order to concentrate recruitment more in the hands of the *Hofkriegsrat* and to reduce the counterproductive involvement of the territorial corps, according to an order of the Supreme Court Council of 30 March 1722, regiments began to be recruited and equipped with horses without any expenses, charges or costs from the regions, districts, lordships and chancelleries, i.e. the regiments were now completely paid for by the imperial treasury.

To enable officers to save on recruitment funds, they were allowed to dismiss a certain number of soldiers, for several months, and from the salaries saved to create a 'recruiting fund', which would be used to replenish the ranks in the event of war, avoiding the need for formal recruitment every year in peacetime. In order to replace the troops, the *Hofkriegsrat, or* on his order a territorial commander, or the *Hofkammer*, or the Commissariat with the regiment could conclude service contracts.

Commanders generally preferred to seek out the '*Land-Recruten*', in the regiment's home territory,[11] or to have so-called replacement troops (*Ersatz-Mannschaften*) rather than have funds to recruit. With those, in fact, many officers were forced to tour the countries, for that particular service, staying away from the regimental ranks for a long time.[12]

As already mentioned, recruitment could certainly not always be called a voluntary act, although an attempt was always made to make it seem so. The regulations of the time expressly stated that:'... *no one could be forced into service by deception or drunkenness, and if one of these complained to the regiment, the recruiting officer would have to recover the recruiting allowance, release the soldier and recruit a new man at his own expense.*

Recruitment was an art, it had to be understood whether the person who showed up did so to escape other punishments, or whether he was a cheater, a thief, an outcast of the country, or a violent man (*Schinderknecht*), it had to be understood that he had no physical defects and that he was not a deserter from other armies, "*because when one was rotten (Schelm), he remained so until the end.*" "*The people to be recruited had to be tall and strong, aged between 24 and 35 and equipped with a suitable uniform and a completely new secondary weapon.*" The tradition inaugurated by Prince Eugene continued in that it was not possible to recruit: "*originally from*

---

11   It was not until 1748 that it was ordered, in order to have a "Continuous Recruitment", "*that the regiments beat the drum and open the signing tables in all the villages in the lands of the regimental headquarters or quartering station, continuing to recruit until the necessary cadres were completed; the local governments were to support and encourage this type of recruitment.* Wrede, vol. I, p. 98.

12   To each recruiting officer, the regiment assigned a quartermaster, a drummer, a surgeon and three or four men.

France, Welschen[13] *, or born outside Germany, because these people unaccustomed to our way of being, could be excellent fugitives or great affabulators, talking over each other, probably seducing and plagiarising even good people ..."* it was then also possible to accept *"known people, from known parents, friends, relatives. They should not be clumsy, naive and talkative, but have a masculine face and a nice physiognomy. No one was to be accepted who had a physical defect..."* Later, the ethnic exclusions were to be even more precise. It was written in the *Reglement* that: *" ... dishonest persons, such as freedmen or Freimänner, servants of executioners or torturers (Schinderknechte), matriculated thieves, persons tainted with infamy, Gypsies, vagabonds, Jews and foreigners, who are natives neither of the hereditary lands nor of the Holy Roman Empire, deserters, unless they originate from some Power with which a Treaty has been established ... are to be excluded from Recruitment."* "*The best nationalities*" for soldiers were considered to be Austrians, Bohemians, Moravians and Silesians.

In Maria Theresa's time, no one could be forced or persuaded to serve under false pretences. Furthermore, their past and the reasons why they might ask to enlist were to be taken into account; the recruitment of professionals, artisans, was desired, as was that of students and young people from the best families.

For the cavalry, they preferred to enlist blacksmiths, butchers, carters, peasants, people generally used to horses and hard continuous work. The same types of people were also sought for the infantry, because of their vigorous build; as well as shoemakers, tailors and carpenters, because of their usefulness for regimental work; finally, students were also sought, because good non-commissioned officers were created from them. *"The private soldier (Gemeine) must be a brave and obedient man, he must always keep his weapons, his musket and his ammunition in good order to receive credit with his officers and to advance in time."*

The regiments were to complete themselves by these means, at the place where they were located, without the need for proper recruitment every year in peace. If it was necessary to completely replace regiments (if they had been taken prisoner before peace) the *Hofkriegsrat,* or the General Command in its power of attorney, concluded a contract with the territory (or the General Commissariat did so directly with the regiments).

A recruited person could not yet feel enlisted unless he had a uniform and a secondary weapon. In this case, he was only entrusted with the cartridge case (*Patronentasche*) and was paid his wages; this was a sign that the recruit was considered an 'obligate' to serve. An 'obligate' soldier' was 'obliged' to serve for life, or possibly for as long as the enlistment specification lasted. The '*unobligate*' *was a* soldier who could resign when he wanted to, but it was a status only for staff personnel, later also passed on to the officer category.

When the recruits arrived at the regiment, the fittest were placed among the grenadiers, then, the right of choice passed to the *Leib-Compagnie*, those remaining were sent to the remaining companies.

Recruitment took place by means of announcements in the public squares, to the roll of the drum. Each recruiting officer was assigned a furier (a table), a field surgeon (for eligibility), a drum and 3 or 4 soldiers to maintain discipline in the recruiting or mustering squares. The commissioned officers had a *Werbe-Patent*, a recruiter's licence given by the *Hofkriegsrat*, with passes and letters of recommendation (*Requisitorialschreiben* to be able to recruit in the imperial territories) addressed to the local princes and rulers.

The *LandesDefensions-Systems* of Charles VI and the attempt to create the Landwehr

The 'calls to arms' continued to be of the same old pattern and were summoned, on various occasions, against Hungarian uprisings, under Emperor Joseph I, or to protect the military border. When, in 1731, the Protestant peasants of Salzburg rebelled against their archbishop in Upper Austria, the militia was summoned to defend the borders of that land against possible invasion, but only on the borders closest to Salzburg. Charles VI, on the other hand, had the idea of creating a plan to put the Austrian lands in a permanent defensive position, taking as an example what had been done for the Tyrol (the *Landesschützen*) and Hungary. The so-called *LandesDefensions-Systems* was an ambitious plan, which never reached the operational phase.

Negotiations took place between the regencies of Lower, Inner and Upper Austria. On 19 May 1734, the for-

---

13   *Welschen* was the term used by Germans to refer to Italians (including the South Tyroleans of Trent) and, in general, to the descendants of Romans, Latins or any people from the south (see the Wallesians in Switzerland, the roots of the terms Polish Wlochy, Hungarian Olasz, Wallachians in Romania, etc.), despite the fact that many authors ennoble it by assigning it a Latin root (a tribe from Gaul - but one could also think of the Volscians and they were south of Rome). Within the Habsburg empire, the term was always very close to derogatory meanings.

mer pledged to field one soldier for every eight houses, to be exercised in a permanent defence of the country with arms. The costs of this institution, until a special fund could be set up, were calculated as follows: 15,000 florins per year for road repair costs. The main weapon was to be supplied by the military foundries and paid for '*in kind*' or 1 florin per piece. For the time being, powder for shooting and practice was to be paid for by the regions.

The militia was to be made up of "*trustworthy and stable subjects, or their children, or, in the absence of such subjects, was to be made up of other honest and honourable men.*" After a few years in the country, they were to be enrolled in regular lists and registers. These mustered troops were to rotate every three years, with an equal number of discharged men being replaced by an equal number of three-year militia. Under this system, almost all subjects would sooner or later receive weapons training, to be used to defend the fatherland.

'*Lower Austria proved to be completely willing to reform. Recruiting one man for every eight houses, it would field 8000 militiamen. The free city of Vienna, instead of its usual contingent of 500 men, would field 4,000 citizens. Throughout Lower Austria, 32 muster places would be formed (8 for each of the 4 Viertels), and, for each muster place, a force of 225, or 1800 men at arms for a Viertel; later each Viertel would have an Oberstwachtmeister, a major with captain's pay (800 guilders), a captain with 500 guilders, etc. For each muster place there would be 5 Feldwebel, each training 45 soldiers, with a daily pay of 6 kreuzer. The corporals would be chosen from the most able people in the rural militia, they would receive two portions of bread and drink during the exercises, the drums would be taken from the young men in the rural militia and trained.*"

The regions of Upper Austria also tried to adhere to the plan for special calls to arms, where their so-called territorial militia (*Landmiliz*) had very similar traits to the Bavarian *Landfahne* in the neighbouring country. Their demands contained the following points: for every ten hearths, one man was drafted, resulting in a corps of just over 4,000 men, who would form the stable contingent of the Upper Austrian *Landfahne*. This regimental-looking formation was not formed and financed by the landowners, but, in order to have more control, by the Land Districts; a bureau took care of everything, the deployment of the troops, the designation of the training site, the armouries and everything else. Invalids were also used for training. Every month, a prize shooting was held. The emperor wanted to provide the country with at least 4000 rifles of the same calibre, bayonets, cartridge cases and powder. Invalids and district court officials could be paid some emoluments annually for their work.

The Plan's greatest difficulties were encountered in Inner Austria. Count von Wagensperg, territorial commander of Styria, said in a communiqué of 26 May 1734 that, according to the opinion, sent to the Emperor on 1 June, of the councillors of the seat in Graz, "*the Entire People*", so it was said, "*were weakened either by higher taxes or by temperament and therefore alarmed and fearful, also because because because of your system of recruitment, they would no longer be able to use the plough.*"

The Styrian land already bore the burden of the costs of the unity of the military border; in any case, the defence offered by the *Grenzer* could also spare them that new territorial militia. The government, however, replied that if there was no stable militia in the provinces of Inner Austria, there would be no training of the population, and that it was therefore important that at least part of the population should be trained in the use of arms, so that they could be mobilised in case of need, in the lands of Inner Austria, for purposes of territorial defence or to serve in the event of disturbances or foreign invasions.

Although Prince Eugene of Savoy had left Charles VI a strong army, this strength was only enough to impose the desired succession. However, a talented leader was lacking after the death of Prince Eugene. Moreover, the army had not only been financially strained and severely decimated by the countless campaigns at the beginning of the century, it had also been plagued and mown down by contagious diseases, brought on by the military overpopulation, right down to the winter quarters; countless soldiers had been wiped out due to diseases, such as cholera in the Balkans for example. New recruitment campaigns, or even measures to improve the living conditions of the armed forces, were only possible to a very limited extent due to empty treasuries. The non-payment of wages and the miserable food further encouraged the disbandment of Maria Theresa's troops, especially in 1740. Furthermore, the supreme military authority, the Curtense War Council or *Hofkriegsrat, had been* left without adequate leadership since the death of Prince Eugene and had become almost unfit for work.

Maria Theresa, born on 13 May 1717, ascended the throne at the age of 23, with no preparation for reforming her ailing military apparatus. The focal points of her education, as she was a female, were more specialised on family planning and good behaviour. Already by 1736, married to Francis Stephen of Lorraine, she was living the life of a mother and a noble wife, rather than that of a future sovereign. These circumstances and the fact that she was catapulted directly into a new war prevented the start of a reform effort that also involved recruitment. But how did people become soldiers in Austria from 1740 onwards?[14]

Maria Theresa, recruitment and war

At first, Maria Theresa did not deviate from the old regulation systems, as there was no time for the major reforms that were to follow in the second half of the century. Numerous regulations on the subject did not change the system much. It was only at the end of the war, in 1748, that she ordered the Commissariat General for War and, in particular, all infantry regiments, at the quarters where they were stationed, to roll the drums again and to open the recruiting tables again *'to maintain the continuity of enlistments with zeal and application until its completion'*.

Regiments-Werbung, regimental recruitment also known as *Ständische Werbung* because it was carried out in the regimental headquarters on the basis of resolutions of the local *Landtag*, persisted among the troops of the crown's hereditary lands (including the Netherlands and anterior Austria). The service obligation was of indefinite duration - in the event of war, it ended with death or disability. In Hungary, from the turn of the century, the *'Aufgebots-Verfassung'*, the Recruitment Act, still existed, whereby the nobility and the clergy were obliged to perform military service 'ad personam', and both were obliged to recruit troops in proportion to their property and assets. The king, with the military force authorised by him, was called upon to defend the country and kept permanent garrisons in the 'public' fortresses and counties; the complements, therefore, undoubtedly also came through the recruitment, sometimes forced, of royal estates and 'public' squares. If the royal military forces were no longer sufficient, the actual feudal militia, the *Banderien* of the *Insurrectio*, stepped in. The petty nobility and low-ranking clergy had to offer their contingents to the banners of the counties. Hungarian calls to arms were total and orderly, even in times of great danger. [15]

The Habsburg historical tradition also included regiments of Italian origin. After the War of the Spanish Succession, only Lombard regiments remained de facto. Although they were equipped as German (in the sense of non-Hungarian) troops, they were called *'Welschen'* or *'Romanischen'*. On enlistment, each soldier gave the regimental scribe, usually a German speaker, the name of his town; the scribe recorded that name according to the vowel forms familiar to him. This gave rise to real *puzzles* and misunderstandings: for example, the names of the Italian towns of Barletta, Pizzighettone, Casale, Guastalla, Biella were entered in the recruitment lists as Parletta, Pizigithon, Quasal, Quastala and Vielle. Worthy of note is the fact that the name of the small (sometimes large) towns of origin was mostly followed by the name of the district or province or state. These designations helped to decipher the geographic cognition of Italian soldiers and how it changed over time. Until 1770, the soldiers in northern Italy called themselves members of a municipality (in Italian it was called Contado). This was closely linked to the historical development process of northern Italy, from the Middle Ages to early modern times.

Thus one could find some markings of the type: *'Casalmaggiore im Cremonesischen* [city district of Cremona]', *'Borgo Val di Taro im Parmesischen'* Parma, *'Venegono im Mailändischen'* for Milan, *'Sabbioneta im Mantuanischen'* for Mantua, etc. In the time of Joseph I, a new type of geographical self-assignment was observed: many soldiers from Pavia, Cremona and other cities in Lombardy registered in the *Musterlisten* as people from *'k. k. Lombardei'. Lombardei'*. This denoted a changed consciousness of the soldiers (or perhaps of the regimental scribe); now the Habsburg imperialregion, i.e. belonging to the state administration, became important.

It is also noteworthy that the Italian soldiers of the imperial army, unlike the Walloon or Croatian soldiers, were not grouped into a single ethnic group in the 18th century. The causes were manifold and it is difficult

---

14 At the war archives in Vienna, the 'military matriculation sheets' and 'enlistment lists' (*Musterlisten*) are almost completely preserved and can be viewed. In peacetime, the matriculation sheets of the Military Confinement, the Imperial Militia and the Hungarian Militia were kept in the local parishes. Until 1768, two *Musterlisten* were created per year, after that date only one per year.

15 The formation of regular Magyar troops had begun in 1688 with the establishment of Hussar regiments, permanently organised in the territory, and then with the formation of the *Hajduken* and Croatian infantry regiments at the beginning of the War of the Spanish Succession. Finally, regular infantry regiments were recruited in Hungary after 1688.

to understand the exact picture of that situation. The low prestige enjoyed by the Italian people, in terms of military capacity, was often highlighted. It was a deeply rooted prejudice that was particularly widespread among German sovereigns and generals. In 1722, the aforementioned Count Khevenhüller advised keeping '*welschen*' and other recruits of non-German origin away from the imperial regiments

Tyrol was a case apart, even though it included a '*Welschtirol*' part of Trentino. The benefits obtained from the *Landslibell of* 1511 and the Ordinance of 1605 were renewed in 1704. The territorial militia had to consist of 10, 15 or 20 thousand men; only in extreme cases could the *Landsturm* or bell alarms be used. Soldiers called to arms were subdivided into companies or *Fähnlein*, with pre-established commanders; the population practised shooting and manoeuvring, instead of the usual signals with fires, the *lighting of which caused more confusion than usefulness*', they trained to be couriers.

The first choices were the strongest men, trained in shooting and precision shooting. As there was already a large number of militia in the country, these were mainly to be used for national defence, the 12 companies *Scharfschützen* and *Scheibenschützen* (two ways of saying sharpshooters), however, had special 'small war' duties. A canton captain (*Viertel*) received 5 gulden (florins) per day for himself and horses, a deputy captain 3 florins, a lieutenant 1 florin and 30 kreuzer, an ensign 1 florin, a sergeant 48 kreuzer, a corporal 24 kreuzer, a ringer 20 kreuzer and a private 15 kreuzer plus the order bread. In Tyrol, in 1745, after many vain attempts, the establishment of a national regiment was initiated and the local standing committee finally managed to allocate the necessary funds. The former Tyrolean territorial battalion was disbanded and in its place appeared a regiment of 15 companies and two grenadier companies, in all 2300 men, equipped like the rest of the 'German' infantry.

The regiment had a special task, however, because if the Tyrol was threatened by an enemy danger, it had to be available for the defence of the country, or else half (or at least one battalion) always had to remain in the Tyrol and the rest employed elsewhere; these 'garrison' battalions rotated every year. When the fund for the necessary support was activated, two battalions and a company of grenadiers were formed; these were created using the most suitable personnel from the old *Landbataillon*, trying to eliminate or dismiss all those less physically fit.

The external dangers, which immediately attacked Maria Theresa when she ascended the throne, gave no time for the 'call to arms' theorised by her father to be organised. All recruitment continued to be carried out as under the old system.

During the period of the first two Silesian Wars and the War of the Austrian Succession, however, the Territorial Selection or *Landes-Aufgebot* was given a new chance. A series of regulations had dealt with the subject without, however, achieving definitive results; These included the Patente of 11 August 1741 on the selection of the tenth man in Upper Austria, the Recall in the Bohemian Lands of 29 April 1742 on the organisation of the *Landsturm*, an Edict on the Estates in Austria of 10 September 1744, Resolutions on the Presentations of 26 December 1744 and 4 January 1745, Edict of the Moravian General Territorial Commissariat of 19 May 1745, Complaints and Proposals of the Moravian Margraviate concerning the Rural Militia (*Landmiliz*) of 27 November 1745 and the Protocol-Note on the Establishment of the *Landmiliz*.

For example, in 1741, the lands of Upper Austria, threatened by the Bavarians, decided that, in the event of enemy danger, whoever owned ten hearths would provide a hunter, a marksman or at least a person capable of shooting. The choice of one man out of ten fell to the landowners only, with the exception of the seven princely towns (those who had to provide their own protection and defence in any case), and had to be made quickly; the designated marksmen knew they were not trained to fight in the open field, let alone across borders, but only to guard the borders and protect their own land. These *Landschützen* (territorial marksmen) were organised into companies in the four cantons of the country and commanded by their appointed officers and non-commissioned officers. The cantonal government paid each man 12 kreuzer per day for food; powder and balls were provided by landowners or the authorities. If a landowner was unable to maintain muskets and second weapons for his territories, the materials were taken from the canton treasury or from the state arsenals, subject to authorisation.

In addition to these local and occasional episodes, attempts were made to arrive at continuous calls to arms, such as those conceived by Charles VI with his rural militia system. The land above the river Enn, Upper Austria in 1744 was asked for at least 2,000 militia men, in view of the dangers that had been encountered in previous years and a contingent of 2-300 hunters (*Schützen*) to be used as soon as possible for the occupation of the Oberhaus fortress in Passau. In the same year, the formation of militias was also ordered in Moravia in the two royal towns of Brünn (Brno) and Olmütz (Olomouc). After the expulsion of the enemy from Bohemia, at the request of the Moravian Territorial War Commissariat, the majority of that militia was left at home, forming, in each of the two towns mentioned, only three district companies and two other private companies, in all 840 rural militia men. In the following years, due to the circumstances of war, the *Land-Miliz* had to grow again. At that time, the militia had six district companies, each of 202 men, and 36 private companies, each of 121 men, a total of 5568 men. To raise those numbers even further, a militia of eight battalions was proposed, half of which were transferred to the fortresses of Brünn and Olmütz, the other half deployed on the Silesian border. As long as this militia remained in effective service, it received its pay from the state treasury and its food from the warehouses in Olmütz.

The daily wage was meagre, a maximum of four kreuzers, for standing in garrison, camping or standing guard on advanced positions. In Moravia, and probably in other lands as well, there were many complaints about this situation and these internal difficulties probably made the institution of the militia unpopular, although they later came back into discussion, especially in 1753. In November 1743, the *Hofkriegsrat of Inner Austria* was dissolved in Graz and replaced by a military directorate, subordinate to the General Command of Inner Austria, Field Marshal Joseph Friedrich von Sachsen - Hildburghausen.

A General Command had also existed in Hungary since the time of Charles VI, and the regimen had entrusted it to Field Marshal Count János (Johann) Pálffy. Under Charles VI, however, another long overdue and urgently needed step had been taken towards improving the military organisation.

In Hungary, under Turkish rule, the traditional militia had all but disappeared until Leopold I's victory had restored imperial order. In the meantime, by means of a *Particular-Insurrectio*, the lands loyal to their king offered wards on foot or on horseback, half of whose food was guaranteed by the peasants' Portale system, but the other half by the wealthy nobility, according to the number of their possessions; the counties on either side of the Danube fulfilled this obligation by providing 10 florins per year for each 'Porta' possessed.

The Hungarian counties had been convinced since 1715 that the conventional institutions for the defence of the territory, the now obsolete feudal militia, were no longer sufficient. As mentioned, the eighth article of the Diet of 1715 had also stipulated that the nobility and all those who wielded power in Hungary were obliged to recruit troops to offer service in the defence of the country, sometimes through the institution of the 'personal' *Insurrectio* or with the *Banderiale*.

The institution of the military border continued to grow. In 1652, the frontiersmen could field 8866 men, compared to only 2282 in 1580. The administration of the Military Border was always subject to the *Hofkriegsrat of Inner Austria*, which was not always welcome and a cause for rebellion. Initially, the border territory (*Grenzgebiet*) was divided into four: *Windische* (Slavic, southern), *Petrinianische* (Serbian), Croatische (Croatian) and *Meergrenz* (coastal) borders. The regions of Styria, Carinthia and Carniola provided the necessary supplies for daily life and the *Hofkriegsrat* in Graz guaranteed the monthly payments to the borderers (*Grenzer*); for the *Windisch* part the money flowed to Varazdin, for the Croats to Carlstädt (today Karlovac) and for the littoral to Zengg. Military exercises were to be held at the border every three years. The former Hungarian borders along the Sava, Tisza and Maros rivers had been organised by Emperor Leopold I, following the Croatian model, by creating the Slavonian border in 1702, this time subject to the Viennese *Hofkriegsrat* and the imperial Chamber of the capital. To increase the valour of the troops on the border and gradually bring them up to standard, Maria Theresa had them gradually formed into permanent regiments. It all began in 1746 in Croatia. The border troops were divided into regiments at district level and also received permanent officers in peacetime.

The excellent services provided by the troops of those regiments led to the recruitment of new ones during the Seven Years' War. The establishment of two bridge boatmen companies on the Danube, *Czaikisten - Compagnien*, in 1747, justified the formation of a *Czaikisten* battalion[16]. On 16 January 1750, the Empress issued

---

16 Although the term *Tschajkisten was a* kind of nickname for the Hungarian foot troop, it must be emphasised that, the *chaika* (in Slavic and Hungarian: czajka, in German: tschajka) was a wooden barge, which could also have a sail and mast, but which was rowing, a small cargo galley. It was used on the Dnjepr by the Zaporozhe Cossacks in the 16th and

a Diploma, for the border lands of Croatia and Slavonia, by which she ceded the authority over the borders of the Banon of Croatia (*Banalisten*) and the right to appoint officers up to the rank of lieutenant colonel.

The Habsburg flag

The foundation of the oldest Austrian regiment dates back to 1619 (what would later become No. 11). It was formed in 5 companies and shortly afterwards expanded to 10; each department had its own flag. Already at that time there was a tradition of loading the flags with images of saints, but especially with that of Mary Help of Christians, '*Mutter von der Immerwährenden Hilfe*' or Mother of Perpetual Help. Our Lady was often accompanied by an inscription such as '*Monstra te esse Matrem.*' or 'manifest yourself as Mother'.

The victory of Tilly's imperial troops against the 22,000-strong Bohemian army at the White Mountain near Prague was attributed, by the strictly observant Emperor Ferdinand II, to the Virgin Mary, to whose protection the troops had been entrusted. From then on, Our Lady was venerated and regarded as the sacred patron saint of the army, and from then on, her image, or 'Muttergottesbild', was emblazoned on the flags of the Austrian army, especially on the reverse side of the Colonnelle (*Leibfahnen*) flags.

Traditionally, the *Leibfahnen* had a pearl-white background, while the other regimental flags (*Ordinärefahnen*)

17th centuries, and the Danube Serbs, whom the Hungarians called Šajkaši. Apart from its river use, it lent itself to wooden footbridges for pontoon bridges over rivers.

preferred to use an imperial yellow background; which was an embarrassment with the advent of Maria Theresa, who could not be represented as Empress of the Holy Roman Empire. Thus every first battalion of an infantry regiment had a white flag with the imperial symbol. Instead, the Virgin Mary began to be depicted standing on the globe, stepping on the serpent and with twelve stars above her head.

To address the extremely complex subject of flags, one must refer to times before 1740. For purely economic reasons, in fact, many regiments born at

Leibfahne   Ordinärefahne

reggimento di fanteria tedesco

the end of the 17th (beginning of the 18th) century retained their original flags for a long time, often loaded with the coat of arms of the owner's family (*Inhaber*). For example, in 1695, a white flag with the image of the Virgin Mary and the imperial eagle (*Reichsadler*) was issued for the First Company of the First Battalion (Guard or *Leib-Compagnie*) at the formation of Infantry Regiment No. 7. The remaining flags of the regiment were yellow and bore the coats of arms of the Houses of Habsburg, Palatinate-Neuburg and the one of the Leib-Compagnie had, in addition to the coats of arms of the Houses, St John as the patron saint of the soldiers. The expansion and reorganisation of the German infantry regiments into three battalions, each with four companies, between 1695 and 1682 led to a considerable increase in regimental flags. One of the most glorious infantry regiments, the future No. 4 Hoch=und Deutschmeister, was also born at this time. During her first review, Her Majesty Empress Eleanor personally donated the white flag of the *Leib-Compagnie* plus eight other 'ordinary' flags for the companies. It was from this time that people began to swear allegiance to the flag, uttering the formula '*Wier Offizier und Soldaten schwören und Globen zu Gott dem Allmächtigen und seinen Heyligen mit diesem körperlichen Aydt ...* ' aloud.

In 1710, the imperial army had 40 infantry regiments, each consisting of 15 companies of musketeers and 2-3 companies of grenadiers. Each infantry battalion had flags of the same colour for its 5 companies, among which were red, yellow and white. The volunteer corps and the Hungarians had green flags. The distinctions of the company flags were now made by a coloured border, 20-25 cm wide, with triangular dowels interspersed, arranged so that all numbered companies of a single battalion had the same border. Those company flags were 2-3 m long and 1.5-2 m wide; they bore the image of the double-headed eagle with a golden sword, over whose heads rested the imperial crown. On the eagle's breast was the imperial monogram 'C.VI'. In 1714 an exception was made for the Osnabrück Regiment (future No. 15), which was allowed to carry the coat of arms of Lorraine on its flag, as there was reasonable doubt as to whether the regiment was imperial or merely in the service of the Empire. On 21 October 1740, Maria Theresa ascended the Habsburg throne but, unlike previous monarchs, was unable to establish a new model for the flags due to the precarious state of Vienna's finances.[17] Almost all regiments kept the old flags, each with 15 Ordinärefahnen and a white Leibfahne, carried by the first battalion company (Colonel) of the regiment. The internal service of the flag now required even more precise tasks from the standard-bearer (*Fähnrich*): "*The standard-bearer had to carry the flag during parades, but the generalship also had the authority to entrust him with ordinance or company services. He was to be well-liked by all as a flag-bearer and was not to be mistreated by anyone, yet he had no right to punishments nor to a stick; he had only a thin whip with a silver handle.* The flag was also present at corporal punishments inflicted

(Heilige Johannes)   **altre immagini della S.S. Vergine Maria**

---

17   Summerfield, Stephen, *Austrian Infantry of the Seven Years War: Uniforms, Organisation and Equipment*, p. 154.

by sentences for acts that occurred in battle, in the procedure of the '*Ehrlichmachens*' (bringing back to the straight and narrow), where the condemned person presented himself to the flag, which was then withdrawn to the perimeter of a circle, formed to carry out the corporal punishment. The provost (*Profoß*) would take the condemned person to the square and put his hat in his mouth, so that he could crawl, using his hands and feet inside the circle, to the spot where the standard bearer with the flag stood; there, after taking three steps, he would pull the hat out, clenched between his teeth, and kneel down to receive the beating '*according to the will of God*'.

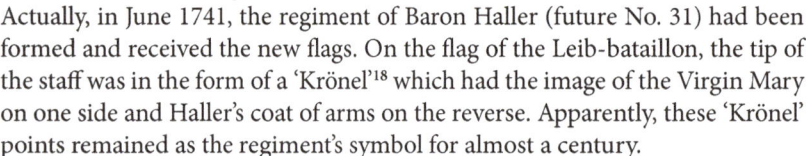

Leibfahne · Ordinärefahne
reggimento di fanteria ungherese

During the first year of the war, Maria Theresa managed to gather considerable support in Hungary: she had herself crowned on 25 June 1741 and, to reaffirm her iron will to rule, assumed the male titles of Archduke and Magyar King. Thus, after the coronation, six new Hungarian infantry regiments were formed; there were only two flags for each battalion, so that a regiment had eight, one white, the colonel, and seven others with a blue background. The same was ordered for the new regiments formed in the Austrian Netherlands.

Actually, in June 1741, the regiment of Baron Haller (future No. 31) had been formed and received the new flags. On the flag of the Leib-bataillon, the tip of the staff was in the form of a 'Krönel'[18] which had the image of the Virgin Mary on one side and Haller's coat of arms on the reverse. Apparently, these 'Krönel' points remained as the regiment's symbol for almost a century.

Ordinärefahne rossa

In early 1742, the manual of the '*Kriegs-Artikuln*' was drafted by Colonel Count Andrássy, owner of the regiment to be No. 33, in Munich during the occupation. The text was displayed in three languages, German, Hungarian and Bohemian, and described how the new flags were awarded and blessed to the regiment, in church, swearing in the sight of God perpetual loyalty "*to the Archduchess of Austria, Maria Theresa, Royal Sovereign of Hungary and Bohemia*", even though the King of Bohemia was momentarily another.

Ordinärefahne ungherese 1743

On 12 May 1743, Maria Theresa was finally crowned Queen of Bohemia in St Vitus Cathedral, thus bearing the rampant lion of Prague in her coat of arms. Particularly noteworthy was the production of new flags with a green field, decorated with gold and silver embroidery, ordered that year by Empress Maria Theresa and her illustrious husband Franz I, whose initials appeared on the flags together with the inscription:
"*Providend providet*!" (Provide, provide!)

According to Summerfield[19] after the election of Charles Albert of Wittelsbach (January 1742) as emperor of the Holy Roman Empire, Maria Theresa was forced to remove all imperial symbols, including all references to the imperial yellow-black colour. Therefore, on 19 October 1743, Maria Theresa ordered that German and Hungarian regiments should be equipped with white *Leibfahne* and green *Ordinärefahnen*. All Hungarian models, so-called of 1743, had alternating red and green flames on a white background as a border. The flagpole 3.16 metres - 3 metres 48 cm high (or 10-11 Viennese feet) was painted in an alternating spiral of green and red. Each infan-

Leibfahne · Ordinärefahne
reggimento di fanteria ungherese 1743

---

18   The Krönel was an ancient tool for cutting stone.
19   Summerfield, Stephen, *Austrian Infantry of the Seven Years War: Uniforms, Organisation and Equipment*, p. 159.

try regiment had a *Leibfahne* and 15 *Ordinäre* or *Compagniefahnen* (a total of 16 banners). The flags measured approximately 190 cm (5 feet 6 inches), according to other sources 170 cm x 120 cm. Summerfield also concludes by stating that regiments continued to use the old flags where possible and that the new rules on colours were largely disregarded.

The *Leibfahne of* 1743: it was white with the Madonna and Child surrounded by sun rays in an oval on both sides or on one side only, with the coats of arms of Hungary and Bohemia on the reverse. At the feet of the Madonna were the coats of arms of Bohemia and Hungary and a small shield of Austria with the initials M and T on the white band. The borders alternated green, white and red 'flames'.

The *Compagniefahne of* 1743 (*Ordinärefahne*) was grass green, bordered with alternating red-white-green 'flames'. In the centre was the 'minor' coat of arms of Maria Theresa (coats of arms of Bohemia, Hungary, Old Burgundy and Tyrol) surmounted

Leibfahne (varianti fronte e retro)

Ordinärefahne (varianti fronte e retro)

by a royal crown. In the centre was a small shield of Austria with the archducal crown. On the sides of the coat of arms were the monograms of the sovereigns: M and T for Maria Theresa and C and F for Co-regent Franz (Corregens Franciscus).

The official ceremony of handing over the flag was a particularly solemn event: '*Here, Mr. Ensign, I award you the flag, which shall be under your custody and life*'!

In 1745 the death of Charles Albert of Bavaria made the imperial throne vacant and, despite some French successes in the Austrian Netherlands, on 13 September the German princes elected Franz Stephan as emperor; Frederick II accepted the proclamation after Maria Theresa acknowledged the loss of Silesia in December 1745. Also due to financial crises in 1745, it was ordered to use the old flags as long as they were in good condition. The Hofkriegsrat, in January, pointed out that in some flags the regimental coat of arms no longer corresponded to the new owners and that old flags were still in use.

All flags of 1743 modelled on the Hungarian flags, which were green in colour, 170 cm long and 120 cm wide, adopted due to the election of the Bavarian Elector Charles VII as German Emperor, and which had the dynastic coats of arms of the crowns of Hungary, Bohemia, Burgundy and Tyrol, were abolished with the election of Franz I as Emperor of the Holy Roman Empire. All flags will be renewed, reverting to the old German model.

Flags after 1745

On 13 September 1745, Franz I of Lorraine, Maria Theresa's consort, was thus elected Kaiser of the Holy Roman Empire. All imperial insignia and colours could therefore be used again. On 22 December 1745, Maria Theresa introduced a new white *Leibfahne* and yellow *Ordinärefahnen*.

Each regiment had a flag for each company (1 *Leibfahne*, 15 *Ordinärefahnen* / *Compagniefahnen*). The regulations of 1743 were repealed. Some colonel-owners, particularly introduced at court and friends of the Sovereign or Consort, were allowed to gloss over the new regulations. Each infantry regiment had a new flag for the regimental baggage train (a Rule of 1749, 174, allowed wives and children to be part of the baggage train). The banner had no border, it was a monochrome cloth, of the regiment's distinctive colour, measuring approximately 179 cm x 127 cm.

The new flag model had borders 15.6 cm (6 Zoll) wide. The cloths were silk and hand-painted, measured 178 cm x 127 cm and had a staff of 261 cm (8 feet 3 inches). The brass tip had on one side the initials 'MT' and on the reverse side 'FCIM' (Corregens Franciscus Imperator Magnus). The wooden shaft had a painted striped ornament.

The *Leibfahne* of 1745 had a white border with alternating yellow and white 'flames' with the tip at the top and red and black with the tip at the bottom. The order of this decoration varied with regiments and sometimes with battalions.

The reverse (left) had the *Doppeladler* or black imperial double-headed eagle with the uniform of Maria Theresa (coats of arms of Austria, Hungary and Bohemia) or the imperial one in which the eagle had a silver sword on the right and a blue globe on the left, together with the shields of Lorraine and Tuscany. In that case the initials were not Me T but CF (Franciscus Corregens) on the left and 'IM' (Imperator Magnus) on the right.

Leibfahne - 1745

Compagniefahne - 1745

The side to the casement had Our Lady above a sky-blue or pearly white cloud, stepping on a serpent and surrounded by a golden ray. Her mantle was blue. It was Emperor Ferdinand III who made the Blessed Virgin official as Patroness of the army. Some regiments had her image on both sides of the flag.

In 1746, to celebrate their good behaviour at the Battle of Rocoux (it seems they had resisted in severe numerical inferiority), Prince von Ahrenberg had the honour of adding the following uniform to the Leibfahne of his regiment (future No. 12), on a band of the flag: '*un contre six*'.

The *Ordinärefahne* (*Compagniefahne*) of 1745 was Empire yellow with a border similar to that of the *Leibfahne*. The measurements of the flag were identical: 179 cm by 127 cm. The most common model bore the imperial eagle with the initials CF and IM on the obverse and the double-headed eagle of Maria Theresa, the reigns of Hungary and Bohemia and the initials MT on the reverse.

In many heraldic variants, Maria Theresa's double-headed eagle was without sword and sceptre, in reverence to her more important consort, whose double-headed eagle had the sword and sceptre instead of the Habsburg globe. In any case, history has always reminded us who ruled the country in those years.

At that time, the most common oath to the flag among regiments was this:

"*We promise and swear, to the most famous, most powerful, greatest and unsurpassable Lord, His Lordship Francis, elected Emperor of the Romans, of the Empire of all different times, in Germany and Jerusalem, King, Archduke of Lorraine and Bar, Grand Duke of Tuscany and also of the "hereditary kingdoms and countries of Austria and co-ruler of the Lands", and of the greatest and most powerful Princess and Lordship Maria Theresa, Empress of Rome, Queen also of Hungary and Bohemia, Archduchess of Austria etc. ...*"

In 1747, a regulation drafted by Count F.W. Esterházy, like all other regulations of the time, expressed an unmistakable offensive spirit. Particularly in the chapter 'Of Battles', this spirit was strongly manifested by stating: "*from the moment that one must advance, one will do so with rifles on one's shoulders, flags unfurled in the wind and sound music, very slowly and with a resolute manner, marching with a constant front.*"

From 1748, the number of flags fell from 16 to 8, effectively halving. At that time, each infantry regiment had 2 grenadier companies and 16 rifle companies divided into four battalions (each carrying two flags). The first battalion continued to carry the *Leibfahne* plus an *Ordinärefahne*, while battalions II-III and IV carried two *Ordinärefahnen* each. In peacetime the flags were one per battalion, with the *Leibfahne* always going to the first battalion or colonel's battalion (*Obristbataillon*).

THE IMPERIAL UNIFORM

There are few sources of useful information on uniforms from the period of the War of Austrian Succession, some collected at the *Heeresgeschichtliches Museum* in Vienna or the Albertina Museum also in Vienna. These sources have already been extensively consulted and examined by numerous scholars of uniformology.

The period of the Seven Years' War, on the other hand, is extensively documented, starting with the writings of Pengel and Hurt and Summerfield. That is why you will find the subject very well covered on the Kronoskaf website, which also has a section devoted to the War of the Spanish Succession.

http://www.kronoskaf.com/syw/index.php?title=Austrian_Army

Another interesting site I would like to point out is:

http://nigbilpainter.blogspot.com/2010/10/austrian-infantry-uniform-differences.html

For sources, we can say that Morier's collection of paintings from 1748 (in the Austrian royal collection) are accurate and believed to be the only official source of images from the period 1740-48. Scholars agree that there were not many changes until 1756. The change to white for robes, corsets and breeches occurred after the War of the Austrian Succession and probably before the outbreak of the Seven Years' War. As can also be seen from reading regimental histories, many commanders reacted very calmly to any instructions from the Vienna Hofkriegsrat, out of a desire to limit expenditure. The rule seemed to be to ignore Vienna, which was no exception. The Seven Years' War, with the contribution of a much more frequent, centralised and organised turnover, ended up changing things, within two or three years, more than in the eight years between the War of Succession and the Seven Years' War.

An observation made by Pengel and Hurt also supports the thesis:

"*In spite of the subsequent regulations issued, there is a definite possibility that some regiments retained the old coloured jackets and robes, which they had previously worn, at least until the 1760s, when the regulations on uniforms became, in fact, stricter. One can, therefore, assume that in the early stages of the Seven Years' War, the old uniforms were seen on the battlefields. The assumption is based on the fact that, in many regiments, the drums kept their coloured jackets for a long time, some even up to 1762.*' In general, the opinion is in line with what can be deduced from the historiography of the 19th century, where the precarious state of the Austrian treasury finances and thus the desirability of using uniforms for as long as possible is always emphasised.

The image of the warrior at the turn of the century had changed. The three-pointed hat (tricorn) became ubiquitous, gradually also in Austria; only the hussars and some Hungarian regiments wore the national headgear, while cuirassiers and dragoons went to war against the Turks still, exceptionally, with the *Zischäge* (typical 17th century iron helmets). The grenadiers began to wear high headgear made of bear hair, with a front plate, different from the pointed, tin plates of the Prussian, British and Russian grenadiers. Long hair was tied back, sometimes even put in a net or hair bag. The jacket became shorter and shorter, but with long, wide sleeves, the sleeveless waistcoat (*Leibel*) became a permanent infantry garment, usually visible and worn with an open jacket. Trousers were tighter, with gaiters often rising above the knee and held in place below the knee by a garter belt, often with a buckle. German type shoes were fastened with a large buckle, Hungarian ones had laces. The owners had a wide margin for manoeuvre in terms of the colour and cut of the uniforms.

By the end of the Seven Years' War (1756-63), the appearance of the Austrian infantry was, for the most part, standardised and similar to what we know from the Napoleonic era - the white *Rock*, with coloured lapels and cuffs. This simple and elegant uniform, however, had been preceded by much more varied and colourful uniforms during the earlier War of Austrian Succession (1740-48). Emperor Charles VI's ordinances of 1720 had only stipulated the fabric and composition of the soldiers' livery, but not its colour - white jackets were traditional, but not formally prescribed - in 1737 it was stipulated that: "*...the imperial regiments on foot were to be clothed in a jacket of good pearl-white cloth* (*Weißperlfarbe*), *retaining the old measurements in length and breadth, and made so that the troop could cover themselves and the weapon, without the need of a coat or cloak* (*Mantel*)."

Lapels, shirts and trousers, on the other hand, could be of the colour ordered by the colonel, however the lapels had to be made uniformly, in the old fashioned way, with three buttons and as many buttonholes, in order to be able to shelter the hands from the cold and rain; "*by which we are led to believe that the type of uniform, so short and narrow, adopted in some regiments, in imitation of foreign troops, may cause the soldier and his weapon, in consequence of the slightest explosion, or in case of rain, an exaggerated exposure without sufficient shelter, and that the new uniform is more suitable, completely suitable, and respectively better*."

Thus, in 1739, the 'Uniform Jacket' or *Uniform Rock*, with folded and sewn hems, was finally standardised.

Also changing was the sourcing of materials and, in particular, the variety of fabrics for uniforms, hitherto influenced by the fact that regiments often purchased fabrics from England and Holland. The Moravian and Bohemian industries were already then equal to foreign ones, and, in particular, 'Iglauer' cloth (from the Iglau weaving mills) was recommended as particularly waterproof and durable.

In fact, it seems that the grenadiers had a *Uniform Rock* as early as 1735, when the lapels of the jacket were folded and sewn together. The uniform was originally double, the robe that was in contact with the body (*Leibel, Camisol, Leibrock, Gilet, Jacke*) and the *Caputrock the actual Oberkleid* or surcoat (vest or *Rock , Röckel* etc.) covered it; in generic language they were therefore divided into "waistcoat or bodice" (*Leibrock*) and main vest (*Caputrock*). In the second half of the 18th century, a third protective garment, the grey cape, was created to protect the soldier from the weather, which was already present in earlier years.

Infantry regiments were to be armed, according to the regulations of 1737, with muskets or pistols of 26 g calibre (weighing 1 ½ Löth) and with senior and staff officers of the Ordinary companies (not the grenadiers) armed with partisans, while the bannermen had lances (*Springstöck*). At the beginning of the 18th century, when the wooden cartridges hanging from the bandoleer were replaced by paper cartridges, the cartridge case (*Patronentasche*) was rather large, made of plain leather, narrow and had a cover of sole or ordinary leather. This always had to be black, with the regimental owner's coat of arms mirrored on it. Tools for cleaning the musket were also kept in the bag. It was hung from a wide strap coming down from the left shoulder, on the right hip (until 1747) to compensate for the pack resting on the left hip; in case of rain it had to be protected under the *Caputrock*.

It was 1735, then, the year in which the majority of the infantry changed the colour of their vests from pearl grey to a military white - the vest itself became more close-fitting, with lapels turned upside down and sewn on or held in place by ornate clasps. The turned-up collar was either absent or barely noticeable, but lapels (*Rabatten*) with buttons appeared in the centre of the chest and the jacket generally had nine buttons, each at the end of three plus three free loops; this system allowed the jacket to be turned upside down, doubling the protection and protecting the weapon in the event of intense cold or bad weather. The Hungarian infantry had a *Caputrock-like* cut, with Magyar national characters and ornaments. They received the white jacket only from 26 April 1749, but the garments remained separate; the robe and trousers were of a different colour, mostly blue. The cuffs, known as hand guards, were made in the old fashioned way, with three buttons and as many loops so that they could be turned over to cover the hands, perhaps even the mechanics of the musket, sheltering it in cold and rainy weather. The infantryman's equipment was as follows a jacket (*Rock*), an underjacket (*Camisol*), a pair of trousers, several German and Hungarian regimentals, a tricorn headgear (high bear hair cap for grenadiers - *Bärenmütze*), two neckbands, two shirts, a pair of socks, a pair of shoes, a cartridge bag with its equipment (oiling vials cleaning needle or pointed iron wire for cleaning the trigger holes of muskets, powder horn and brush), the bayonet together with its hooks, the backpack (*Tornister*) made of calfskin or *Zwilch* (a very dense fabric made from flax or hemp) - sometimes also called a sack (*Schnappsack*) or bag (*Ranzen*). The backpack was covered with calfskin only on the flap closure, and existed in the infantry as early as 1700; it was a canvas-lined sack, longer than wide, with a flap lid. According to the 1747 regulations, it was tied with two straps, and had three containers, one for bread and provisions, one for linen, the third for tools and brushes. A wide strap held it down from the right shoulder to the left hip.

As there were no collars, military regulations and ordinances from the end of the 17th century prescribed red collar bands (*Halsbinden - Halstücher*) for the German infantry and cavalry and, from 1741, also *red* "*Turkish cloth* bands *for the* newly formed *Hungarian infantry*". The Esterházy regulations of 1747, mentioned the red collar, to be worn during parades and also a black one, worn on duty, reprimanding the custom of wearing it over the robe. Collar and buckle were to be, if at all, attached to the shirt under the robe.

The trousers were covered by long socks (in the future by gaiters), there were black and red ones. Since the shoes covered the instep, the sock (or gaiter) had to protect it. In the beginning, the shoes did not have right and left feet; both pieces of the pair were the same and the soldier had to change shoes every day, from the right to the left foot. Hungarian shoes were originally open and laced at the instep, a tongue covered the slit of the string holes and the shoes reached down to the ankles. According to the Esterházy regulation of 1727, the shoe had to last one year and six months - a sole, thick and solid, at least eight weeks.

In 1739, in addition to the riflemen, the *Uniform Rock* was also assigned to the Dragoons; it was quite long with folded and sewn lapels. The Dragoons of the Khevenhüller regiment wore the tricorn, rainproof, with a silver braid, a red jacket with hand guards and blue lining, a shoulder cord, a blue robe and blue trousers. They also had a white cloth cloak with a red collar and red lining, a pointed Pallasch, boots with spurs, which should be made of genuine Russian-tanned leather; muskets and pistols[20].

The cuirassiers and dragoons wore the black felt tricorne (until 1720 the cuirassiers wore an iron headdress with a defence on the nape of the neck and one on the nose - *Nasenfeder*), they had a white 'horse' cape with coloured distinctions, their vest went down to their knees. The dragoons had red, green or blue jackets with distinctions of other colours for the hand guards and buttonhole laces, a white or blue robe, a white or black neck band, red trousers like the cuirassiers. All wore protective gloves. Carabinieri and grenadiers on horseback usually wore gaiters and light boots, grenadiers wore bear hair caps and on the plate the symbol of a burning grenade. The carabinieri and grenadiers could also be hairstyled in a more ostentatious manner; this depended on the coffers of the colonel who owned them.

From the 1700s, German cavalry boots were heavy, tubular boots (*Kappe*) made of double leather, lined with canvas on the inside (*Faschine*) and ending in a forefoot with a heavy sole. At the instep stood a buckled binding that held the spurs (*Anschnallsporen*). The lightness of the boots increased very little over the years, in 1740 the boots still looked similar, although the wide, flared part above the knee was now much reduced. The hussars wore boots made of leather, naturally tanned yellow, light, adapted to the foot, called *Czismén*. The body extended to the lower half of the leg, having a front leather tongue higher than the back edge; only from 1754 did the *Czismén* become black.

The cavalry had the rolled sack (*Mantelsack*) instead of the knapsack. It remained virtually unchanged throughout the period from 1700 to 1867; it had a cylindrical shape and was 65-75 cm long, with a diameter (when filled) of 25 cm. At both ends it had two fabric discs, approximately 17-18 cm in length. On the upper side, the *Mantelsack,* which was sewn on both sides, had a slit about 45 cm long, which could be closed by a drawstring and covered with a zipped cloth, with 7 cloth-covered buttons or sometimes even buckles for closure. The sack was made of cloth of a specific colour for each type of weapon, and especially for each regiment, and lined with linen cloth. It was mounted on the saddle with three straps (*Mantelsackanschnallriemen*) according to the desired position, generally almost always behind the rider.

The hair, which until then had been loose on the shoulders, was tied back in a braid. Moustaches began to conform to the habits of the past. when they first appeared in 1705 among the grenadiers of the Wallis Regiment and in 1722 also among the riflemen of the Browne Regiment. They had the form described in a 'Manual' (sic, in Italian) of 1735. They were then passed on to the cavalry and riflemen in accordance with the 1739 drawings in Khevenhüller's *Observationspuncte*.

Equipped with such equipment and clothing, the recruits were presented to the war commissioners for absento[21] (enlistment). The costs were between 17.5 and 18.5 florins, and were included in the recruitment penny. The officers' uniforms were made of the same sturdy fabric while bearing gold embroidery. Among them they were distinguished by the different types of staffs, the different types of partigiana and the typical gold-black silk sash a waist. Note that, from 1743 to 1745, the sashes or sashes (*Schärpen*) worn at the waist were grass-green or *grassgrühn* in colour.

---

20   Khevenhüller, *Observationspuncte*, 2 vol, pag. 176 e s.
21   *Absento* was a voice borrowed from the Spanish Habsburg period, as in Spain it denoted a kind of contract made between a state and a private individual or company of private individuals, who undertook, for a fee, to keep a certain number of ships permanently ready for war purposes. In the Austrian army it became synonymous with a contract of enlistment with the regiment (or, rather, with a successful recruitment - *Werbung* - after fitness examinations) .

The uniforms of the new Hungarian regiments of 1741 and the Military Boundary

The new Hungarian regiments adopted the national costume in 1741. In practice, they were dressed 'Hussar-style' with national garments: *dolman* with frogs' wings, Hungarian trousers of blue cloth decorated with yellow laces, two Hungarian shirts and underwear. On their heads the troop wore felt hats, on which, during parades and in battle, an oak or fir twig was always placed (autumn-winter). The weapon was a rifle with flintlock percussion and wooden (later iron) ramrod, they had a Hungarian sabre, carried in a holster. The leather cartridge case was held by a wide strap, white or yellow, which went down from the left shoulder to the opposite side; the powder horn was attached to the cartridge case, in front with a strap. The *Patronentasche* contained 40 cartridges with their corresponding balls.

The officers' uniform was similar in colour and cut to that of the troop, but was more richly decorated with gold frogs, studs and silver buttons (depending on the regiment). As headgear, officers were provided with a felt tricorn with a wide gold border and cockade. Officers and troops wore white wigs, braided and with a final braid, and a wide curl at the temples. From the colonel downwards, all senior and staff officers, with the exception of the Obristwachtmeister and the Ensigns, wore muskets, and German partisans.

The future No. 2 regiment, at the time Ujvári, was equipped with the following uniforms. The officers wore a *Czako* edged in gold, with a gold plaque depicting the Hungarian crown, a short white *pelisse*, lined in black and imperial yellow, with gold frogs and yellow buttons, a blue *Dolman,* sometimes with gold frogs and white (or yellow) buttons, blue Hungarian trousers adorned with gold fringes and studs, Hungarian boots (*Czismen*), below the knee long and of yellow leather, and, on the leg, a yellow band with gold buttons. As early as 1744, the officers' distinctions were abandoned in the manner described here: "For the *whole troop the dominant colour was green, so the officers' sashes also became grass-green in colour, sometimes enriched with golden or yellow scales, as their rank as officers permitted.*" As a weapon the officers had a Hungarian sabre, with a yellow hilt and golden ornaments; from these hung a holster finished in gold.

With the exception of the *Obristwachtmeisters* and *Fähnrichs,* each officer had a brass-finished flintlock rifle with a set bayonet and a cartridge box that had a gold plaque with the Hungarian crown. The troop, from the *Feldwebel* downwards, wore felt, black, visorless colbaks, a long white Hungarian cape, a dark blue dolman with brass buttons, blue Hungarian trousers with yellow stripes, shoes with laces and a yellow belt with blue buttons. Their weapons were a curved sabre with a yellow leather holster with black trim (the golden hilt was worn over the *dolman*). They had a flintlock musket, which in soldiers of average height came up to eye level, including bayonet and with wooden batons. The ammunition consisted of 40 cartridges with 26 g balls (1 ½ Löth), they kept the powder in a powder horn, attached with a strap to the cartridge box. These, made of yellow leather, hung on the right, while on the left was a calfskin backpack, the yellow straps mentioned above crossed over the soldier's chest.

The uniform of the Hungarian infantry, which had started the war with national costumes, changed in 1748, becoming more similar to that of 'German' troops. This is, for example, what happened to the aforementioned Ujváry regiment. (The change of infantry uniforms would not actually become official until autumn 1751 with the issue of the first *Adjustierung-Vorschrift).* In it was stipulated that the officers were to dress like the troop, with the same fabrics and keeping the felt tricorns, which had already been in place since 1744. Instead of the Hungarian *Oberkleid* (*Pelz*), the infantry were given white jackets with gold buttons on two-finger wide frogs and gold buttonholes. Instead of the *Dolman they had a* blue robe with worked braids running through it. The *Csiszmén* were replaced by shoes with laces and gaiters, the trousers remained unchanged. As mentioned, the clothing of the troop remained the same except for the colbac, which was initially retained (the use of the tricorn for the troop seems to have been introduced later, although many illustrations relating to 1748 show it. In reality, not all regiments had identical changes in dress). The non-commissioned officers also obtained partisans, as well as muskets with iron batons, model 1744.

The matter becomes even more complex when talking about the border troops: the *Grenzer*. Always used to keep their national costumes, with the establishment of the first regiments the uniforms gradually changed their appearance, becoming, in fact, uniforms. Regarding the *Grenzer*, from the years 1740-1748, we have some pictures of paintings by Martin Engelbrecht and one, in particular, in Trakošćan castle, in the former territory of the Szluin regiment, dated 1749/1750.

The uniform of the border soldiers was extremely varied, both in cut and colour. The only thing they had in common was the headgear, the "*Klobuk*", made of felt, in the shape of a blunt cone, which was the same style for all. There was a serious problem within the military border. The *Grenzers* were obliged to dress at their own expense, so it was difficult to convince them to give up their colourful costumes. The borderers were strongly averse to all innovations in clothing and equipment, because they increased their expenses. For this reason, starting with von der Trenck's colourful Panduri, uniformity in uniformity was not achieved for many years. Only when the field uniform (*Feldmontur*) provided by the treasury prevailed could uniformity in clothing be achieved. The *Grenzers* had, with the formation of the regiments, two kinds of uniforms, named by the purpose for which they served. For service inside the Borders they had the so-called territorial uniform (*Hausmontur*), paid for by themselves, while, for use outside the Borders (in the event of war), they were provided with exchequer uniforms (the aforementioned *Feldmontur*) kept in depots (it is unclear whether these uniforms delivered in the countryside were made of white fabric as for the infantry).

From the research of Prof. Vladimir Brnardić we learnt that the new Bano regiments, (*Banalisten*) formed after the period under review, as the 1st and 2nd regiments, had their first real *Grenzer* uniform in June-July 1750, when they were summoned for exercises in Ptuj (today in Slovenia) together with 5 other regular infantry regiments: Hoch-und Teutschmeister (Viennese), Forgacs, Molck, Kheul and Hildburghausen. This was quite logical, as the two regiments were entirely new, as new were the administrative divisions into which they recruited. The *Grenzers* hoped to have finally solved the long-standing problem of the uniform being free of charge, with the cost being borne by the treasury, but this was not to be. Paying for the uniform had always been a major headache for the Border Infantry, a territory where not much money circulated, due to a predominantly agricultural economy with relatively little purchasing power of the population. There was yet another serious rebellion, in 1754, when Maria Theresa announced that she would visit Croatia and the Military Border in the following year. It all originated at the Generalate in Varazdin, where it was deemed right to have new uniforms for the imperial visit, the cost of which would be charged to the military themselves. The latter, however, felt that they were still presentable in their old uniforms from a few years earlier and did not want to shell out money for new uniforms. So a rebellion broke out and a few officers were killed. After the inevitable crackdown, a special commission of enquiry was set up to investigate the facts and to set a basic uniform cost. Unfortunately, until 1769, when uniforms similar to those of the regular infantry were introduced, unease reigned among the soldiers of the Border and uniform confusion (often borrowed from Insurrectio models) continued.

Distinctive colours

The distinctive colours (abbreviated to 'badges') that became typical for a given soldier's membership of a certain corps or regiment were a purely accidental thing, derived from 17th century customs. The so-called hand guards were simply comfortable long sleeves of the jacket that, in hot weather, were turned inside out so that the colour of the inner lining could be seen. By the end of the 17th century, it became evident that some colonel-owners required different coloured linings for the various companies in their regiment, and later requested a simplification by indicating a single lining colour for their unit. In 1666, the Austrian Empire prescribed that the knight and infantryman should have the same linings, but by 1683 individual regiments with different coloured linings were already appearing. By 1708, it seemed that the main arms of the army had become accustomed to different coloured distinctions, but still in 1751, in a phrasebook on army colours, there was no mention of collars and breastplates, but only of '*Doubleurs*' or *Rabatten*, a word meaning lining. It was not until 1767 that the first table of Habsburg colours of distinction officially emerged; until then, regiments had arbitrarily determined the inner lining of their jackets (*Rock*). There were also some curious cases such as the blue linings of the white armour jackets of the cuirassiers, when all their regiments had red Boy linings[22]. Stockings of different colours and garters were used as distinguishing marks for the comrades until the introduction of gaiters, or distinguishing marks were limited to cockades on tricorns and pom-poms. As a matter of principle, however, it was almost always assumed in Austria that the distinction of companies was unnecessary and that therefore, in contrast to the German and Russian armies, distinctions (*Aufschlag*), collars (*Kragen*), lapels (*Rabatten*) (the two inverted breast flaps), and jacket bottom flaps (*Revers*) or jacket tail edges

---

22   Boy was a light, hard-woven, pressed flannel-like fabric, usually red, woven in England, Germany, and France. In the case of the blue regiment, it is likely to think of an Auszeichnung i.e., a "merit" grant commemorating the regiment of a famous 17th-century Field Marshal.

(*Frackschosseinfassungen*) were all of the same colour - the colour of the regiment. Considering that many infantry regiments in the mid-century had white jacket tails, it almost suggests that, to save money on uniforms, only the upper parts of the jacket were lined in Iglauer fabric.

To be precise, not only the colours were taken into account, but above all the shape of the badges, which, conventionally, the military costume divided into three types: the Swedish or German badge, straight and parallel to the line of the forearm; the Polish or Hungarian badge, of a different width, narrower towards the hand, typical of the costumes of those nations; and finally the Brandenburg badge, with a shape very similar to the German or Polish model, but with a flap - in Germany often of a different colour - called *Patte*. This *Patte* was nothing more than the remnant of the old protective flap on the cuff. In the Hungarian infantry, by ancient tradition, that flap had taken the form of a lace, which was fastened by a button to the cuff.

The distinctive colours of the Austrian regiments (especially the hand guards, which were turned upside down and unbuttoned to protect the hands from the cold and rain, the breast flaps or *Rabatten*, which were also unbuttoned and turned upside down to protect the musket from the rain, and the lapels at the bottom of the jacket) presented quite a few problems, considering their shades. We know that the basic colours to match the ivory white of the jacket (after the pearl-grey period at the beginning of the century) were red and blue, with only two infantry regiments sporting distinct greens. According to Bleckwenn there were basically three shades of blue at the beginning: light blue also called sky blue or *Lichtblau*, *Himmelsblau* was the blue, which we would later call azure, also called *Bleumorant,* in the French manner, and finally dark blue or *Dunkelblau*. Light blue or *Lichtblau* is documented for the Baden-Durlach regiment (future 27) at the Battle of Prague, where General Schwerin was killed in front of that regiment, identified by the light blue hand guards.

Although Bleckwenn is sure that Austria had only one shade of red, uniformly of the 'madder red' or *Krapproth* type, we know that there were a few rare shades of bright red (*Scharlach*) an aurora red and dark red (*Dunkelroth*). The uniforms that have come down to us in museum collections, prints and paintings often present completely unprepossessing shades, due to deterioration over time.

Other oddities come in much later times. One witnesses the fact that the de Ligne Regiment (future 38) in 1762 wore pink gaiters, and notes this while parading in Schweidnitz. Others testify that an officer, who died, of that regiment wore pink breeches, half-leg boots, and a pink 'Soubise' (ornamental flat braid). So either they were discoloured paintings or they were non-standard uniforms. Bleckwenn, in fact, gave Seven Years' War infantry the option of wearing long black or red gaiters, both common and regulation.

Armament

Literature, in the past, has not dealt much with portable weapons in the 18th century. In fact, technological and scientific advances began to take hold around the second half of the 1700s (although still scarcely). What could be improved was more a refinement of individual parts.

The imperial army entered the 18th century armed, still, unevenly; in general, the fuse musket, proposed by Lieutenant-Colonel Franzen in 1657 according to the Dutch model and produced in Wiener-Neustadt, still prevailed. However, as this 'firearms factory' could only supply a relatively small number of muskets, carbines and pistols, the regiment's owners were allowed to purchase weapons directly, at least until 1744 (1750).

Flintlock muskets, known as '*Flinte*', already existed in Montecuccoli's time; this general had equipped his regiment with 2,000 rifles which, in addition to fuse ignition, also had a flintlock, the latter, it seems, to be used only for night actions, where the glittering fuses would easily betray the soldiers' presence. Mass production, however, did not begin until 1699, in Switzerland, after weapons colonel Karl Ernst Graf von Rappach procured a model rifle and delivered it to rifle manufacturers. The factories were mainly the 'Wiener -Neustädter Armatur-Gewerkschaft', the 'Benedict Schöffler', the 'Entzinger zu Entzingen' and 'Anton Penzeneter' in Hainfeld and Steyr.The weapon that dominated the scene, therefore, was the flintlock musket with bayonet. The army's first stone muskets were assigned to the 12, 14, 15, 16, 29, 41 and 51 infantry regiments. They were of calibre 18.8 and 21 balls, together barely weighing a Viennese pound. The musket was shorter than the fuse musket by a palm length, had no rings, but the barrel was fixed to the shaft with chains, and there were three slots for the ramrod. The rods were made of wood.

Iron rods, which had already been prescribed for musketeers in Austria in 1426, had been replaced by wooden rods, and were only reintroduced by Royal Resolution of 5 December 1744; not, as one usually reads, after the

Colori distintivi dell'armata austriaca XVIII secolo
1740 - 1790

- **Dunkelrot** - Dark red - rosso scuro
- **Krapprot** - Madder red - Rosso robbia
- **Scharlachrot** - (Ponceau) Scarlet - Rosso
- **Rosenrot** - Rose red - Rosa antico
- **Schwefelgelb** - Sulphur yellow - zolfo
- **Lichtblau** - Bright blue - celeste
- **Himmelblau** - Sky blue - azzurro
- **Dunkelblau** - dark blue - Blu
- **Grassgrün** - Grass green - verde erba
- **Weiß** - White - Bianco
- **Schwarz** - Black - Nero

Colori accessori dell'armata austriaca a fine secolo

- **Kirschrot** - Cherry red - Granata
- **Amarantrot** - Amerante red - Rosso amaranto
- **Blaßrot** - (Gris-de-lin) Pink - Rosa
- **Krebsrot** - Crab red - Aragosta
- **Carmoisinrot** - Crimson - Cremisi
- **Rotbraun** - Terra cotta - Mattone
- **Bordeauxrot** - Claret - Bordeaux
- **Dunkelbraun** - Dark brown - Marrone
- **Lichtdrap** - (Lichtbraun) Hazel - Nocciola
- **Orangegelb** - Orange - arancione
- **Kaisersgelb** - Imperial yellow - giallo impero
- **Stahlgrün** - Steel green - verde acciaio
- **Apfelgrün** - Apple green - verde mela
- **Paperlgrün** - Poplar green - verde pappagallo
- **Meergrassgrün** - Sea grass green - alga
- **Meergrün** - Sea green - acquamarina
- **Hechtgrau** - Pike grey - grigio metallo
- **Aschgrau** - Feldgrau grey - grigio cenere

battle of Czaslau (1742 - Chotusitz). The wooden batons had the bad habit of breaking, especially in the most chaotic battles, leaving the soldier defenceless, only with bayonet and sabre.

The year 1722 was epoch-making for the armament of the Austrian army; on 16 May the application for a uniform armament was submitted. *The Oberst Land- und Hauszeugmeister* (colonel of the central arsenal, curtense rank of artillery) Field Marshal Count Wirich Daun (father of the victor of Kolin) had 4000 rifles produced at the famous weapons master Hans Spangenberg, of Suhler, which were to be copied from the French M.1717 rifle, with the difference of having beech wood instead of walnut wood: the famous *Ordinäre Flinte* mod. 1722. This 'ordinary rifle' was imitated throughout the country and became the common weapon of the Austrian infantry until 1754. Its calibre was 18.3 g (*anderthalblöthig*, 1 ½ Löth or the weight of a ball) according to the Vienna weight (to be noted as some manufacturers used the Nuremberg weight, which was different). Furthermore, the ordinary rifle M1722, was similar to the 1657 rifle, only it had a so-called round flintlock: i.e. the large castle plate was curved, in contrast to the future flat plate of 1748; the hammer had a so-called snake-neck shape. It weighed 4.8 kg and was 157 cm long, costing 3-15-5-50 florins, depending on the manufacturer.

In 1745, the Commissioner for War Accounts and Artillery Innovations, Johann Schmied, presented a new rifle which, after three years of painstaking testing, was adopted on 11 March and 8 April 1748 'for *useful and constant use*'. It was similar to the rifle of 1722, but had three rings, the middle one a round strap, at the bottom

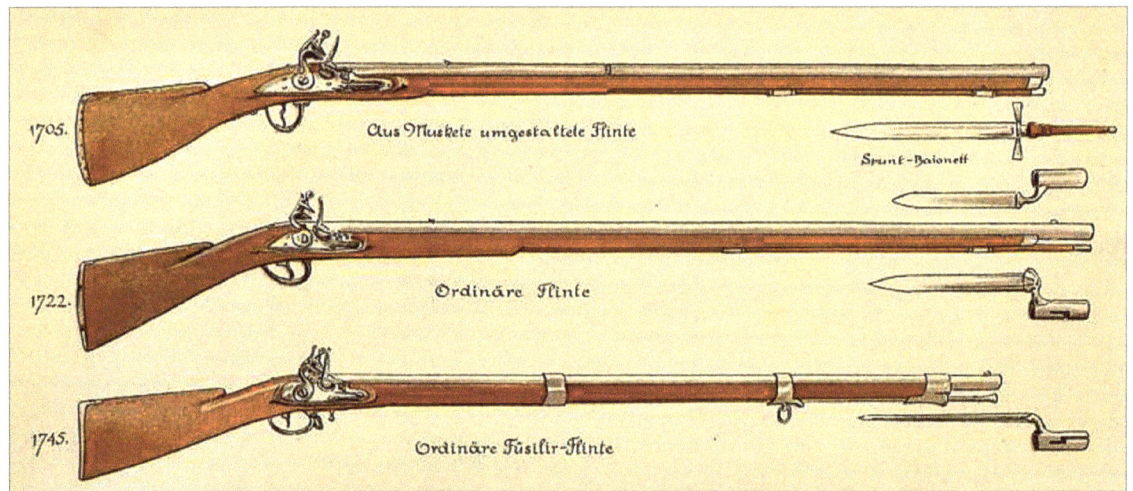

a spring to hold the iron rod. The flat flintlock clasp and had a snake-neck hammer. Every year, six regiments were to be armed with these new rifles. Prince Liechtenstein's reforms led to new models of the Schmied musket, until the 1754 model was adopted. That old model variously called the 'old type musket', 'cylindrical musket' or 'rural people's rifle' remained in service, used to arm second-line formations or militias.

The dominant white weapon was definitely the bayonet of the flintlock musket (*Steinschloß=Bajonett*). The shape of the muskets of the various armies were largely similar, thus the so-called 'swan-neck' bayonets for the attachment to the barrel of the musket.

The length of the bayonet, without primer, was 48 cm, had three cutting surfaces and was hollow. Initially, the bayonet was not very popular. In fact, many years elapsed before the Swedes and Prussians proved that it was possible to use the bayonet-holstered musket. Then in 1740, Austrian sceptics adopted the bayonet as a secondary or 'flanking' weapon (*Seitengewehr*). At the time, moreover, Austrian infantry tactics combined the use of the bayonet with that of the short sabre, i.e., when attacking with the bayonet, the third ranks, on either side, charged with the sabre, in order to catch the enemy in the flank. After 1722, the old mount was abandoned in favour of using the rectangular outer mount, which was attached to the barrel. The blade was still shaped like a knife, but from 1748, all imperial infantry and dragoons adopted the triangular blade of the 30-40 cm long French bayonets (the dragoons had longer bayonets but abandoned them in 1769).

When it was decided that the regiments were to be equipped with 1 ½ Viennese Löth calibre muskets (approx. 18.3 mm) of the Flinte M 1722 model; there was also an Ordinance that the staff officers and superiors of the *Ordinary* Companies (*Ordinari-Compagnien*, not grenadiers) were to carry Partisans.

The introduction, at that time, of ready-made cartridges greatly increased the loading speed and thus the importance of the gunfight. The shooter no longer needed to put the balls in his mouth, pour the powder from the powder horn, take the cap from the brim of the hat and then introduce the ball. The cartridge was torn off and the paper was pressed at the same time as the bullet.

What we call cartridges today were not made of paper, but of pig gut. Then they were made of thick paper (hence the name cartridge) and in both cases the ball was fixed at the bottom. The priming powder, which was still necessary, was placed either above or below the ball, so that it ended up in the centre of the cartridge. The end of the cartridge was formed by a special high-edge flap that had to be torn off with the teeth, due to the thickness of the paper (at the time of cantonment recruitment, one reason for military exemption was the absence of incisors). The *Jäger* carried powder in their horns and loaded in the old-fashioned way, putting the cap in the hat and putting the ball in the barrel. The Sharpshooters of the Military Boundary, on the other hand, had special cartridges, brass cylinders open on both sides, containing charge and ball.

In 1726, a soldier carried 16-24 cartridges in a cartridge bag (*Patronentasche*) and next to it, on the front of the belt, a bottle of gunpowder. Around 1739, Lieutenant Oettner proposed the '*Postenschuß*' or '*Kartätsch-Patrone*'. This consisted of a charge of 13 grams of powder, separated from 8 pellets by a wooden foil, all sewn into a canvas bag. In 1741, each man received 8 of these cartridges, along with the others, and their use in the Battle of Kesseldorf was attributed a devastating effect. That unusual calibre was first used by the Prussians and directly desired by Prince Leopold of Dessau, after bitter struggles with his subordinates within his regiment, formed in 1702. The Austrians fired 26 g lead pellets. Austrian light troops also used *Doppelflinten*, double rifles or carbines with two barrels, one smooth and the other rifled.

The senior and junior officers of the grenadier companies were also armed with bayonet rifles. In addition to the bayonet, grenadiers also carried a sabre. They were named after the hand grenade, the use of which, often more dangerous for the person throwing it than for the opponent, had become obsolete (if not forbidden). The arsenals of the time still possessed large stocks of hand grenades, full or empty. One of these, usually made of cast iron, weighed two to three pounds (1-1.5 kg) with the explosive charge.

Another typical infantry weapon of the time was the *Schweinfeder* [23], i.e. the pole used to make Frisian horses (at the time called Spanish knights or *Spanische Reiter*). The infantry regulations of 1737 prescribed the use and specific training for '*Schweinsfeder*'. In the Austrian army, these were poles made in the shape of a pike and 1.73 m (5.5 ft) long, ending in an iron point, which were attached, by means of prepared holes and in a predetermined number, to beams 9 ft (284 cm) long and 8 cm thick, creating the so-called portable 'Spanish Knights', which could be hooked together and served as protection against cavalry attacks.

The beams were transported by the regimental train on their own wagons (*Balkenkarren*). With the beginning of the War of Austrian Succession, however, the '*Schweinfeder*' disappeared from the infantry inventory. In December 1740 and at the beginning of 1741, regiments marching from Hungary to Silesia were ordered to deliver the '*Schweinfeder*' to the arsenals closest to the route of march; they were later translated and assigned to the troops in Silesia in 1741 together with their wagons.

Weapons of distinction

Staff officers (apart from the *Oberstwachtmeister* - future Major - who commanded with unsheathed sword) and senior officers of the rifle companies always carried a sword on and off duty, but on duty they used a six foot (189 cm) long pike. That of the colonels was all gold-plated and had a gold *Quaste* (fringed plume); that of the lieutenant-colonel was gold-plated only in the upper half and had a gold and black silk *Quaste*; the superior officers (*Hauptleute* or captains) had the same plume, but was gold-plated in the lower half; the lieutenants' pike was not gold-plated and had no *Quaste*.

Non-commissioned officers and infantry officers therefore no longer had seventeenth-century pikes, but shorter weapons, the blade of which was of a random type, extending 15-25 centimetres from the attachment. The initial, conventional form of those blades, called '*Hellebarden*' or halberds (*Helmbarten* = *halbe Barten* literally half-beards) remained for German infantry and artillery until 1759-1769. The Hungarian infantry, officially formed only after the abolition of the pike, did not have such weapons at all, or did so only rarely.

tipi di Partigiane e Springstock (a destra)

In 1722, the custom of adapting the shape of the blade to the charge became established. The non-commissioned officers had shorter '*Helmbarten*', what are today known as Partisans.

The Alfieri used the half pike or *Springstock*, a pole about 2 m long, equipped with iron points on both ends. The partigiana (*Partisan*[24]) was a long spear of Italian origin (the ancient originals measured about 210-280 cm, of which 60-80 cm were the tip and interlocking), in use since the 15th century. Partisans were Ranseurs (*Runka*) with a central ox-tongue tip and shorter side spikes, called ears (*Runka* were similar to flat-bladed pitchforks that disappeared after the 16th century). Partisans were also in use among the officers of the Lansquenets. In the 17th century, the partisan was still a popular weapon in Germany and the Netherlands, becoming the weapon of superior officers. The oldest partigianas still had longer lengths, becoming shorter as the years went by. Particularly rich in engraved iron and gilt decorations were those used by the German Guard regiments

---

23 The *Schweinfeder* was an old weapon used in wild boar hunting (literally, the pig's bristle), an 8 cm steel-tipped skewer with two hooks attached to a 30-35 cm long pole, used to hook the hunter's wounded wild boar.

24 The etymology derived from the French Partisan, weapon of faction, does not seem credible. It seems that the name may derive from the Italian Pertugiana (which creates pertugi - which pierces).

(*Leibgarden*). These spears were mainly used to 'stimulate' the soldiers to keep their ranks tight by poking them, sometimes quite firmly.

The non-commissioned officers' partisans were officially called *Kurzgewehr* (short weapons similar to the traditional German spikes or *spontons* - with a 23 cm tip - instead of the old 4-5 m long pikes). Corporals had a straight, spear-shaped blade, '*Stosseisen*', at the base of which was a half-moon blade on one side and, on the other, a pointed leaf, which acted as a support hook, followed by the attachment on a pole of about 50 cm; it had to be carried with the

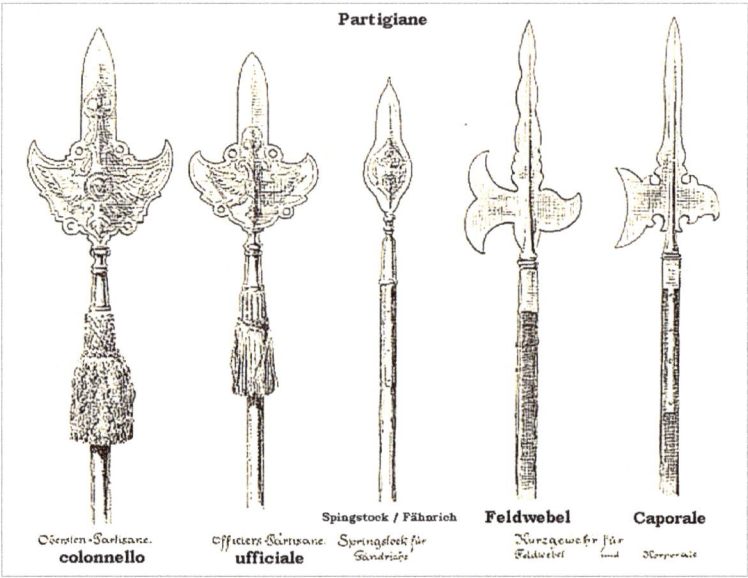

left hand. Sergeants and provosts had a straight blade and a double half-moon with supporting hooks pointing downwards, NCOs of the lower First Plana, if able to fight, had two hooks pointing downwards; these weapons had to be carried with the right hand.

The artillery partisans were similar and short; each artificer had an ignition pole; a pole about 2 metres long on which two protruding fuses were fixed, with locking screws; the NCO wore it similar only the fuses were only carved as ornamental figures.

Partisans and *Kurzgewehr* disappeared from the Austrian army after the Seven Years' War, while during the War of Succession officers were rarely seen brandishing rifles. Then, around the end of 1748, Partisans and *Kurzgewehr* were expressly prescribed for all officers and non-commissioned officers of the *Ordinari-Compagnien*, 'instead of rifles'; and so they became the norm.

In the 18th century, the adopted *Kurzgewehr*, or short partisanship of the non-commissioned officers of the German armies, were also called *Sponton*. The name was clearly derived from the Latin *espietus*, *spedus* (spit), and the early Renaissance *Spetum*. These shorter spears were favoured by colonels and lieutenant-colonels, captains and lieutenants. Around 1770, however, the Spetums were replaced everywhere.

Cavalry Weapons

The cavalry was also equipped with firearms. After the Battle of Mollwitz (10 April 1741), the watchword became the obligation to 'produce iron batons' and cavalry outfits. The Penzenter company in Steyr had produced 10,000 carbines and 12,000 cavalry outfits (one carbine plus two pistols) sold at 4.30 florins and between 9.30 and 10.50 florins, depending on whether the outfit was for hussars or cuirassiers; all had to be equipped with the new iron rods, as well as other minor modifications (iron rods, however, only became regulation after 1744). The cavalry used ¾ Löth calibre (20 balls made a pound of Vienna, or 17 mm in diameter) and there were carbines for cuirassiers or dragoons, made of iron; then there were slightly shorter ones, for hussars, which were made of brass, like pistols. Until 1768 the carbine for dragoons also had a bayonet.

 The best known cavalry weapons, however, were certainly those used in assaults. Cavalry possessed secondary weapons or *Seitenwaffen* that were in fact destined to become main weapons. Among the white weapons, a wide variety of blades (*Cavalry-Klingen*) were widespread and, at the beginning of the century, were of the type desired by the colonel owner. From 1722 onwards, greater uniformity in cavalry swords was demanded, while as far as hips, sheaths and scabbards were concerned, the arbitrariness of the regimental owners remained unchallenged. It was not until 1769 that all white cavalry weapons were regulated in a uniform fashion. The rules of 1722 spoke only of correct proportions for the length of the blade (it had to reach up to the navel), without any particular conformations in length, such that the enemy could be skewered on the ground, directly from the saddle.

The *Pallasch* was a single-edged straight sabre, which German knights carried in the time of Prince Eugene, instead of the double-edged heavy sword previously in use. It was 82-86 cm long without tang, with different types of shanks. The hilt, its shape and the material of the handle varied depending on the regiment. In the period between 1736 (?) until 1748, blades had a single narrow tang, while those after 1748 had a double one. Some *Pallaschs* retained the double-edged blade (they were to be the main assault weapon of the Austrian cavalry until the 20th century). They were of two types:

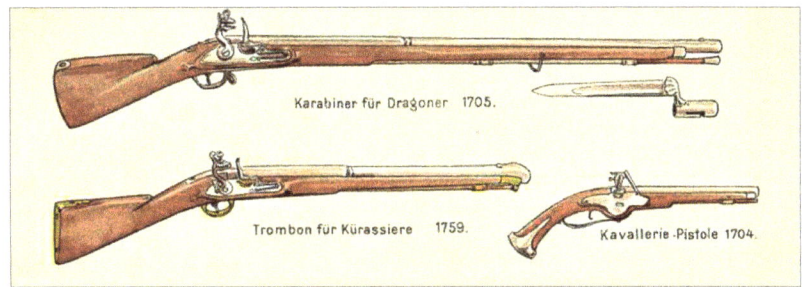

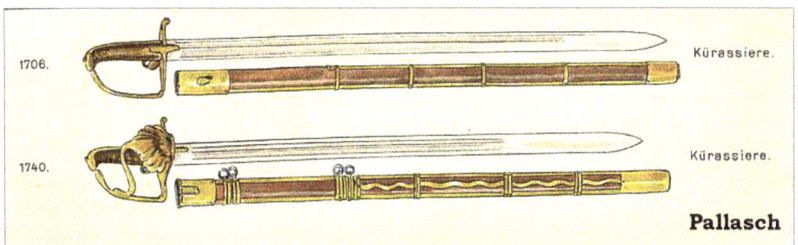

1) Saddle Pallasch (16th-18th centuries), complementary weapon (second weapon to the right of the saddle) of the Hungarian hussars, a purely cutting weapon, considered to be a sword;
2) Military Pallasch, (18th-20th centuries), main weapon for cuirassiers and dragoons, firstly a slashing weapon, then a blowing weapon, also a blow and cut weapon, finally a *Stoßwaffe*, i.e. a bludgeoning weapon, assimilated to the sword.

Several decrees, such as the one of 13 March and 8 April 1748, specified the need to purchase Pallasch exclusively from domestic factories (such as Pottenstein, Wiener -Neustädter Armatur Gesellschaft, Eisengewerkschaft in Waitz).

Until 1758, when two light cavalry regiments were temporarily organised, the Austrian light cavalry was represented only by hussars, some volunteer corps (*Freikorps*) and the Frontier *Grenzer*. The dragoons (also the future light cavalrymen and dragoons) carried the Pallasch, while the hussars, already since 1700, had their own curved sword, unsuitable for cutting blows, better as a striking weapon. The older hussar sabres - also called *Hajducken* (the Hungarian *Hajduk* infantry also carried it) - or *Huszarsabel*, until 1748 could be of 4 types, distinguished by the curvature index of the blades. The length ranged from 72 to 84 cm. The blade was always single-edged and 3-4 cm wide. The word sabre apparently derived from the Old Hungarian Säbel[25] (but also from the Hungarian word szablya, Polish szabla and medieval German sewel). In the early years of the century, the sabre was also carried by mounted grenadiers.

The *Armschiene*. It was a second protective weapon of the Hungarian irregular cavalry that consisted of a piece of rough iron, about 44 centimetres long, which the rider wore strapped to his left forearm and whose plate also protected his hand. This improper weapon - which remained in use until 1738 - shielded the hand that held the reins and was dictated by the Ottoman tactics of the time, since, in battle, the Turks always tried to strike the hand that held the reins.

Armour. In the German cavalry, a double breastplate (breast and back) forged in iron and supplied by contract by the '*Armatur - und Waffengewerkschaft in Wiener -Neustadt*' at the agreed price of 4 guilders was in

---

25 According to Kilidsh & Shamschir as cited in Seifert Gerhard, Fachwörter der Blankwaffenkunde www.seitengewehr.de on p.49.

use. The shape of the early armour was slightly different from its later appearance, as it was more linearly cut in its lower half. The generals wore a shiny, sometimes silver-plated, richly ornamented and gold-plated breastplate; the general staff and senior officers also wore an opaque breastplate, crossed by a band of gold-plated metal plate, on the midline of the chest. This plate extended only to the middle of the chest for the junior officer, while for the *Rittmeisters* (captains) it reached to the lower edge, and, if it was a staff officer, the plate indicating rank was accompanied by one or two strips, carved in silver, depending on the officer's rank. The soldier's breastplate was painted black, with a strip of brass plate passing through the middle of the chest in the case of *Wachtmeisters*, a strip of brass plate reaching only to the middle of the chest in corporals, with bands always shiny for military ranks.

The *Hutkreuze* or iron crosses were protective reinforcements for the cuirassiers, dragoons, cavalrymen and were the same as those with which the infantry would be equipped from 1769, to protect themselves from sabre blows. The old 16th-17th century helmet, called *Zischäge*, but also helmet or *Kasket*, was apparently still in use by the Hungarian heavy cavalry, combined with a plate armour. German-speaking troops had long since abandoned that headgear, although it appears that dragoons still wore the *Zischäge* in the war with the Turks in 1788 - 1789.

The Supreme Command and the Imperial Guard

Observing the development of standing armies, as support for absolute sovereign power to be imposed on reluctant lands, it was customary that the supreme command of the entire army, of a state, was always entrusted to the prince of the country. Thus, like his predecessors in the reunified Habsburg lands (German line), Charles VI was the supreme warlord; he bequeathed this position to his daughter Maria Theresa, although shortly after her accession to power, the latter appointed her husband Francis Stephen, the Grand Duke of Tuscany, as co-regent. Nevertheless, from 1741, the 'queen' always had the absolute general direction of the state and the supreme right to dispose of the army. In fact, one rarely found resolutions and decisions, in military matters, that were signed by the former Grand Duke of Tuscany, being penned with the formula '*nomine reginae*'.

Rarely, and probably always only in accordance with special events, relations or advice were shared with the Grand Duke, without, however, excluding his direct influence. But in spite of what was known and in spite of the compulsory information coming from the *Hofkriegrat*, it really seemed that the brilliant daughter of Charles VI, had a memorable flair for handling political and military matters, always hitting the decisive point; a property of synthesis that could only be possessed by those who had before their eyes the numerous comments on the records in the archives of the Supreme War Council and the k.k. *Hofkammer*[26]. Even if it was generally assumed from the everlasting cliché that '*women* were *more easily adaptable to intercession than men*', it should be emphasised that this '*masculine spirit in a feminine shell*' was very intransigent, always favouring the good of the state, and of the army in particular, without ever deviating from her great sense of justice and fairness, showing preference only when she felt she could benefit from an individual; and she had the greatest support from the military precisely when her throne was contested by the whole of Europe.

The exercise of military supremacy was concentrated in the hands of the princes of the empire, who were still in 1740 the managers of the rights and duties of the hereditary lands, as far as recruitment, supplies for the troops on marches and lodgings, and the raising of funds for the army were concerned. Count Haugwitz had ascertained the consequences caused by this situation and had already written in 1742, in a memorandum addressed to Maria Theresa shortly after the Peace of Breslau, that all ordinances relating to the military system were to be taken out of the hands of the territory and brought into those of the central government. In this sense, a first reorganisation of the army was to be started after the Peace of Aachen.

In the exercise of the Supreme Command, the monarchy had at its disposal: the so-called courtly council or, better, curtious war council (*Hofkriegsrat*), the court chamber (*Hofkammer*), both of these organs were in a singular and dual relationship with the General-Kriegs-Commissariat or General War Commissariat, formally subordinate to both of the above, but in fact endowed with a great deal of autonomy, and in the end almost

---

26   The so-called 'Court Chamber', in absolutist and monarchical states, was the authority that administered the princely estate (the Treasury). Under the rule of Maria Theresa, the chamber obtained an even more prominent role in the centralisation of the monarchy, being entrusted not only with the financial system of the Empire, but also with trade, economics, mining and traffic, remaining in this power until the 19th century when, from 1848, these competences were divided among a series of ministries.

equated to them. This trinity could be regarded as the Habsburg Supreme Command. Then there was the Sovereign and there was the need to defend his person at the palace.

In 1740, there were, as imperial palace guards, the *Arcieren-Garde (Hartschier)* horse guards and the *Trabanten-Garde* foot guards. Both corps were managed by the court command office (*Obersthofmeister-Amte*) guaranteed by large appropriations (19,296 florins[27] under Charles VI and 18,600 florins under Maria Theresa in 1747). The *Arcieren-Garde* (which from 1763 was to be renamed the 'German Noble Guard', since the 'Hungarian Noble Guard' had been formed three years earlier) had the following formation in 1740 a captain (who was actually a Feldzeugmeister, Count Heinrich Daun), a lieutenant, an upper quartermaster, a lower quartermaster, an adjutant, five *Rottenmeisters* (a kind of lead sergeant, 5 in 1747 then 4 in 1748), 95 *Arcieren* (78 in 1747, 50 in 1748), six trumpets, a kettledrum, a field surgeon, a blacksmith and a guard servant (*Wachtknecht*).

The *Trabanten-Garde* on foot had: a captain (the General of Cavalry Count Cordova), an upper quartermaster, a lower quartermaster, ten *Rottenmeisters* (1747 but 9 in 1748), 90 *Trabanten* (89 in 1747; 68 in 1748), a drum, a fife, and a guard servant. Every soldier, of both companies of the Guard, had, from the very beginning, the so-called 'Privilege', i.e. they could drink wine or beer in their quarters '*ad libitum*' and even cede 'drinking' rights for a fee. Since, however, Vienna's bourgeois restaurateurs felt aggrieved by this practice, the city, with the court's approval, paid each man of the Guard 60 florins each year as '*Zapfengeld*' (in theory '*cap pay*'), in lieu of the *Privilegium*. Each soldier of the *Arcieren-Garde had* to buy and manage the horse alone, having only a common '*Pferde-Adjutum*' of 25 florins.

In 1745, the 'Swiss Guard' of the Grand Duchy of Tuscany, quite similar to the Vatican's today, passed into imperial service. The officers had halberds, the troop had halberds, and everyone had a sabre. The *Schweizer-Garde*, whose 'colonel' was still Count Cordova, had in 1747: a captain, a lieutenant, a sub-lieutenant, an ensign, a chaplain, a secretary, a corporal (*Wachtmeister*), a quartermaster, a field surgeon, a provost, 4 corporals, 4 musicians and 81 men. Each year it cost the treasury 15710 florins and a half.

In Brussels, two companies of the Guard served the Governor-General of Flanders: the „*Trabanten der adeligen Leibwache Seiner Majestät*' and the Halberdier Company. Their strength and costs are not known today.

The Hofkriegsrat or War Curtain Council

After the dissolution of the Inner Austrian War Council (*innerösterreichischen Hof-Kriegsrates*) in Graz in 1705, in order to "*avoid greater disconcertations*" („*zur Verhütung grösserer Disconcerten*') and the Upper Austrian War Chamber in Innsbruck (*oberösterreichischen Kriegs-Stelle*), the only central body, responsible for the operational conduct of war and the management of the army, remained the *Hofkriegsrat in* Vienna, which came into being under Emperor Ferdinand I. After the death of Charles VI, as was always the case during the period between the death of a Habsburg emperor and the election of the next one, the Vienna Hofkriegsrat took the title of: "imperial *Hof-Kriegsrat* left by His Majesty Emperor of the Romans", and more succinctly "*Hinterlassener kaiserlicher Hof-Kriegsrat*". Only after the Peace of Füssen (22 April 1745), when Maria Theresa recognised the election of the Bavarian Charles VII as Emperor, did the *Hofkriegsrat* have to take the name 'Royal War Council' („*königlicher Hof-Kriegsrat*'). With the election of Emperor Franz I (13 September 1745) it became imperial again and called itself 'imperialregio' as did all army units (k.k.= „*kaiserlichköniglich*')[28].

The last instructions for the courtly council, issued before the death of Charles VI, dated from 1650, and in them the following points were made:

1. Mediation of arrangements between emperor and field commanders and troops.
2. Management of all organisational arrangements.
3. Proposals for the appointment of generals and their staffs, fortress commanders and regiment holders. Constitution of special forces in case of necessity. Military justice from staff officers upwards, and leave of absence or resignation.

---

27   The most valuable coin was the Thaler, which was worth two Gulden (Dutch guilder or forint in Hungary) in Austria, while one Gulden was worth 60 kreuzer. A three-kreuzer coin was called a Grosso or Groschen.

28   Not to be confused with the prefix k.u.k (imperial AND royal) assumed by the army in 1867 after the Ausgleich. Before leaving Frankfurt on 6 September 1745, Maria Theresia herself had given orders that, after the much hoped-for 'happy election', both the *Hofkriegsrat* and the army were now to be called 'Imperial-Regi' by all. Hence the nickname 'Kaiserlicchi', which was to accompany the Austrians until 1866.

4. Organisation and military supplies in agreement with the *Hofkammer* and the *General-Kriegs-Commissariat* (with this also control of the entire territory).
5. Compilation of directives for taxes and commissions in conjunction with the *General-Kriegs-Commissariat* and the *Obrist-Proviant-Amte* (higher commission office).
6. Control of all artillery and parks by mediating between field, territorial and curtilage supplies.
7. Fortresses and military constructions through the Fortresses Construction Office (*Fortifications-Bau-Zahl-Amt*) by specially appointed engineers.
8. Issues concerning navigation and bridges through the *General-Kriegs-Commissariat* and the Higher Navigation Office (*Obrist-Schiff-Amt*).

In addition to these military tasks, from 1720, the *Hofkriegsrat* also dealt with diplomatic relations with Russia and Turkey, but, after the establishment of the State Chancellery (*Hof- und Staatskanzlei* - 1742), only with diplomatic relations with Turkey.

il conte Ludwig Andreas von Khevenhüller

The *Hofkriegsrat was* and remained, however, an advisory body, completely incapable of making important decisions, unless, at its chairmanship, there was a dominant personality, as there had been Archduke Eugene (who, in fact, was in charge of the empire's foreign policy). Over the years, then, a real conflict of competences between the *Hofkriegsrat* and the *General-Kriegs-Commissariat* arose, which lasted even after the equalisation of the two state bodies in 1746, so much so that, in 1750, the Court Council was already being accused of having lost its authority. For instance, in earlier years, the Italian *Hofrat* in Milan had, on occasion, issued ordinances completely contrary to those in Vienna, repeatedly contradicting them. The *Hofkriegsrat of* Inner Austria, Graz, had also done the same with 'sharp oppositions' hindering, for instance in 1736, the passage of troops from Italy by not giving them access to supply depots. Then, in 1735, the entire Graz Council had even directly opposed the imperial resolutions on borders. Unification had not resolved the criticism, sometimes even bitter, of the consulate system, where (military) experts reproached the 'laymen' for talking about things that were outside their competence or, even worse, for acting in their own interests.

In the years 1740 and 1741 the *Hofkriegsrat* had the following composition: the president was, since 1738, FM Joseph Count Harrach, the vice-president was FM Count Ludwig Andreas Khevenhüller); 25 (later 29) councillors were drawn from the local lordships, of whom, according to the instructions, only the five most senior (those not appointed by a command or territorial service in Vienna), were allowed direct management and, as such, directly paid - among them was always the commander of the city of Vienna; there were 11 (later 15) Godfathers, not always of noble lineage, (including four "secret Referendari: Count von Lachawitz, von Wöber, Ignaz von Koch and O. Weingarten); finally, there was the staff including 28 (later 27) secretaries, 1 curator of the registry, 2 curator's assistants, 3 registry clerks, 2 protocol clerks, 2 dispatchers, 2 dispatcher's assistants, 16 (later 15) aspiring registrars 2 would-be casual clerks, 17 (then 16) registrars, 20 (then 25) would-be casual clerks, 2 (then 1) ushers, 4 registrar's clerks, 1 heating clerk, 1 archivist, 1 assistant archivist, 1 register clerk, 1 archive clerk. The clerical staff was completely civilian.

There was no lack of friction between the bodies. A letter from the staff of the *Hofkriegsrat* to the *Hofkammer,* dated 20 August 1743, stated that many troops had not received any pay since the end of October 1741 due to the non-receipt of Hungarian contributions, paid to the *Hofkammer* and totally used to create the six new *Hajducken* infantry regiments.

The matters dealt with by the Court War Council were divided into '*Publica*' and '*Judicalia*'. The latter were, for the most part, processes instituted by its legal organs, *Hof-Kriegs-Justizrate,* until 1745 not yet separated from the rest and able to burden its work. The '*Publica*' were strictly military and economic-administrative affairs, the latter being subject to the decisive influences of the *Hofkammer* and the *General-Kriegs-Commissariat*.

There were standing commissions for the questions of supplies and quartering, for weapons and ammunition, for the affairs of the Hungarian garrisons and the stationary occupation troops, for the questions of invalids, for troop redundancies in the winter quarters. In particularly important matters, such as troop reductions at the end of the war, expert opinions were requested from eminent generals, either by imperial order or at the suggestion of the *Hofkriegsrat*, and then a final report was drawn up for the emperor.

The Kurdish War Council, in peacetime, had no regular way of communicating with the highest military authorities and the troops, yet managed to interact with the regiments, directly, on all matters. It could not, of course, be described as a rapid communication system. Thus, in Prague, in December 1740, FZM O'Gilvy asked the *Hofkriegsrat* to directly contact the Royal Court Chancellery of Bohemia (*Hofkanzlei*) about the defensive preparations of the fortress of Glatz, because the reports sent to Vienna occasionally wasted a lot of valuable time and prevented the normal activities of the troop from taking place.

The numerous criticisms of the institution forced Maria Theresa to revise the competences of the Council not new instructions in 1744. For matters '*in publicis*' (everything that did not concern the College of Justice) only three referendaries remained at work: Wöber, Lachawitz and Weingarten. The former remained, once again, the most important person in the courtly council, because he was explicitly assigned '*das Universum, als da ist : die Militär-Systemata, Regulamente, Repartition und in's Feld bestellenden* Armeen *zu besorgen*', i.e. the entire military universe, systems, regulations, apportionments and field armies. If one of the three had died, only two referendums would have remained. The Court *Schematismus of* 1746 showed, in comparison with that of 1740, a reduction of noble councillors from twenty-five to three, common councillors from eleven to eight, secretaries from twenty-eight to six, four of them for the '*Publica*', and the total of the remaining personnel from seventy-eight to forty-eight employees.

In future, the entire military court system was to be separate. A separate 'special and separate office' was to be appointed under the supervision of the president of the *Hofkriegsrat*; four '*Hof-Kriegsräthe für Justiz-Angelegenheiten*' or War Councils for Judicial Affairs and their auxiliary staff.

"*According to the former Observances*" remained or were subordinated to the *Hofkriegsrat*: the office of the War Commissariat (*General-Kriegs-Commissariat-Amt*), the superior field artillery section (*Obrist-Land-Zeug-Amt*) and the similar curtense section of the Central Arsenal (*Haus-Zeug-Amt*), the Supreme Court (*General-Auditoriat*), the Higher Navigation Office (*Obrist-Schiff-Amt*) and the Field Pontoon Service (*Feld-Schiffbrücken-Stand*), „*everything in any case pertaining to the military*', including the general and/or military directors in the provinces, the commanders of the fortresses, the National Militia and the Military Boundary. Now all decrees for the army, commanders, generals, fortress commanders at home and of the Border, in war even those for lower-ranking generals, required the queen's signature. The delegation to the War Council was limited to a few cases, compared to the past. All copies of the ordinances, with the exception of those that were secret, had to be made in the war chancellery (*Kriegskanzlei*).

Officers were only allowed to write directly to the *Hofkriegsrat* in special cases (e.g. if it was a matter of recruiting, reassembling etc.), even if it was a matter of complaints by officers directed against the regimental commander or the owner, or complaints by the latter against the commander. For all other cases, the hierarchical path was, ascending, from the regimental command, to the commanding general (army).

The general 'field commander', the chief, supreme commander (also '*capite*'), was appointed by the monarch at the suggestion of the Vienna War Council. Since, only the latter body had links with diplomacy and the higher military spheres, the basis for drawing up a war or campaign plan could come from it and, in addition, the Council itself had a general staff, in the modern sense of the term. In peacetime, there was usually not even a General Quartermaster (the so-called 'Minor General Staff'), and in any case only a very small part of the General Staff worked. It is clear, therefore, that the *Hofkriegsrat* always had a very significant impact not only on the planning of the war or campaign, but also on further operations. The supreme commander was not only directly answerable to the monarch, but was also in charge of mediating his orders and presenting them to the *Hofkriegsrat* when they concerned war material and all kinds of campaign needs. Even in Maria Theresa's time, therefore, the Council's long-standing influence on war and operational plans remained active, with very few exceptions. In other cases, the situation was less rigid. Not only Prince Charles of Lorraine or other higher commanders, such as Field Marshals Lobkowitz and Khevenhüller, were often advised by the queen and also by the courtly council to act at their own discretion, since the circumstances could not be judged correctly from Vienna, but even generals of independent lower command, such as Lieutenant Field Marshal Browne in Silesia, Field Marshal Bärnklau in Bavaria and others. The Prussian General Staff itself, while contesting the fact that campaign plans were drawn up in Vienna, admitted that "*around, in the other states, it is not as if there was anything better.*"

For the written reports of a supreme commander or army commander, to the emperor and the *Hofkriegsrat*, each larger corps of an army was called a 'war expedition' (*Feld-Kriegs-Expedition*) (or *Feld-Kriegs-Kanzlei*), as it often had its own chancellery director, or only one campaign secretary (*Feld-Kriegs-Secretär*) at the organisational head, perhaps assisted by six (up to fifteen) collaborators. The proposed reforms of the Viennese War Council of 1740 - 1741 required that only people who had successfully served in the field chancelleries serve in it. The cost of an imperial 'war expedition' was estimated in 1739 at about 33579 guilders.

For the normal connection between armies and the *Hofkriegsrat,* each army corps in the field had a field post office (*Feld-Post-Amt*) with two post officers, several couriers or field postmen who maintained contact with the common post (*Ordinari-Post*), riding to and from Vienna, to the corps. Their lines of communication had to be safeguarded by soldiers, as were the order lines between the various corps of an army. For example, in June 1745, between the main army and the Hungarian *Insurrectio* the road connection touched the following villages: Neustadt, Ziegenhals, Freiwaldau, Altstadt, Linsdorf, Opocno and Jaromir.

IMPERIAL COMMANDS

General (Generalate) and Fortress Commands. Since the Spanish Netherlands had come under the rule of the Austrian sovereigns, the peculiar political conditions of these provinces and their remoteness from Vienna necessitated a General Command in Brussels, which was subordinate to the *Hofkriegsrat* in Vienna, both for the funds allocated to the stationed troops, managed by the Imperial Governor(-regium), and for military power in the country. Around 1740, Field Marshal Duke Leopold zu Arenberg was the commanding general in the Austrian Netherlands. The government of the armed forces in Lombardy and the Austrian Duchies was in a similar position, with Field Marshal Count Otto Ferdinand zu Abensperg-Traun in charge of the *Gubernium ad interim* in Milan; under him, his subordinate FML Wachtendonck commanded the imperial regiments in Tuscany.

Also in Bohemia, Moravia, Silesia and the Siebenbürgen there were General Commands, those of the most important fortresses and towns. In 1740 in Prague the FZM Count O'Gilvy commanded, in Brünn (Spielberg fortress) the FML Count Sinzendorff commanded, in Gross-Glogau there was the FML Count Wenzel Wallis, in Hermannstadt in Transylvania the famous FM Prince Lobkowitz. They were the local representatives of the *Hofkriegsrat* and the military interests in the territory, responsible for the discipline of the soldiers in their quarters, the elimination of troop excesses, as well as the regularity of food, the organisation of marches and accommodation, for which the interests of the territory were safeguarded by the local war commissioners (*Land-Kriegs-Commissäre*). After the loss of Silesia, that general command passed to the Moravian command in Brünn.

A special case was the General Command of Slavonia, which resided at the fortress of Esseg (today's Osijek). From 1733, the command was held by the FM, Count von Khevenhüller, later replaced by his representative, Marquis Guadagni, when the field marshal was sent to war in Italy, Serbia and the Upper Danube. The Slavonic generalship was of great importance, not only for the defence of the Borders against the Turks, but also for the importance of the '*developing Slavic-Syrmic military border*'.

As was the case with Slavonia, after the Peace of Carlowitz, the Banat of Temesvár (today Timisoara in Romania) was not annexed to Hungary after the Peace of Passarowitz, but had its own administration organised there, dependent on Vienna, at the head of which was Count Mercy, the commanding general of Temesvár. After the Belgrade peace agreement, Field Marshal Suckow took over the leadership of the General Command, which, on 13 March 1741 was entrusted to FML Baron von Engelshofen, together with the administration of the garrison, on an *interim basis*, until a true commanding general was appointed, and, '*so that he himself might share in its splendour*' he was given 3000 guilders annually, in addition to his personal endowment. *General-Feld-Wachtmeister* (abbreviated GFWM) de Scotti was appointed as his deputy and representative. There too, as with the Slavonic generalate, the most important military task was the planned establishment of the *Grenz,* the Military Condîfine. Thus, at the time of his death, Charles VI could say that he had general commands in all his lands, except Hungary.

It was Maria Theresa herself who, on 24 October 1740, entrusted the General Command of Hungary to the statesman and warrior FM Count Johann or János Pálffy. With that appointment, the Hungarian field marshal was given command over all the regular troops stationed in Hungary, the *Grenzer*, the volunteer and national militia companies (*Frei-Compagnien* and *National-Miliz*), all the fortresses, artillery, naval offices and supply depots. He was to have close contact with the General Commands of the Siebenbürgen, Temesvar, Slavonia and also the military apparatuses of Inner Austria, exchanging information and news, but only responding to direct orders from the Queen or the *Hofkriegrat*. The FM Count Alexander Károlyi, then the FML Römer and the *General-Feldwachtmeisters* Saint-Ignon and Philibert were assigned to support him. Pálffy was also given a small field chancellery (*Feld-Kriegskanzlei*) with a secretary and two chancellors.

Immediately after the death of Charles VI, the FZM Prince of Sachsen-Hildburghausen was appointed Commander of the Varazdin Generalate. By a curious twist of fate, the prince had more disagreements with the Styrian authorities in Graz than with the Turks on the border. He succeeded, however, in creating two *Grenzer* regiments of regular infantry in the Varazdin generalate, which, from 1744, were also employed in battle. Opposition from Graz, Carinthia and Carniola, however, succeeded in boycotting a similar project, extended to the Carlstädt generalate. The promotion of those territorial, 'shopkeeping' interests did not please the sovereign. Thus, at the end of 1743, the military apparatus of Inner Austria was dismantled and, at the beginning of the following year, Prince Sachsen-Hildburghausen, now FM, was appointed *Militär-Ober-Director* and general commander of all the lands of Inner Austria, as well as of the Varazdin and Carlstädt generalates. The *Militär-Ober-Directorium* also functioned as the second appeal instance for the *Grenzer* generalates' court cases (the third and final appeal was, of course, the *Hofkriegsrat*). In Inner Austria, and in the border generalates, only the artillery and its arsenals remained autonomous, entrusted to the new *Land- und Haus-Zeugmeister*, Prince Wenzel Liechtenstein, who was to be the future promoter of the Habsburg artillery reform.

In fortresses, senior officers or generals were often retained as commanders, usually enjoying the pay of their military rank. In fact, they ended up in the fortresses because they were no longer fit for field service in war; in general, therefore, the granting of a fortress command was an excellent benefit for soldiers who would otherwise have retired directly. During the discussions on the plans to reduce the army, the proposal repeatedly emerged to abandon the institution of the fortress commander, to no longer hire new ones after the death of those already in appointment, and to entrust the command of the fortress to the commanders of the garrison troops. The proposal, however, was only successful in the Tyrol, namely in 1745, when the country and territory regiments were formed.

Only half of the garrison could be taken to church and Mass; during the 'divine service' the other half had to remain in the quarters, on guard. The guards had their muskets loaded and twelve to twenty-four precision bullets with them. On each side of the fortress, on the ramparts, in peacetime, two cannons were to be loaded with fire, one with bullets and the other with blank cartridges. The most important aides of the fortress command were the square major and the square lieutenant. They were responsible for the routine, exercise and supervision of the entire fortress service. By Act of 12 April 1743, the Vienna Fortress Staff had the now senior FM Count Khevenhüller as commander, who had a pay of 10,000 florins (if he led a regiment, he would only get 8,000 florins); the square major had a pay of only 1,000 florins.

The General-Kriegs-Commissariat or Central War Commissariat. The central office, established in 1650, was entrusted to Count Nesselrode from 1726. Leading all the armies in the field with the *Hofkriegsrat* and the *Hofkammer* meant working with the various commissions; often too much time was lost even in settling non-urgent requests or trivialities. In order to supervise and remedy the large number of these necessary commissions, to guide their choices and make them efficient so as not to harm the common good, the Emperor appointed Count Nesselrode as war commissioner, recommending that he remain subordinate to the *Hofkriegsrat* and the *Hofkammer*. The body was, from the outset, contradictory and obviously tended to be independent, despite imperial recommendations. On the death of Prince Eugene, who was able to hold the political-military regency together thanks to his charisma as a leader, the disharmonies became apparent.

The discord and jealousies between the *Hofkriegsrat* and the Commissariat, which Maria Theresa often witnessed in person, were known to the army and were detrimental to the image of the War Office. The *Hofkammer*, however, also complained about the Commissariat. In 1746, she was forced to admit that she had not received any correspondence from the Commissariat for three years and that she no longer knew anything about military allocations. The service was accused of not doing what it should. At a session of the ministerial deputations in 1742, it was accused of *"having no discipline, of always doing what it pleased, and of making the troops suffer so much from that attitude that they were forced to make up for it in the territories."* What was most worrying was the confusion in the counts for the partition of funds between territory and military; no one knew what they had to pay anymore. The queen had to intervene herself. Reform was a pressing necessity and the occasion was the resignation of Count Nesselrode (end of 1745) with the appointment of his deputy, Count Salaburg, as General War Commissioner. The latter, supported by the regima, but hated by the other two superior bodies, forced drastic solutions. An Instruction of the Queen, dated, 28 December 1746, intended to transform the Commissariat into a collegiate body, had influence only on the last years of the war. On 6 January 1747 a *Rescript of* Maria Theresa closed the *General-Kriegs-Commissariat* and immediately transformed it into a *Hofstelle* (which we would call a Ministry today).

The Lands-Kriegs-Commissariat. Despite their almost similar name, they had nothing to do with the Central War Commissariat. They were bodies present in all crown lands and had the task of assisting troops, whether in the district or on the march. Depending on the geographical area, there were general (*General-Land-Kriegs-Commissäre*), cantonal (*Viertels*) or local (*Führungs-Commissäre*) territorial commissars; in Hungary, the commissars were provincial. Their task was identical everywhere: to protect the country from the damage caused by the soldiers and to claim compensation during military marches and transports of all kinds, long periods of quartering and recruitment. As a result, of course, the Central Commissariat often came into direct collision with the organs of the territory. They did not get along well; in 1741 in Bohemia, the two bodies did not want to be subservient to each other, they insulted each other and prevented each other's transports, kept the stocks administered by one or the other body secret, even went so far as to accuse each other, in bad faith, of the quality of the supplies. From the point of view of bureaucracy, Austria was indeed a loser.

The Obrist-(Feld-)Proviant-Amt.[29] - It was the supply office in the countryside and was, in effect, a projection of the *Hofkammer*. As its name implies, it had to ensure the control of supplies to the fortresses (especially the Hungarian garrisons) and the armies in the countryside. It checked the supplies, partitions, storage and preservation of all things needed by the soldiers. The transport sector (which would become *Militär-Fuhrwesen* or Train Arms) and the bakeries, both in peace and war, reported to this office. As a rule, the Provisions staff, the food carters and the 'bread bakers' company, were rounded up in war, while in peace only the strongest remained on duty. The service was the link between the central *Obrist-Proviant-Amt* with the warehouses and fortresses. With the Prussian invasion of Silesia, of course, a Feld-Proviant-Stadt was formed for supplies in the countryside. This *Feld-Proviant-Stabes had* personnel in varying numbers, which depended on how large the army served. At the head of the Central Office was a Lieutenant-Colonel who, since the War of the Spanish Succession had been Baron Georg von Harrucker; after his death in 1742, the post was taken by *Proviant-Ober-Commissär* Ferdinand Bosch.

There was also often discord and jealousy between officials of the Commissariat and the Provisions Department; the latter did not want to be subordinate to the Commissioners, as was correct. In the late autumn of 1743, Prince Carl personally complained to Maria Theresa about the poor state of the commissariat system.

The Obrist-Land- und Haus-Zeug-Amt.[30] - Technically it was the Central Arsenal or the Central Artillery Department (*Haus* = central and *Land* = territorial, of the forts), which also became *Feld-* campal, in war. The direction of the fortress artillery and the park of pieces was the responsibility of this centralised office in Vienna, headed by the *Obrist-Land- und Haus-Zeugmeister*. In 1740, he was not in control of the situation due to the dispersion of personnel and materials: in Inner Austria, artillery material depended on the War Department of Inner Austria; in Upper Austria and Upper Austria, the artillery functioned in a few regional groups and was led in 1740 by an official based in Innsbruck, the *Feldzeugmeister* Count Montrichier, who was however subordinate to the *Militär-Directorium* in Vienna; in Italy and Holland (as well as field artillery detachments) there was still a national artillery, formed by the previous rulers, now under the control of the regional authorities. This disorder was certainly not tolerable. Thus the task of unifying all artillery under one

---

29 *Obrist* here has the literal sense of superior or central, rather than colonel.
30 *Zeug* was a medieval term for armaments in general, later used to refer to cannons, artillery parks, foundries and piece restoration workshops. From the word derived the rank of *Zeugmeister,* an ancient entry for artillery officer and Feldzeugmeister the current entry for an infantry army general.

department in Vienna was completed in 1741, without, however, the central office still being operational. The Instruction, drawn up on 7 August 1741, by FM Count Lothar Königsegg (in place of the late Field Marshal Count Wirich Daun) appointed *Obrist-Land- und Haus-Zeugmeister*, was still bound to the same restricted areas mentioned. Like his predecessor, he was totally subordinate to the *Hofkriegsrat* and could not communicate directly with any other court office. His duties were 'to *catalogue all types of artillery, rifles and weapons of all kinds, large and small, with all war equipment, so that everything always has a name*'. From the office, the need for supplies was justified and communicated to the *Hofkriegsrat*, without whose authorisation it was not permitted to change the stocks of individual arsenals (mostly for fortresses). All central and territorial artillery personnel were under his command and he exercised disciplinary rights over them; even here, however, he had to report the most serious legal cases to the *Hofkriegsrat*.

With Königsegg's retirement, the cavalry general Prince Joseph Wenzel Liechtenstein was called in from the Netherlands to hold the position of *Obrist-Land- und Haus-Zeugmeisters*. One of his instructions, dated 3 June 1744, recommended a single central leadership for the artillery, a decision that was on the verge of breaking with the *Hofkriegsrat, which was* opposed to the solution. In it, a single inventory of all artillery was recommended for all regional branches, such as the *Haupt- und Filial-Zeughäuser in* Hungary and Bohemia, in all Austrian crown lands, in Italy, and even in the Borders; only the Netherlands was excluded.

Apart from two articles on field artillery, Liechtenstein's instructions did not differ much from Königsegg's. Later, due to the expansion of the department's scope, in 1745, Maria Theresa issued an ordinance to rename the office as „*General-Feld-Land- und Haus-Artillerie-Zeug-Amt*', in practice replacing the term *Obrist*. At that time, Vienna was endowed with its own chancellery (*Zeug-Amts-Kanzlei*), its own paymaster's office (*Zeug-Zahlamt*) and its own general staff (*Zeug-Amts-Stab*), which it had in 1740, was confirmed: a *Zeug-Lieutenant*, a *Stuckhauptmann und Ober-Feuerwerkmeister* (a captain at the piece and master artificer, the famous gunsmith Anton Penzeneder), a scribe for the office, 4 messengers, 1 smelter (*Stuckgiesser*), 1 cannon engraver (*Stuckverschneider*), a corporal gunsmith (gunner), 15 gunsmiths, 9 arsenal workers specialised *Zeughauswerkmeister*. There was also a fort-building paymaster's office or *Fortificationsbau-Zahlamt* in which a number of military engineers were in charge of planning and fund-raising, again by delegation of the *Hofkriegrat*.

The Obrist-Schiff-Amt or navigation office. The *Obrist-Schiff-Amt* was a department that not only had military purposes, but also took care of the court's civilian cruises to Pressburg, hunting expeditions, etc. It was also responsible for tax matters, such as the transport of salt on the Danube and Tisza rivers, the collection of transit taxes and tolls on the Danube and Tisza. It also dealt with fiscal matters, such as salt transports on the Danube and Tisza rivers, the collection of transit taxes and bridge tolls; finally, it directly provided the river police service. During the war, it served almost exclusively to assemble boats and pontoons to build military bridges. Of course, it also took care of boats that sailed and draft animals to be used in navigation against the current. In addition to the installation of the field bridges, the department supervised all water transport of 'men, materials and everything useful in war'.

The **General-Feld-Kriegs-Auditoriats-Amt or Superior Court Martial**. - This Austrian Supreme Court was organised by the *General-Feld-Kriegs-Auditor* von Summ, in 1740, and was the referent of the *Hofkriegsrat, which was* spared the '*Judicalia*'. He was in charge not only of military trials, but also of civil trials, which crossed competences with the Court War Council. It consisted of a judge, called Lieutenant-General Hearing Officer (*General-Auditor-Lieutenant*), flanked by a secretary (*Feld-Gerichtsschreiber)* and a personal chancellery. In 1740, there were also lieutenant-general auditors in Graz, Raab, Esseg, Hermannstadt, Temesvár, Szegedin, Milan, Brussels and Tuscany; one step below them were the territory auditors in Ofen, Komorn, Kaschau, Peterwardein and Innsbruck. In the countryside, each major army had its own Lieutenant General Uditore who managed every trial, which was the responsibility of the commands, according to the '*jus gladii*'. The Imperial Court Martial (*kaiserlich Kriegsgericht*) and the Regimental *Schulteissen-Amt (Regiments-Schulteissen-Amt*[31]) in Vienna were subordinate to the Auditor General. The same power was exercised over the magistracy of the military in the Vienna area, insofar as they were not subject to the judicial power of a regiment; in particular, investigations into the faults of senior officers, civil actions against the army, such as administrative actions, supplies and invoices.

---

31   Schultheiß (German: Schultheiß, Schulte or Schulze) indicated, until 1832, the person who held the legal-political power in a municipality (corresponding to today's mayor). In our case in the regiments.

The Officers of Maria Theresa

At the beginning of the 18th century, the precarious situation of the Austrian commands seemed to be changing. The prevalence of siege warfare, conducted with increasingly refined means, soon brought to light the lack of suitable professionals. In addition to the appeal for suitable officers to command, there was also the appeal by the President of the Curtense War Council, Prince Eugene about the disastrous situation of military engineering and the lack of suitable specialist officers. This also led to the foundation of the '*k.k.-Ingenieurs-Akademie*' on 24 December 1717.

They were only drops in the ocean. For Count Leopold Daun, one of the young Maria Theresa's closest advisors, it was clear from the outset that this could not be limited to technical troops, but that action also had to be taken on the officers of the main weapons, the infantry and cavalry, who needed uniform and specialised training. Artillery was still more of a siege skill than a field skill. Of course, the disastrous situation of the Austrian army at the outbreak of the War of Austrian Succession had soon convinced the inexperienced Maria Theresa that only a total reform of the military system could benefit the Austrian Empire. The thought of removing the dominance of the private, business connected to those who held the regiments, the landlords, and to think about creating a true national army slowly made its way in.

One of Maria Theresa's main achievements was to continue the reform of the military administration initiated by Joseph I, who had abolished the Curtense War Council in Graz. From then on the curtense war council in Vienna, *Hofkriegsrat*, was really the supreme command of the entire army. From 1756 it united the heads of all departments 'the Collegia', with a supreme president (*Ober=President*), the first being Lacy, then Daun. The '*Collegia*', which were part of the war, said Johan Heinrich von Justi: '*... could be of three kinds. One such collegiate body could devote itself to directing war operations; another could only administer the necessary economic resources and a third could only direct justice. In reality, the Hofkriegsraths=Collegium in Vienna was dedicated to all three of these branches, although it is true that the supervision of the economic aspects were under the direct responsibility of the General- Kriegs-Commissariat*'.

Maria Theresa had also provided for the establishment of a *Hofkriegsraths=Collegium* in legal matters, while maintaining links with the other Collegia. Among the functions of the *Hofkriegsrat* was also the approval of campaign plans. Almost all members of the *Hofkriegsrat* held the rank of Field Marshal (FM). At this point, a digression clarifying the different ranks of the high commands of the Habsburg armies is appropriate.

Generalissimus. - In the first half of the 17th century, or rather at the time of the Thirty Years' War, at the top of the pyramid of Generalships stood a *Generalissimus*, sometimes called *Oberster* Feldgeneral (Colonel General), *Generalobristfeldhauptmann* or *Obristfeldhauptmann* (General or Captain Colonel of Campaigns), in the Italian style in a type of rank inherited from the 15th century, the '*Capo über alles kaiserliche Volk*' (Chief *über alles kaiserliche Volk*) (Chief sic. of all imperial nations), or the army commander, *Armeekommandant*, the general commander *Generalkommandant,* etc. The *Generalissimus* par excellence was Wallenstein (in the years 1625-1630 and again from 1631), then it was King Ferdinand (1634-1637), later Kaiser Ferdinand III, or Archduke Leopold Wilhelm (years 1639-1643, and 1645-1646), the brother of Emperor Ferdinand II. Then there was a very long pause until 1806 when, having abandoned the ranks system of the Holy Roman Empire, a new *Generalissimus* returned: Archduke Charles, the main reformer of the Austrian army.

From the 17th century onwards, however, the representative of the imperial high command in the field, the '*Stellvertreter of the Kaisers im Oberbefehl*' was called **Lieutenant General** '*Generallieutenant*' or LG. A lieutenant-general already existed in Wallenstein's time, as an intermediate rank between field marshals and the Generalissimo, at least in the Habsburg monarchy, just as it should be pointed out that the rank of generalissimo was not a true permanent general. The Lieutenant General's powers were clearly limited compared to those of the Generalissimo. He could in any case be the supreme army commander (*Armeeoberbefehlshaber*). Some famous examples of LG at the turn of the 17th to 18th century were: Tilly (1630), Gallas (1633-1639, 1643-1645, 1645-1647), Piccolomini (1648-1656), Montecuccoli (1664-1680), Charles V of Lorraine (1680-1690), the '*Türkenlouis*' (Louis the Turk) or Ludwig Wilhelm of Baden (1691-1707), the famous Prince Eugene of Savoy, who was above all the epitome of multifunctionality, Field Marshal of the Empire, President of the *Hofkriegsrat* (1703), Field Marshal General of the Catholic Empire (*Reichsgeneralfeldmarschall*) (1707) and finally Lieutenant General of the Emperor's personal force *Immediattruppen*[32] (1708). From 1738 the De-

---

32   They were the imperial forces of the Holy Roman Empire or Reichsarmee, considered by some authors in the

puty *General-Lieutenant* (*Stellvertreter des obersten Kriegsherren*) on the death of Prince Eugene was Maria Theresa's own husband, the Grand Duke of Tuscany, Franz Stephan of Lorraine.

A General Staff (of the Supreme Command) with the functions we associate with it today only existed for the Habsburg monarchy from 1758. Previously, the General Staff meant the generals assigned to the army, thus, to some extent, the Grand Headquarters (Great General Staff) together with the auxiliary staff of the General Headquarters (Small General Staff). Until then, the Quartermaster General was a subordinate officer, who had relatively little to do with practical tasks: selection and preparation of directions of march, depots and river crossings, reconnaissance directions, billeting, etc. It was not until the beginning of the 19th century that there was to be a Chief of Staff, also in office in peacetime, who was to become one of the central figures in the Habsburg military system. The theory, on the other hand, i.e. the classification of the rights and duties of the entire generalship and not only of the General Staff, will take place in 1769, with the so-called 'Generalsreglement'. Starting from the bottom, the ranks of the commanding generals were:

1) the **Generalfeldwachtmeister** (*Obristfeldwachtmeister* or also *Generalwachtmeister*) more commonly known by his initials GFWM, which after the mid-18th century became Major General or GM (*Generalmajor*). In the campaign he was the brigade commander.

2) The **Feldmarschall-Leutnant** (Lieutenant Field Marshal or FML) was originally, in the old armies, the acting Field Marshal (FM), the rank dates back to 1632, but in the 18th century he commanded 2 or 3 brigades in the order of battle; in some cases he could command a wing. Later, at the end of the 18th-19th centuries, he was the commander of Divisions, hence the nickname Divisionary.

3) The **Feldzeugmeister** (FZM or also *Generalfeldzeugmeister* or *Obristfeldzeugmeister*) was a high rank that revealed its artillery origins (the supreme artillery commander, the superintendent of the park and workshops, *Zeug* the artillery 'things'), but was always used, even, and especially, for generals coming out of the infantry academies. His equal rank for the cavalry was the General **der Kavallerie** or GdK. In the 18th century, FZMs and GdKs commanded the corps of the order of battle (the wings or lines), subordinating troops of all types to them.

4) Above them all stood the **Field Marshal** (*Feldmarschall* or *Generalfeldmarschall*), who was originally the supreme commander of the cavalry (*Obrist Feldmarschall*) or *Befehlshaber der Reiterei*; the name was derived from an ancient medieval Latin root *mariscalcus / marescalcus*,[33] who, in the 15th-16th centuries, was only a cavalry officer, like a *Stallmeister*. From the 17th century he had the rank of Supreme General.

The above-mentioned designations are quite indicative to define the levels of hierarchy, mentioned above, as, simply, functions or offices, exercised only for campaign time. Until the beginning of the 17th century, they were apparently not permanent in the military hierarchy, the

Feldzeugmeister

General Feld-Wachtmeister

19th century to be a standing army. This is not technically correct, as the term k. k. was never used for the standing army of the Habsburg Empire at that time.

33   Actually, the Latin was derived from the Frankish *marhskalk 'servant (skalk)' 'horse attendant (marh)' from which mariscalco and marshal. The form farrier, blacksmith, derives from the combination of the Latin 'manus', hand. In the Middle Ages it had the same meaning as constable; which is derived from Comes Stabulae or chief of the stables (of the king) and still exists today.

highest rank of which remained the colonel or *Obrist (which is* why the army commander of Rudolf II's 'Long War of the Turks' - 1592-1606 - was referred to as 'colonel general' (*Generalobrist*) and his representative in his absence, was called lieutenant of the colonel general (*Generalobristleutnant*). In 1620, the commander of the cavalry was called Colonel General of the Cavalry (*Generalobrist über die Reiterei*), referred to in Latin as '*universi equitatus nostri generalis capitaneus*', but also (*Obristwachtmeister über alles Kriegsvolk zu Roß*) Master of the Colonel's Guard for all mounted people. A special rank was coined for the legendary Croatian general Isolani (1632) who was described as (*Oberkommandant über alles Kriegsvolk zu Pferd kroatischer* Nation) the supreme commander of the entire cavalry of the Croatian nation.

Until the beginning of the 17th century, the higher commands were various persons, mostly colonels, regimental commanders, who in the field, i.e. during a campaign, issued 'general' orders or created staffs known as 'general offices' (*Generalämter*) or war offices (*Kriegsämter*), in some chronicles referred to as '*Ämbter im Veldt*', field offices. Over the years, those service definitions gradually turned into ranks and grades. At the end of the Thirty Years' War, it seems that the evolutionary process was completed, leaving only the ownership and command of the regiment to the colonel. A large number of high ranks in the Habsburg army also owned a regiment. The situation of the high ranks in the Austrian army (armies one should say) was more or less as follows at the outbreak of Maria Theresa's War of Succession.

Austrian - Bohemian and Hungarian generalities of the War of Austrian Succession (FM by seniority)		
1723 FM	Harrach zu Rohrau, Johann Joseph Philipp Graf von (conte di)	1716 FZM
1723 FM	Königsegg-Rothenfels, Lothar Joseph Dominik Christian Graf v. (**presidente dell'Hofkriegsrat**)	1716 FZM
1723 FM	Starhemberg, Maximilian Adam Graf v.	1716 FZM
1737 FM	Arenberg, Leopold Philipp Karl Joseph de Ligne, Duc d´Aerschot et Croy	1723 FML
1737 FM	Wallis Frhr. v. (barone di) Karighmain, Georg Olivier Graf v.	1723 FZM
1737 FM	Khevenhüller zu Aichelberg u. Frankenburg, Ludwig Andreas Graf v.	1735 GdK
1739 FM	Seherr-Thoß, Johann Christoph Frhr. v. (barone di)	1735 GdK
1740 FM	Lothringen u. Bar, Karl Alexander Hzg. v. (duca Carlo di Lorena)	1738 FML
1741 FM	Althann Gundacker Ludwig Joseph, Freiherr auf der Goldburg Graf zu Murstetten	1723 GdK
1741 FM	Cordova de Comares, Don Gaspar Fernández de Córdova y Alagon, Conde de	1723 GdK
1741 FM	Csáky v. Keresztszég u. Adorján, Georg I. Emerich Graf	1735 GdK
1741 FM	Hessen-Kassel, Maximilian Prinz v.	1735 FZM
1741 FM	Neipperg, Wilhelm Reinhart Graf v.	1735 FZM
1741 FM	Lobkowitz, Georg Christian Fst. v.	1735 GdK
1741 FM	Hohenzollern-Hechingen, Friedrich Ludwig Fst. v.	1735 GdK
1741 FM	Traun, Otto Ferdinand Graf v. Abensperg u.	1735 FZM
1741 FM	Nesselrode zu Roth u. Grimberg, Johann Franz Hermann Graf v.	1728 FZM
1741 FM	Károlyi v. Nagy-Károly, Alexander Graf	1723 GdK
1741 FM	Schmettau, Samuel Graf v.	1735 FZM
1741 FM	Daun, Heinrich Dietrich Martin Joseph Graf u. Herr v. u. zu	1723 FZM
1741 FM	Sachsen-Hildburghausen, Joseph Maria Friedrich Wilhelm Prinz v.	1736 FZM
1741 FM	Esterházy de Galántha, Joseph Sigmund Graf	1739 GdK
1741 FM	Vasquez de Pinos, Johann Jakob de Vasquez y de la Puente, Conde de	1735 GdK
1744 FM	Marulli, Franz Xaver Cavaliere di	1735 FZM
1745 FM	Hohenembs, Franz Wilhelm Rudolf Graf v.	1741 FZM
1745 FM	Liechtenstein, Hzg. v. Troppau u. Jägerndorf, Josef Wenzel Laurenz Fst. v.	1739 GdK
1745 FM	O'Gilvie, Franz Karl Hermann Graf v.	1735 FZM
1745 FM	Batthyányi, Karl Joseph Fürst von	1739 GdK
1745 FM	Diemar, Hartmann Ernst Frhr. v.	1741 GdK
1746 FM	Waldeck u. Pyrmont, Karl August Friedrich Fst. v.	1741 FZM
1745 GdK	Aspremont und Lynden, Ferdinand Karl Graf von	1741 FML
1748 FZM	Baden-Baden, Ludwig Georg Simpert Wilhelm Markgraf v.	1728 FML
1745 GdK	Balaira, Ludwig Graf von	1737 FML
1748 GdK	Berghe gen. Trips, Adolf Sigmund Karl Frhr. v.	1745 FML

1742 GdK	Berlichingen, Johann Friedrich Frhr. v.	1737 FML
1745 GdK	Bernes de Rossana, Joseph Karl Anton Graf v.	1739 FML
1745 FZM	Botta d'Adorno, Anton Otto Marchese	1735 FML
1746 FZM	Braunschweig-Lüneburg, Ludwig Ernst Hzg. v.	1741 FML
1745 FZM	Browne, Baron de Camus and Mountany, Maximilian Ulysses Graf v.	1739 FML
1748 FZM	Callenberg, Heinrich Graf v.	1733 FML
1745 FZM	Chanclos, Sg. de Leves, Karl Urban Graf v.	1738 FML
1748 GdK	Czernin v. Chudenitz, Theobald Martin Graf	1737 FML
1745 FZM	Damnitz, Wolfgang Sigmund Frhr. v.	1737 FML
1745 FZM	Daun, Fst. v. Teano, Marchese di Rivola, Leopold Joseph Maria Graf v.	1739 FML
1748 GdK	De Fin, Alexander Anton Frhr. v.	1745 FML
1744 FZM	Diesbach, Fst. v. St. Agatha, Johann Friedrich Graf v.	1723 FML
1748 FZM	Dungern, Karl Ludwig Johann Frhr. v.	1745 FML
1748 FZM	Engelshofen, Franz Leopold Anton Frhr. (Ponz) v.	1741 FML
1741 GdK	Esterházy de Galántha, Franz VI. Graf	1734 FML
1748 GdK	Esterházy v. Galántha, Paul Anton I. Fst.	1747 FML
1748 GdK	Fesztetics de Tolna, Joseph Graf	1741 FML
1748 FZM	Feuerstein v. Feuersteinsberg, Anton Ferdinand Frhr.	1745 FML
1745 FZM	Gaisruck, Franz Sigismund Hieronymus Felix Graf v.	1739 FML
1749 GdK	Guadagni, Ascanio Alessandro Marchese di	1737 FML
1748 FZM	Helfreich, Christian Frhr. v.	1745 FML
1748 GdK	Hennin-Bossu, Johann Franz Joseph Graf v.	1745 FML
1748 Gdk	Holly, Johann Joseph Maximilian Frhr. v.	1744 FML
1748 GdK	Kalckreuth, Georg Christian Frhr. v.	1746 FML
1748 FZM	Keuhl (Kheul), Karl Gustav Frhr. v.	1745 FML
1748 GdK	Koháry v. Csábrágh u. Szitnya, Andreas Joseph Graf	1741 FML
1748 FZM	Kökenyesdi v. Vettes, Ladislaus Frhr.	1742 FML
1748 FZM	Kolowrat-Krakowsky, Kajetan Franz Xaver Graf v.	1741 FML
1748 FZM	Königsegg-Rothenfels, Christian Moriz Graf v.	1741 FML
1748 FZM	Lalaing, Vicomte d´Audenaarde, Maximilian Joseph Graf v.	1733 FML
1748 FZM	Lannoy de la Motterie, Eugen Graf v.	1733 FML
1744 GdK	Ligne, Ferdinand Prinz de	1743 FML
1748 Gdk	Löwenwolde, Friedrich Kasimir Graf v.	1741 FML
1748 Gdk	Lucchesi d´ Averna, Joseph Graf (morto a Leuthen)	1745 FML
1748 FZM	Luzán, Johann Emanuel Graf v.	1744 FML
1748 FZM	Marschall v. Burgholzhausen, Ernst Dietrich Graf	1745 FML
1748 FZM	Mercy d´ Argenteau, Anton Ignaz Graf v.	1741 FML
1745 FZM	Moltke, Philipp Ludwig Frhr. v.	1739 FML
1748 GdK	Nádasdy v. Fogáras, Franz Leopold Graf	1744 FML
1741 FZM	O'Nelly, Johann Graf v.	1734 FML
1741 GdK	Orsini, Marchese di Roma, Egidio	1723 FML
1745 GdK	Pálffy ab Erdöd, Paul Karl III. Engelbert Graf v.	1739 FML
1745 FZM	Pallavicini-Centurioni, Johann Lukas Graf v.	1741 FML
1748 GdK	Pertusati, Christoph Graf v.	1744 FML
1746 GdK	Pfalzgraf bei Rhein, Prinz v. Zweibrücken-Birkenfeld, Wilhelm	1743 FML
1740 FZM	Pignatelli d´Aragona, Fernando, Principe di Strongoli, Duca di Tolve, conte di Melissa	1733 FML
1741 GdK	Podstatzky, Karl Maximilian Graf v.	1733 FML
1748 GdK	Preysing, Ernst Friedrich Frhr. v.	1741 FML
1744 FZM	Prié-Turinetti, Marchese di Pancaliere, Johann Anton de	1733 FML
1741 GdK	Römer, Karl Joachim Frhr. v. (morto a Mollwitz)	1737 FML
1745 GdK	Sachsen-Gotha, Johann August Hzg. v.	1738 FML
1745 GdK	Salburg, Franz Ludwig Graf v.	1739 FML
1745 FZM	Salm, Hzg. v. Hoogstraeten, Nikolaus Leopold Fst. v.	1739 FML
1748 GdK	Schmertzing, Friedrich Hannibal Frhr. v.	1746 FML

1745 FZM	Schulenburg-Oeynhausen, Ferdinand Ludwig Graf v. der	1739 FML
1748 GdK	Splényi v. Miháldy, Gabriel Anton Frhr.	1742 FML
1748 FZM	Stentzsch, Georg Leonhard Frhr. v.	1741 FML
1739 GdK	Styrum, Otto Ernst Leopold Graf v. Limburg zu	1735 FML
1741 FZM	Thüngen, Adam Sigismund Frhr. v.	1734 FML
1748 FZM	Tornaco, Arnold Franz Frhr. v.	1745 FML
1748 GdK	Trivulzio gen. Galli, D. Antonio Ptolemeo, Fst. v. Misocchi	1741 FML
1740 FZM	Wachtendomk, Karl Franz Frhr. v.	1735 FML
1745 FZM	Wallis, Frhr. v. Karighmain, Franz Wenzel Graf v.	1735 FML
1741 FZM	Walseck, Otto Anton Frhr. v.	1734 FML

abbreviations: Frhr. = Freiherr (baron); Fst. = Fürst (prince); Graf - Conde = count; FML = Feldmarschall-Leutnant (lieutenant field marshal); Wing commands; GdK = General der Kavallerie; FZM = Feldzeugmeister; FM = Feldmarschall or field marshal. V. = von

Greater States, Lesser States and Major States

The number of field marshals, cavalry generals, FZMs, FMLs and major generals was not limited. Unless the generals were, themselves, commanders of an army or army detachments, they were under the orders of the superior general commanding the army, to whom they were assigned according to need and desire. The original meaning of the rank designations had already become considerably generalised; the designation no longer indicated a specific field of operation, but a career move from general.

Higher order army corps (large tactical and strategic units) did not yet exist and therefore generals were included in the Battle Orders as Line (*Treffen*) or Wing commanders, and as their aides. Contrary to the belief of many, the 'brigade' did not even exist, although this term was often used to identify a gathering of six to ten battalions; it was, to all intents and purposes, only a temporary formation, created on the spot. The entirety of all generals of an army constituted the 'Great General Staff' (*grossen Generalstab*). Its members were part of the 'Army War Council', which the army commander was obliged to convene in important cases, without, however, being bound by their vote. In peacetime, the service of the General Staff was entrusted mainly to the *Hofkriegsrat*, possibly in conjunction with several senior generals, appointed on a case-by-case basis.

There was no General Staff at all, as there had been in the Napoleonic wars, and the

1751
General Feld-Wachtmeister

1751
Feldmarschall Leutnant

1751
General Feld-Wachtmeister

1751
Feldmarschall Leutnant

field service fell entirely to the Grand Staff and thus to the generals themselves. For some time, however, a Lesser General Staff, also known as the 'minor' General Staff (but here the words 'major and minor' clashed somewhat), which included generals as well as other positions, had been established for less important tasks in battle. The main players in these minor staffs were the *Adjutant-Generals (General-Adjutanten)* and the Quartermaster-General (*General-Quartiermeister*); The latter included the lieutenant of the quartermaster-general, the quartermaster-general of the General Staff (possibly also with a lieutenant), the general director of transport (*General-Wagenmeister*), with his lieutenant, the captain of the guides (commander of the *Wegweiser* or road markers, of the relays or *Boten*, of the informers or *Kundschafter*), the attorney-general (*General-Gewaltige*) commander of the field police, also serving with a cavalry escort, the provost of the General Staff (also with his lieutenant).

The services of these posts could be deduced from their names and mediated between the army and the General Staff. The Adjutant General was not the Adjutant General of the Napoleonic wars, but precisely the aide-de-camp of the commanding general, the order bearer who passed on commands to both the Quartermaster General and his organs, i.e. the generals and troop commanders. The Quartermaster General had the task of finding the place and building the camps and establishing and winter quarters (quarters) according to the general instructions of the command; he was also responsible for the knowledge and development of the assigned areas in terms of food and land use. The 'junior' staff was essential for the marches, taking care of supplies and quarters.

Other organs of the Small General Staff, known as the Lower General Staff (*kleiner Generalstab*), such as the Medical Staff (Doctors of Medicine), whose most senior member acted as Army Doctor (*Chef-Arzt*), also gravitated within the ranks of the Small General Staff, the General Staff of Surgeons (*Stabs-Chirurgen* or by the old term *Stabs-Feldscherer*), the Commissariat offices, the commissariat office, the Field War Office, the Auditors, the Field Pharmacy, the Field Post Office, a few Engineers and the *Pater Superior,* a kind of Field Bishop, head of all chaplains.

One could immediately see the similarity between the Lower General Staff and the 'Lower First Floor' of the companies (then still called *Fähnlein*) and regiments. The table shows the service equivalences.

Army Headquarters	Regimental Staff	Company
Adjutant General	**Lieutenant-Wachtmeister** (Adjutant)	**Feldwebel**
Quartermaster General or his lieutenant, State Quartermaster Maj-Gen. and Captain of the Guides	**Regimental Quartermaster**	**furiere**
General-Kriegs-Commissariats -Amts -Feld - Substitution	**Quartermaster as Rechnungsführer** (Chief Accountant)	**furiere**
Lt-Gen Uditore	**Auditor**	(the company commander was in charge of discipline)
Feld-Kriegs-Expedition	**Secretary** (the Uditore himself)	until 1740 **Musterschreiber, then furior**
Pater superior	**Chaplain**	compulsory service by bishops and sergeants or Führer
General - Wagenmeister or his Lieutenant	**Regiments-Wagenmeister**	(two soldiers guarding the cars)
General- Gewaltiger (General Prosecutor) and General Staff Provosts	**Regiments-Profoss**	(corporal)
Stabs - Medicus **Stabs-Chirurgus** **Feld - Apotheker**	**Regiments - Feldscherer** (surgeon) with the '*Medicamenten-Kasten*' medicine box	**Feldscherer-Geselle** assistant surgeon with bandages (*Verbandzeug*)

Officers in country

The Habsburg officer corps was mainly drawn from the old landed gentry. The great magnates were the top of the pyramid mainly due to their economic abilities, they had palaces in the capital and multitudes of 'servants'. Looking at the list of "promoted" generalities between 1740 and 1748, one can see Hungarian magnates in large numbers compared to previous years. The Habsburg nobility were notoriously generous, maintaining entire regiments at their own expense and initiating their scions into military careers, not always with warm approval. The future officers of the army had no dedicated schools, they ended up attending generic *Ritterakademien* or even studying the equestrian and martial arts abroad.

As far as the fighting corps was concerned, it must be emphasised that the officer corps of the Austrian army was by no means homogenous, both nationally and socially, but differed greatly, not only in terms of different cultures and languages, but especially in terms of promotions and careers. Thanks to the privileges of regimental owners, patents for officers could be acquired or obtained due to high social position. Many young nobles, who had never smelled gunpowder, started their military careers immediately, as staff officers. On top of that, nepotism and political influence prevented officers from advancing in their careers, 'from the pike to the service', becoming so-called 'soldiers of fortune', despite their military qualities and achievements; it was almost impossible to reach the ranks of the General Staff or even the Generalships.

In this regard, according to an opinion on the disastrous state of the military, but in particular that of the infantry, which a commission set up in 1738 presented to the Emperor, the main problem was: "the *exchanges and the 'market' of ranks in the regiment (the Stellenkauf), the desire to aggregate and the desire to seek one's fortune more in Vienna than through diligence and application to the regiment, causing the good officers to become demoralised, ending up subordinate to the younger ones ... they no longer reviewed the companies, the hospitals, the kitchens, nor did they devote themselves to camaraderie and the care of the uniform.*"[34]

There were also classes of officers of acquired military nobility or from wealthy families, especially on the borders of the empire, who were often disliked and treated as '*parvenu*'. Thus, for example, the ancient Italian nobility was certainly a nobility recognised, in rare cases, as equal to the counts of the empire (certainly not to dukes and princes of high rank), but remained, nevertheless, more 'Italian' than nobility. Maria Theresa, moreover, was very generous in awarding *Nobilitätsdiplomen* to officers who had distinguished themselves through fine deeds or long periods of service, creating, in effect, a new social class, those of the landless nobility. The trend was observed from the very beginning, with the need to obtain Hungarian war support, and was later mitigated with the foundation of the Military Academies, where the old nobility once again had control over the cadets.

A large number of officers came from the empire or foreign states. Prince Albert of Saxony was clear in stating that Austria '*was the first German House in which serving was considered an honour*'. Of course, all this was connected with the great pool of the Holy Roman Empire, with the associated principalities, grand duchies and duchies proudly maintaining entire regiments at their own expense. Many officers of the Lutheran or Calvinist religion were accepted as long as they practised their beliefs privately. Curiously, there were apparently entire regiments of Protestants, which caused some concern in the larger states, especially having to deal with Prussian propaganda. Despite the low class of nobility, Italian officers were highly regarded, especially the Lombards and Venetians (these, however, were not part of the empire); Montecuccoli's legacy was still alive in the traditions. The officers of Naples and Sicily were less highly regarded, now left to their own devices, like the Spaniards, after the death of Charles VI. Many were still in the imperial ranks, many others were against Maria Theresa on the Italian fields from 1745 to 1748. Other important nationalities were above all the Dutch, the Walloons and the Lorraine (whose land had been ceded to France in exchange for Tuscany in 1738), serious and well-prepared officers who knew how to distinguish themselves at numerous junctures. A large number of generals and officers began their service as teenagers in the 'family' regiments (those who could). There was a certain competition in enlisting young noblemen and making them cadets of one's own regiments. First and foremost, a good constitution and good looks were required, perhaps even intelligence; no one would dare criticise them in the regiment if they were sons of the empire's best-known families. The *Inhaber* or owners of the regiments were allowed to admit the *Regiments-Cadeten* as they passed through the various locations in the empire. This, of course, generated special training at each regiment, which was not always homogeneous

---

34 Jähns Max, *Das XVIII. Jahrhundert seit dem Auftreten Friedrichs des Grossen, 1740-1800, Geschichte des Kriegswissenschaften vornehmlich in Deutschland*, Oldenbourg, München 1891, p.2289.

with the rest of the army; this was also the reason for the establishment of the Military Academies, which will be discussed later.

Regimental recruitment involved the incorporation of volunteer Cadets (*Volontäre*) or Ordinary Cadets, usually sons of serving officers. There were also Regiments *Cadeten,* already incorporated, the most senior of whom were *Fahnen Cadeten.* These were the officers who attained the first rank of Ensign (*Fähnrich*) in infantry and Cornet in cavalry. They were in fact non-commissioned officers, by whom they were followed and trained. In 1748, the number of ensigns dropped to eight per regiment and the rank was destined, in time, to disappear with the advent of second lieutenants.

As far as the fundamental disciplinary aspect of the army is concerned, which is closely linked to the degree of culture and training of the officer corps, it is necessary to emphasise how everything still functioned thanks to the rules of the colonel-owners (it was a tradition dating back to mercenary armies when contracts were made with the colonel, with penalties also being made explicit in them).

In the 17th century, the disciplinary articles underwent a substantial change in their interpretation and meaning. No longer necessary to renew a contract with a colonel at the start of a new military campaign, the articles gradually became collections of unilaterally imposed rules that served exclusively for the administration of criminal justice.

The Holy Roman Empire had its legal basis in the *Constitutio Criminalis Carolina,* which was not a court-martial code, containing only a few articles concerning the army. The Holy Roman Empire supplemented the existing rules, those promulgated by various Habsburg emperors, with a *Reichsartikelbrief* of 1682 (which remained in force until 1806). The disciplinary rule, created by Leopold I, only covered mercenaries serving under the empire, not regular Austrian troops.

The legal concept in force was not only to judge the unvirtuous behaviour of the individual, but also to judge it from the perspective of a direct injury to the honour of the regiment; a kind of subjective responsibility. Particularly harsh and consistent punishments were to remove the criminal from the unit and restore the honour of the regiment.

The main office, for carrying out the investigation against a crime and for constituting a court of war, was, from the 16th century, the Regimental Provost (*Profoß*). His function, according to the current interpretation of the law, combined the duties of a police officer and a prosecutor. When a soldier was accused of a crime, the court martial could be assisted by a Hearing Officer (*Auditor*), whose task presented considerable difficulties, since in the 18th century there were still no legal texts. The regulations of 1737, in fact, merely indicated to which persons military criminal procedure applied.[35]

In the regiments, as mentioned, the law of the owner was in force. The stricter the discipline, the harsher the penalties. Cash fines were not given to soldiers; however, officers could have their pay suspended for 2, 3, or more months. Small offences such as theft, quarrels or insults were sometimes punished using the old system: small gibbets in which the soldier's neck and wrists were threaded, and he had to carry all his paraphernalia on his shoulder for one or more hours.

Among the old military punishments that were still in use was the *Spitzruthen* or *Gassenlaufen,* a punishment initially popular with the army of Gustavus Adolphus of Sweden, but presumably derived from the ancient *Spießrecht,* a law dating back to ancient German soldiers (Lanzichenecchi or *langen Spieße,* long spades) who had the power to judge and punish mutineers and those who caused the loss of a comrade's life. The condemned man, bare-chested and with his hands tied in a cross, had to walk, from 4 to 16 times (depending on the seriousness of the crime), along a narrow path surrounded by two or three rows of several hundred men, where each common soldier, equipped with a stick or pointed canes, beat the unfortunate man on the back, every time he passed.

In capital punishment, the *Gassenlauf* was extended to death; sometimes with punishments of 36 passes through the crowd, in some cases extending the execution for two or three consecutive days; the street was thus called 'Life or Death'. The execution was solemn, rythmed by fifes and drums, with the soldiers intoning, to the tune of the melody, the following words: *"Because Thou didst run away, here Thou must walk the way, here is where Thou didst wrong!"*

---

35   A step forward was taken on 25 June 1754 when Maria Theresa issued the '*Norma wie bei unseren Regimentern zu Fuß und zu Pferd in Justiz-Sachen künftighin fürgegangen werden solle',* commonly known as the 1754 Norma, which gave insights into military law. The Norma was completed by the *Theresian* reform of 1768 with the publication of the *Constitutio Criminalis Theresiana.*

In the cavalry, instead of using pointed canes, in the 'alley race' blows were inflicted with stirrups, breastplates or pack straps, in a less bloody manner. People gradually came to prefer flogging to *Gassenlauf*, due to the fact that in the run they were struck haphazardly, as one witness asserted: "*the corporals made the soldiers punished, disabled or lame, or deficient, if they were beaten awkwardly on the head.*" Flogging was less damaging. In the Austrian army, however, the 'stroke of the canes' was regulated by the 1752 Rule, with the exact allocation of passes through the caning. Minor offences in the infantry were punished by 2 strokes and 300 men with canes, in the cavalry by 150 men with pack-straps; more serious crimes were punished by 4 strokes and if even more serious by the death penalty or something very close to it. There was also a heavier punishment in infantry with 6 rides between 300 men and, similarly, in cavalry 6 rides with 150 men with pack-straps. The 'stick race' was mitigated by Emperor Leopold's rule in 1790, but was not abolished. The punishment of the cavalry 'belt race', on the other hand, will only be abolished in 1808. *Feldwebel* or *Wachtmeister*, corporals, *Gefreite* or Vice-captains, and all non-commissioned officers who had suffered such punishment were demoted to private soldier, with sentence announced by trumpet and drum roll.

The mildest corporal punishment took place in training and exercises, when the soldier was considered an 'automaton'. Officers were beaten with sticks, non-commissioned officers with bayonets or sabre blades, but this was considered part of the system. Non-commissioned officers and cadets themselves were punished for minor offences by officers with sabres or swords (it was good for an officer to know how to handle a blade well). It was thought that it was not possible to train a recruit without him receiving an occasional good thrashing.

As early as the first half of the 18th century, the 'stick regiment', as it called itself, played a leading role, so much so that several bans were issued due to the mistreatment of soldiers. It cannot be said that Habsburg officers were particularly popular. 'Standing under someone's cane' was like going down the hierarchical ladder. Already at the turn of the century, the staff of the Small Staff (*Regiments Adjutant , Regiments - Feldscherer , Proviantmeister , Wagenmeister, Profoß*) were 'under the stick' (in the sense that they could be punished with the stick) of the senior staff officers or the commander, at least in most regiments. Only the Quartermaster and the Auditor were considered exempt from caning. In sequence they could cane the Regimental Adjutants all those who, by service, were subordinate to them and, in addition, all the troop from the Feldwebel or Wachtmeister downwards; the Regimental Surgeon (*Regiments-Feldscherer*) all his assistants (*Unterfeldscherer*) or affiliates; the Quartermaster and *Proviantmeister* could beat the furiers and scribes; the Auditor could beat the Provost and his subordinates; the Captain and Lieutenant could beat all the troop from the *Feldwebel* or *Wachtmeister* down in their company; the *Feldwebel* all the corporals and soldiers; and, finally, the corporals only the soldiers. Only thanks to an Ordinance of the *Hofkriegsrat*, dated 20 June 1752, "*the Regimental Helpers otherwise called Wachtmeister-Lieutenants, as well as the Regimental Surgeons, who from Regiments-Feldscherer in the future are to be called Regiments-Chirurgus, shall henceforth no longer be - under the staff - of the Regimental Commander.*"

From Count Khevenhüller's regulations of 1734, we borrow the following text: '*No soldier should use insulting or immoral words, or even mention his name in such a way as to offend the honour of an officer, because if this were to happen, an officer would bear the heavy responsibility of having what he said publicly retracted in front of the soldiers. Any such misconduct must be punished, because the officer must command honest and good people, and because every commander has sufficient means and ways to exercise his authority, without the need to use harsh and unnecessary words. If punishment is necessary, he may inflict 25 beatings, for minor offences, and 50 for more serious offences. But no more than this number, because exceeding 50 beatings already becomes a regimental punishment.*"

Returning to the tune '*Why did you want to run away,...*' (*Warum bist Du fortgelaufen*) one could point out how this brought to the fore a major scourge of the time: deserters. The subject of desertions was, as mentioned, a plague in Maria Theresa's army. The large number of measures enacted during the war and the Final Patent of 1749 attest to the importance of combating the phenomenon. An initial regulatory approach was only created, however, with a Patent of 26 May 1749 entitled '*zur Behandlung eines Desserteurs*', how to treat a deserter, later called the 1749 Patent. Although this patent contained only four pages of text, the provisions it contained must be considered comprehensive and far-sighted. Especially important was the introduction of a financial reward for the capture and extradition of the deserter. The amount of the reward varied depending on whether he escaped on horseback or stole a horse to escape. This put an end to the phenomenon of refugees in the 'neighbouring duchy' and, in this way, it was much more difficult for deserters to hide in the country or receive assistance during their escape. The finding of financial resources for the payment of rewards - in spite of depleted treasuries - showed the great importance Maria Theresa attached to this issue.

Italian nobles as imperial officers

Italian historiography has lively debated the problem of military careers in the armies of the absolutist states of the 17th-18th centuries (in particular, the Savoy State), trying to understand whether these experiences had changed the traditions of the ancient nobiliary conscience, founded on principles of civilisation, by introducing a new hierarchy based on professional merit, or whether the hierarchical supremacy of the nobility within the State had in fact been consolidated and strengthened. Maria Theresa forcibly imposed military meritocracy with the creation of the most famous Habsburg honour, on 18 June 1757, the day of the victorious Battle of Kolín, effectively severing any internal hierarchy based on more or less influential or wealthy nobility with the crosses of knighthood. The sources give us an ambiguous picture, even after the spread of state military schools in the 18th century, when technical skills and knowledge were the basis of a successful officer's career; many nobles still considered entry into the army a privilege and hereditary recognition, which allowed for important advantages in the state and local administrative system.

But there were also other tensions within the Italian nobility. After the extinction of the Spanish branch of the Habsburgs in 1700 and with the dispute between the Gallispani (the followers of the Bourbons) and the Ghibellini (the followers of the German emperors of the House of Habsburg), the relations of the Italian nobility, in terms of political-dynastic loyalty, changed profoundly.

Until the beginning of the 18th century, Italian noble families regarded the Spanish monarchy, the emperors of the house of Habsburg and the papacy as a kind of trinity of similar governments, an almost unitary federation; in other words, the triad was Spain-Habsburg-Rome, a north star in the stormy sea of politics. At the time of the Thirty Years' War and the campaigns against the Turks, many Italian nobles had served in the imperial army, either as volunteers or officers in search of adventure, especially also as general officers and entrepreneurs. Prominent among them were Ottavio Piccolomini from Siena, Annibale Gonzaga from Mantua, Raimondo Montecuccoli from Modena, Enea Caprara and Ferdinando Marsigli from Bologna, Antonio Carafa from the Kingdom of Naples and, of course, the cosmopolitan Eugenio di Savoia-Soissons (Eugene of Savoy, as he usually signed himself). The biographies of those Italian warlords showed that a career in the service of the emperor did not contradict loyalty to the Spanish monarch, the so-called 'Catholic king'. In fact, they participated in wars against the enemies of Catholicism (heretics and non-believers). The breaking of this dogma, following the War of the Spanish Succession, caused a deep shock to many Italian nobility.

The impact was particularly hard on all active officers, although it is likely that the subsequent reshaping of European politics ended up mitigating the traumatic effects of the break. The vicissitudes of the Este family of San Martino, a secondary branch of the ducal dynasty of Modena, demonstrate the significance of the division of that centuries-old alliance. At the end of the 17th century, the Este family of San Martino owned properties and fiefdoms in the Duchy of Modena, Lombardy and Savoy. In December 1701, Marquis Gabriele d'Este was a colonel in the service of the Savoy duke Victor Amadeus II, an ally of King Philip of Bourbon of Spain. But after two years, the Duke of Savoy left this alliance, with the Gallispanians, and came to an agreement with the Emperor of Austria, Leopold I. It was then that Gabriele decided to leave his regiment and flee to the territory of the neutral republic of Genoa. This was prompted by honour and the well-founded fear that the Spanish governor of Milan would confiscate his '*goods of my right*' in Lombardy. Many nobles from Lombardy and, curiously, also from Veneto continued to serve under the flag of the double-headed eagle, some becoming famous Habsburg generals until the century that followed; especially the nobility of Friuli and the Littoral, who were often entrusted with the control of the military border.

Another trauma that profoundly influenced the attitude of the Italian nobility towards a military career was the transformation of a cosmopolitan imperial army into a great national and military power under the monarchy of the house of Austria; but this happened later, in the second half of the 18th century, in 1760.

It is no coincidence that in the same time period, the number of Italians in the imperial officer corps began to decrease significantly. While officers from Lombardy, but also from Piedmont, Tuscany, Venice and Naples were very numerous, in many regiments in the mid-18th century, their numbers decreased drastically, after the 1960s; so much so that, in the 1980s, even the two Italian infantry regiments, No. 44 (Belgioioso) and No. 48 (Caprara) had only half of their captains of Italian origin.

If we then consider the genealogies of twenty-one aristocratic families in Milan, we discover the following development: in the 17th century, thirty-three Milanese nobles were in the service of the kings of Spain as soldiers. From the beginning of the 18th century until the end of the Seven Years' War, twenty-four Milanese nobles chose a career in the Austrian Habsburg army, but in the following thirty years there were only six Milanese. A reading of the generalities of the imperial army between 1747 and 1797 corroborated this trend. In fact, the number of senior officers of Milanese origin also decreased, from seven (one *Field Marshal*, one *Feldzeugmeister*, three *Feldmarshalllieutenants*, two *Feldwachtmeisters*) to only one (Lieutenant Field Marshal Count Ludovico Belgioioso di Barbiano).

The 'white' army of the Austrian monarchy was on its way to becoming a German army, even though it started from a strong Hungarian base with Maria Theresa. This Germanisation, which was to be associated with the compulsory knowledge of German, or at least of a large command base, was to be a major obstacle to the aspirations of the Lombard, and later Emilian and Tuscan, nobles to undertake a military career in the service of their Viennese rulers. It would suffice to read the memoirs penned by Count Pietro Verri ('*Memorie sincere del modo con cui servii nel militare e dei miei primi progressi nel servigio politico*'), one of the most famous Milanese illuminists, who participated in the 1759 campaign in Lausitz and Saxony '*where he could learn in great measure what the profession of war is*' to have an eloquent testimony of this transitional period.

The birth of the Academies

Maria Theresa earned great merit by creating military training schools. Her purpose was twofold: to care for the children of officers and soldiers and the offspring of the army. First, in 1744, she built the Kremsmünster Cavalry School in Upper Austria, two years later the *Theresian* Academy of Chivalry (the famous *Theresianum* in Vienna), placed under the supervision of the Jesuits, which, after the abolition of the Order, was merged with the Savoy Academy, founded by Theresa of Savoy and handed over to the Piarists (the German name for the Scholopian Fathers). In 1752, the Empress founded a) a war academy for a few nobles (similar to the military academy in Berlin), b) the military 'nursery' school for 200 student cadets in the old *Chaosstifte*[36], and c) the military academy in Wiener-Neustadt, which became famous. The military 'nursery' school served as a preparatory institute for the military academy in Neustadt and was attended by corps of noble cadets.

The forerunner of Prince Liechtenstein's Artillery School was the large *Haupt-Artillerie-Depot* or Army Park, which was located, from 1744, in Bergstadl, a village near Budweis. The students were non-commissioned *Stückjunker officers* (equivalents of the infantry *Feldwebel*) and veteran artificers (officers) who were initiated and qualified to become officers. The subjects taught were: mathematics and mechanics, artillery (calibre, drawing of pieces, examination of pieces and ammunition, use of all types of weapons, ballistics, *laborier*, i.e. service work on the piece), High Artillery Honours (and secret subjects, the dissemination of which to unknown people was forbidden by the 1757 regulations), the art of war building, fortifications and encampments. The Engineering School, on the other hand, pre-existed as early as 1735 under the name of the Academy of Military Engineering, in Vienna.

A direct impact on the army and the entire Habsburg monarchy as a result of the War of Austrian Succession was the rethinking of a new idea of state. During the collapse of the ethical-political values associated with the crown of the Holy Roman Empire, with the House of Habsburg from 1740 to 1745, a new idea of the nation-state, different from the generic idea of the *Reich*, had slowly begun to emerge. With the increasingly strong identification of the House of Habsburg with its countries, the awareness arose to work for the total defence of those regions, also by standardising the military, administrative, justice and interior structures of the Austrian monarchy. The experienced threat in foreign policy, therefore, ended up fuelling an internal tension towards unification, which would reverberate in future reforms of the army.

Taking stock of the conduct of the War of Succession we could agree that it did not significantly change the borders of the Reich. Although Maria Theresa did not manage to gain any territorial gains, she did manage to restore imperial dignity to the House of Habsburg and defend the empire from division. Maria Theresa, as

---

36   The Chaos Foundation for Orphans was established in 1663 by Baron Richthausen von Chaos. In the course of time, the Foundation had numerous buildings built in Vienna, including the Chaos Foundation and the Stiftskaserne, which are still standing today.

regent, was very adept at disentangling political weaknesses, the disastrous condition of the army in terms of leadership (officers), training, organisation but above all discipline. The loss of Silesia and the failure in numerous battles, increased levels of desertion, coupled with the greed of her soldiers, were all decisive factors for Maria Theresa to renew and improve the military penal system in order to create a disciplined and well-functioning army. The introduction of a new 'national' discipline, no longer entrusted to the 'rules of the landlords', and the improvement of the officer corps were not objectives at odds with the desire to retake Silesian lands, indeed they were perhaps the means to a legitimate aspiration.

The army at the beginning of the War of Austrian Succession

Maria Theresa was forced to go through two major conflicts: her own succession to the throne and the Seven Years' War. Apparently she was so popular among the military ranks that, already in the third year of her rule, the enthusiastic army asked for a coin to be minted for 'their godmother' on which the motto '*Mater castrorum*', mother of the camps, was engraved. It had not all started so well, however. When his father, Charles VI, died, defeatist inscriptions had appeared on the walls of Vienna such as:

"*Vivat! The emperor is dead,*

We have dry bread.

The Lorenese does not please us at all,

The Bavarian fits us well."

Speaking of religion, the number of Catholics living in Silesia was very large and there were few troops to protect them, lest, sooner or later, foreign intervention should occur. In Lower Austria and Tyrol, the Elector of Bavaria had a large following, as did the Elector of Saxony in Bohemia. There were also riots and small uprisings. For example, a Viennese journalist wrote on 1 December 1740: '*The bad people from time to time commit acts of debauchery. A few days ago, they wanted to defenestrate the Count of Oedt, but the dragoons of the Alt-Hanisch dispersed that senseless crowd.*"

In spite of everything, the queen (actually the king because the Hungarian title was male), who had only started ruling as Grand Duchess of Austria, went on her way. In her efforts to improve the army in the war, Maria Theresa was helped by her son, the future Emperor Joseph II, from 1765. Joseph, a pupil of the distinguished Field Marshal Count Lacy, an expert in the theory of the art of war, made many journeys through the regions of the monarchy, assessing, with his own eyes, the state of the troops, fortresses, provisions, etc. He was then the architect of all those reforms, which the war had experienced in the field, under his mother's rule, the many antecedents of which would project him as the creator of a great reform. Thus Maria Theresa, and Joseph II, will form the two administrations decisively involved in the modernisation of the Austrian military apparatus.

MARIA THERESA'S FIRST INFANTRY

It is not an easy thing to deal with the army of Austria, so cosmopolitan and international was its capital, Vienna. This is how the jurist von Loen described it in 1740: '*The way of life in Vienna is amusing, free, euphoric, indulgent, unchanging, serious and natural. You can be pleasure-loving and in love, but never to the point of despair. One laughs and jokes, and one does not break one's head to be lucid and delicate. You eat and drink, you fast and swarm in the streets, you pray and swear, you do everything and the opposite of everything ... The hustle and bustle in Vienna is even louder than in Paris, this is because the city is not large at all. The streets always full of people, horses and carriages endanger the lives of those who walk. The coachmen and valets are always shouting, 'Schauts auf! Look up!" And by dodging one, one collides with the other. So if you want to visit Vienna, you have to take the carriages. Here you see people from foreign places and from all over the world: Hungarians, Hussars, Aiducs, Poles, Muscovites, Persians, Turks, Moravians, Spaniards, Italians, Tyroleans, Swiss, in short, from all European peoples. It would be nice to know how many tailors there are and where they live, as they have to make a lot of types of clothes; that's for sure, it's not done anywhere in the world except in Vienna.*"

At the death of Emperor Leopold I (1705), Austria inherited 37 infantry regiments, his successor Joseph I added three more, so that by the time Charles VI ascended the imperial throne (1710) there were 40 infantry regiments. Their staff was as follows:

Staff of an Austrian infantry regiment (1710)			
Colonel Commander Owner = Inhaber		Colonel Commander (Obrist)	
Lieutenant-Colonel = Obrist-Lieutenant	Obristwachtmeister (future Major)		Regimental Quartermaster
Regimental Aide or Wachtmeister-Lieutenant	Auditor	Secretary	Chaplain
Transport Commander or Wagenmeister	Regimental surgeon		
Supply Commander or Proviantmeister		Provost (Profoß) cum suis (6-8 bodyguards)	
Regg. drum			
Composition of an Austrian Musketeer Company (1710)			
Officers of Prima Plana			
Captain	Lieutenant	Bishop (Fähnrich)	Feldwebel	Führer (sergeant)
Furies	Musterschreiber (compiler)		Feldscherer (sanitary) = total 8 men	
Troop			
6 Corporals (Korporal)	4 Fourierschützen (Fourierschützen)	4 musicians	12 Gefreyte (elite soldiers)
for a total of 140 men			

Staff of a Hungarian infantry regiment (Hajducken) (1710)			
Colonel Commander Owner = Inhaber		Colonel Commander (Ezredes)	
lieutenant colonel = Alezredes or Oberslajdinánt	Obristwachtmeister (Főstrázsamester) future = őrnagy or major		
Regimental Aide or Wachtmeister-Lieutenant	Joggyakornok (Uditore)	Secretary - Titkár	Chaplain (Káplan)
Kocsi Gondviselő - Wagenmeister	Ezred tábori orvos = Chief Surgeon	Kvártély-csináló = quartermaster	
Élés-mester		Provost (Prépost) cum suis (6-8 guards)	
Ezred dobos			
Composition of a Hungarian Hajducken Company (1710)			
Captain or Kapitán	Lieutenant - Főhadnagy	second lieutenant - hadnagy	Strázsamester- Feldwebel*	Őrmester (sergeant)
Furír	Musterschreiber (compiler) or Irnok		Standard bearer (Futár o zászlótartó)	
Tábori orvos (sanitary) but also Seb-orvos or Sebész = total 8 men				
6 Corporals (Káprál or Tizedes)	4 Fourierschützen (Fourierschützen)		4 musicians	12 Őrvezető (elite soldiers)
a total of 178 men or Hajduck and a blacksmith (Kóvacs)				
* - Főtorzomester in another source.				

By the time of Prince Eugene, victorious in the campaigns of Peterwardein, Temesvár and Belgrade, the Habsburg army had occupied the territories of the Banat of Temes, parts of Serbia, Bosnia and Wallachia, with a total force of 53 infantry regiments, 22 cuirassiers (mounted regiments), 17 dragoons and 5 hussars. Although the fifteen years following the Peace of Passarowitz (Požarevac) were not entirely devoid of fighting, the times of relative peace allowed for multiple reductions in the number and strength of regiments, mainly due to the general precarious financial situation and Habsburg land holdings.

At the beginning of the 18th century, the Austrian imperial army had the following troops: infantry (initially called Foot Regiments and Hayduckenregimenter or Hayduck regiments of the Hungarian crown), cavalry (cuirassiers, dragoons and hussars), artillery (including a miners' company). The foot regiments were officially renamed '*Infanterie-Regimenter*' (initials IR) in the year 1718 and the '*Hayduckenregiment*' did not officially become Hungarian regiments until 1743. Until that year the Hungarian infantryman was not called *Gemeine* but *Hayduck*. A speciality of the infantry were the grenadiers who formed 1-2 companies per regiment and, from the reign of Charles VI, had lost the ability to throw hand grenades, becoming more and more an elite troop.

Under Leopold I, at the beginning of the war in Italy in 1701, all infantry regiments had 17 companies. For a long time everything remained the same under Charles VI, the only difference being that each regiment had 15 companies of musketeers and 2 companies of grenadiers; previously a regiment had 4 battalions, each of 4 companies, but now it had 3 battalions, each of 5 companies. It was in the period of 1717-1718 that the foot regiments (*Regiment zu Fuß*), as mentioned above, were given the name *Infanterie-Regiment (Infanterie-Regiment)*, denoted by the lineage of the colonel-owner or *Inhaber*; their numbering came much later, in 1769. In the spring of 1727, many regiments (most of which were stationed in Hungary) were urged to locally recruit 4-5 *Auctions-compagnien* each, of 83 soldiers, with the purpose of creating an irregular battalion (IV Battalion) that would be assigned territorial defence tasks (Slavonia Cordon and Military Borders). This was a practice already used in Habsburg recruitment and the companies were recruited at the expense of the local nobility, being only formally part of the regiments (to which they could be attached in the event of war, to complete the ranks). The imperial disposition (*kaiserlicher Entschließung*) of 5 November 1731 dispersed all those IV battalions, assigning the companies to other regiments, and completed them with discreetly trained recruits.
At the end of that 'relative peacetime' (circa 1732), the Habsburg army had 'immediate' (ready) troops, i.e. 47 infantry regiments, 20 cuirassier regiments, 12 dragoon regiments and 3 hussars. During the War of Polish Succession, there was a momentary need for cadre extensions. Between 1733 and 1735, eight new infantry regiments had been formed (of which the Moltke regiment, formed in 1733, had been disbanded the following year), two of dragoons and six of hussars. After peace, three infantry regiments were disbanded (among them the two Neapolitan regiments Monteleone and Spinelli) along with two regiments of cuirassiers.
In 1733, each infantry regiment had 15 musketeer companies (also called riflemen or „*Füsilier-*" or „*Ordinariers-*" of 140 men) divided into three battalions, plus two grenadier companies (100 men). Thus, each battalion had 700 men and the regiment 2300 men, including the '*completen*', e.g. the prescribed number of men. Each regiment, which was based in the Holy Roman Empire, was given a provisional fourth battalion in 1733, bringing it up to around 3,000 men.
The planned disbandment of two more infantry regiments at the beginning of 1736 and the prescribed reduction of each regiment to 2,000 men (cuirassiers and dragoons to 800 men and 440 horses, hussars to 600 men and 300 horses) were never completed due to the outbreak of war against the Turks. Even before the start of that war, however, on 18 October 1736, an imperial resolution stipulated that '*all infantry regiments were to be increased to 2,300 men, out of three battalions and two grenadier companies; if the 4th battalion was still present, it was to be disbanded, as of 1 November 1736*'.
At the end of the war against the Turks, the strength of the Austrian infantry was 52 infantry regiments or 118700 men, which, with the 40962 cavalry, brought the army to a total strength of 159662. This figure was not real. In reality, the number of soldiers left was much lower, due to the losses suffered, the efforts made on the marches and in the countryside, the unhealthy climate and often swampy terrain, and finally, the plagues and other diseases, which were endemic at that time on the southern borders of the kingdom. A status table of the imperial army in Hungary and Slavonia (20 October 1739) spoke of only 74 battalions and 56 grenadier companies of infantry, a presence of 20508 men against the planned level of 57400 men, i.e. only 35.7 per cent, a little more than a third. The exceptions were three infantry regiments stationed in the Netherlands, Los Rios, Prie and de Ligne, each with their 2000 men.
In matters of regulations, for many years, the 'laws' had been made by the regimental owners. The first *Vorschrift* or regulation for the entire army was only published in 1737. According to the *Reglement* of 1737, the infantry regiments were divided into three or four battalions, in proportion to their strength, so that each battalion had five '*Ordinari-Compagnien*', while the two grenadier companies were free, deployed on the two wings of the regiment. Each battalion was divided into three divisions, each division into two *Theile*, called platoons (*Züge*) or *Pelotons*, in the French manner.

The Force Reduction Project in the years 1739-1740

Peace with the Ottomans was made on 18 September 1739 in Belgrade. The emperor's first concern was to heal the wounds caused by the unfortunate war, striving to alleviate the suffering of his subjects by reconciling the political and military position of his court. The most common way was to reduce the armed force, but this was not an easy task. Some influential generals, such as Prince Joseph zu Sachsen-Hildburghausen, even considered it necessary to increase the strength of the army to avoid external aggression. Others, such as FM von Khevenhüller agreed with the need to reduce military expenditure.

The first preparatory step was taken on 3-24 October 1739, ordering all regiments on foot and horseback, not to replace vacancies in the major states, and among superior and inferior officers. The financial budget provided for only the sum of 8 million florins per year to be allocated to the army, of which six and a half million were allocated to the regiments in the hereditary lands (German, Bohemian, Hungarian), the rest for further military needs. The regiments stationed in Italy and Holland were to be financed from the income of those provinces. The first reduction project began in October 1739 thanks to the FMs Count von Khevenhüller and Seckendorff (at the time stationed in Graz). The latter had been more concerned with the general political situation, rather than the concrete issue, and therefore, his project, although noteworthy, was never considered. Khevenhüller reworked his design up to the first half of 1740, together with four other projects by the FM Counts Harrach and Königsegg, the FZM Prince zu Sachsen-Hildburghausen and the Koch *Hofkriegrat*. The common summary of the plans was that they all favoured cavalry (especially cuirassiers) at the expense of infantry. Khevenhüller even planned to disband 12 infantry regiments and reduce the officer corps. The proposals of the five experts were combined in a later compilation.

Although times were unhappy, it turned out that Charles VI, in his planned reorganisation, not only took into account the efficiency of his lands and their sufficient protection, but also gave due consideration to the possible succession of his daughter and the role the army would have to play in the event. Reducing the infantry too much would have left gaps in the country, which could only be filled with regiments still in the field, when peace had just been concluded. After peace, in fact, the army deployed against the Turks had been transferred to winter quarters, which stretched from Transylvania to Croatia and across Hungary. It would have been complicated in peacetime to make the troops make long winter marches to change garrisons. The plan, therefore, was moving towards the proposal to authorise a number of 52 infantry regiments, 18 cuirassiers, 14 dragoons and 8 hussars.

Thus, throughout the winter, the entire army remained in Hungary and the neighbouring countries; only with the arrival of spring did the marches begin. Parts of the two hitherto active garrison regiments, O'Gilvy and Wenzel Wallis, headed for Bohemia and Silesia; the rest of the regiments went to front Austria, where there were only two battalions of Salm and Walsegg, with the Jung-Daun and Damnitz infantry; to the Netherlands, which was then protected by only five infantry regiments and two dragoon regiments, three more infantry regiments, Salm, O'Nelly and Heister, and, to Italy, the infantry regiment Gyulai. infantry regiment Gyulai.

The other troop redeployments in the summer of 1740 were mainly carried out with the aim of re-establishing a balance between Hungary and its neighbouring countries with respect to having agile supply lines. In the middle of 1740, more than half of all war power was still stationed in the Hungarian countries, including eight infantry regiments and one/three dragoon regiments, to be transferred to the hereditary lands of German Bohemia. Despite all the pressure from Hungary, which still felt threatened in the south, however, the *Hofkriegsrat* opposed any further postponement, at least until it had been definitively determined how many and which regiments would be disbanded; it would have been pointless to move some regiments back and forth.

The Emperor, in his Resolution of 10 June, had finally agreed to the protocol of FM Count Harrach's reduction project, but had also decided to disband three infantry regiments (instead of two). Furthermore, three companies in each infantry regiment were to be reduced.

Harrach reduction project					
Infantry regiments	50	2000 u.	12 comp. 150 u.	2 cp. grenadiers 100 u.	
Cuirassiers Regiment	18	800 u.	10 comp. 70 u.	1 cp. Carabinieri 100 u.	400 cav.
Dragoon Regiment	12	800 u.	10 comp. 70 u.	1 cp. grenadiers 100 u.	400 cav.
Hussar Regiment	4	600 u.	8 comp		300 cav.
Regs. to be dissolved	2 infantry		2 of dragons	4 of hussars	

On 22 September, however, it was still uncertain whether to reduce six infantry regiments instead of three, in which case they would be transferred to the Bohemian hereditary lands, less than eight infantry regiments. In fact, Khevenhüller's draft showed that the Grand Duke of Tuscany had voted for the disbandment of eight infantry regiments; he was the most outspoken supporter of Khevenhüller's drastic vision. With the unque-

stionable influence of such strong opponents to the Harrach plan and the politically equally important opinion of Hildburghausen that the army should be increased rather than reduced, it had become very difficult for the emperor to come to a final decision. In fact, by 15 October (five days before his death) he had still not come down to report to the *Hofkriegrat*. The trend was towards the disbanding of regiments as confirmed by regulations given, on 9 July to all regiments stationed in all hereditary lands, on 8 October to those stationed in Italy and on 19 October to those in the Netherlands, according to which each company was to eliminate one corporal, two Gefreites and two assistant furiors, regulations which had not been passed on to the regiments 'to be disbanded'.

After the infantry regiments Botta, Browne and Harrach and the Liechtenstein Dragoons had already been marched into Silesia and Moravia in August and September, presumably in the certainty that they would not fall into the meshes of the 'Reduction', finally, between 15 and 19 October only a few days before the Emperor's death, the 'General Tables for the year 1740' with the orders for changes of headquarters, of the General War Commissariat, came out, which then, on 5 November 1740 (a month before Frederick II of Prussia invaded Silesia), indicated the future distribution of regiments, as in the following table.

Regions	Regiments			
	infantry	armourers	dragons	hussars
Lombardy and Tuscany (Italy)	13	2	1	2
Holland	8	-	2	-
Hungary, Croatia, Slavonia and Banat	12	13	7	5
Transylvania (Siebenbürgen)	4	3	2	1
Bohemia	5	-	-	-
Moravia	1	-	1	-
Silesia	4	-	-	-
Lower Austria	-	-	1	-
Inner Austria	1	-	-	-
Tyrol	1	-	-	-
Front Austria	3	-	-	-
TOTAL	52	18	14	8

No reduction had time to materialise, therefore, and the changes, caused by the regulations of 15 and 19 October, to the previous dislocation, which had been decided upon at the time of the death of Charles VI, only related to the main infantry group in the hereditary lands and still took a long time to complete. The Königsegg infantry regiment was moved to Tyrol, where it arrived in mid-November, while at the same time the Alt-Daun infantry was in Styria. The Harrach regiment entered Silesia, in the first half of November, was followed by the Browne and Botta infantry regiments, am only in December, and, at about the same time, the Moravian infantry, with part of the Liechtenstein Dragoons heading for Silesia. In November the Grünne infantry had yet to march, the Kolowrat and Carl Lothringen infantry regiments marched to the Bohemian hereditary lands in December; only the Franz Lothringen infantry regiment was on the march. The table above shows what the deployment was supposed to look like: little concern for possible Prussian threats, none for Bavarian threats. The final troop presentation, on the other hand, shows the approximate deployment of the Habsburg army at the time of the Prussian invasion (16 December), which, in Vienna, from 10 December onwards was not considered possible. Thus it was that, in December, relays left with urgent orders to several regiments in Hungary to march hastily to Silesia, Moravia and Bohemia.

But even if the number of regiments had not been reduced, the hesitations of the emperor and his advisors had indicated a lack of unified vision. Fortunately, the moral damage to the army was marginal, because at least the traditional tactical procedure of regiments had been maintained. Many historians have wondered whether indeed, during Maria Theresa's rise to power, the military apparatus had been as impoverished as claimed: almost 50,000 men (31.3 per cent of the effective strength) and 9421 horses (23.8 per cent), against a theoretical effective strength of 157,000 men and 39,102 horses. These figures could probably be correct, considering that the Supreme Resolution of 10 June had been completely scuttled by the sudden death of Charles VI. Maria Theresa did, however, want to follow in her father's footsteps, adhering to the "Harrach Reduction" as can be seen from the *Hofkriegsrat*'s circular of 31 December 1740, when the regiments sent to the Neipperg army were given the limits of 2000 men for infantry and 800 for cavalry; only the hussars were not raised to 600 per regiment and retained their previous numbers.

The situation of the Austrian army at the outbreak of war was this:

type of field weapon	Expected force		Effective force		difference		diff. lost %	
	men	horses	men	horses	men	horses	men	horses
infantry	108400	-	75653	-	32747	-	30,2	
chivalry in its entirety	33480	33480	32239	29741	1259	3739	3,8	11,1
armourers	14800	14800	14594	12998	206	1802	1,3	12,1
dragons	11800	11800	11818	11289	-	511	-	4,3
hussars	6880	6880	5827	5454	1053	1426	15,3	20,7
TOTALS	141880	33480	107892	29741	34006	3739	24	11,1

The Silesian Wars

The infantry of the 1740s consisted of the regular infantry regiments, the Tyrolean battalion (*Tyroler Land-Bataillon*), the garrison and garrison troops, to which the *Grenzer*, the militia of the Varazdin and Carlstädt military border, the Sava, Danube, Tisza and Maros militia were added in peacetime; in wartime, the territorial militia and volunteers (Frei-Corps) would be added.

At the beginning of the Silesian War, however, the total number of Austrian-Hungarian troops was 52 infantry regiments, 18 cuirassiers, 14 dragoons and 8 hussars. In addition, there was a Miners' Company and 5 Artillery Companies, the Corps of Engineers with a *Haus-Compagnie* and the Bridge Corps. This agglomeration of troops formed the bulk of the standing army, together with a number of Volunteer (or garrison) companies, with a strength of 107,892 men and 29,741 horses compared to an expected 157,082 men and 39,162 horses. On the other front, the numbers were more variable: 52 regiments of 2308 men for a total of 120,016 soldiers. To these were added a significant number of irregular troops, which could be used as territorial (*Landsturm*) or recruiting sources, territorial selections and the Hungarian portal militia. The fact that this army needed much improvement was widely recognised.

At the time of the First Silesian War, the Austrian infantry still had the strength of previous years. Grenadiers and musketeers formed the heavy infantry, people from Hungary, Croatia and Slavonia formed the light infantry. Of the 52 regular infantry (or Line) regiments - from a table of 1740 - 31 were from Austrian, Bohemian and Hungarian lands, 13 were in Italy, including Tuscany, 8 were from Brabant and Luxembourg. There were 44 German regiments (understood to be recruited in the hereditary lands of the empire), 3 were Hungarian (Kökenyesdy de Vettes, Leopold Pálffy, Gyulai), 3 Dutch (de Ligne, Los Rios, Prie-Turinetti), 2 northern Italians (Vasquez, Marulli), 1 (but it was still a battalion) was Tyrolean - although nationality was still a meaningless concept, because there was still no connection between nations and languages. Their official designation had always been the name of the owner; even after the introduction of numbering in 1769, the rule remained that imperial regiments were named after their owners.

Of these 52 regiments, at the end of 1740, those in Italy (thirteen) had a strength of 2300 men, the others (with the exception of O'Gilvy with 2400 and Wenzel Wallis with 2100) one of 2000 men. All consisted of two 100-man grenadier companies and three battalions (600 or 700 men), made up of five rifle companies or 'Ordnaries'. The infantry regiment of the Royal Hungarian-Bohemian Army (as it was called in 1740), therefore, theoretically had 15 rifle companies (of 140 men) and 2 grenadier companies (of 100 men), the former divided into battalions. Together with the 8 members of the General Staff, the regiment could count, on paper, on 2308 men. For internal service and administration, each company had 6 *Korporalschaften*, wards made up of *Kameradschaften* (squads) of 6 men, in practice those who slept in the same tent, entrusted to the command of the chosen soldiers, Gefreyte.[37]

---

[37] When an officer assigned a private soldier a special task, that soldier was free (befreyt) from the usual duties and services. The rank of Gefreyte or Gefreite comes from the word befreyte (gefreit). The figure originated from the ancient

The companies had the following composition:

company grenadiers	*Ordinary'* company		grade	breakdown	
	Reg. at 2300 U.	Reg. at 2000 u.			
1	1	1	captain (Hauptmann)	officers	First Plana
1	-	-	lieutenant (Ober-lieutenant)		
1			second lieutenant (Unter-lieutenant)		
-	1	1	Lieutenant		
-	1	1	bishop (Fähnrich)		
1	1	1	Feldwebel (NCO)	Small First Plana	
1	1	1	furiere (Fourier)		
-	(1) (0)	-	scribe (Musterschreiber)		
-	1	1	sergeant (Führer)		
- (1)	(1) (0)	1 (0)	surgeon - barber (Feldscherer)		
4	6 (5)	5	corporals (corporal)	Troop	
2	4 (2)	2	Fourierschützen (Fourierschützen)		
-	12 (10)	10 (12)	selected soldiers (Gefreite)		
2	4 (3)	3 (2)	musicians (Spielleute)		
87 (86)	106 - 112	92 - 95	soldiers (Gemeine)		
100	140	120	**TOTALS**		

The ranks of *Oberlieutenant* and *Unterlieutenant* of the grenadier companies were equal to those of Lieutenant and Ensign of the rifle companies. Depending on the moment, some figures could be eliminated, such as scribes, company surgeons (also called assistants or -*Gesellen*), some corporals, Gefreite, Fourierschützen or musicians, in which case the strength of the company was increased by four soldiers. Each company had two soldiers enlisted and paid by the regiment („*auf Regimentsunkosten*") who were carpenters or bricklayers (*Zimmerleute*) by profession.

The regimental staff, in peacetime, consisted of the colonel-owner (*Oberst-Inhaber), the* colonel-commander, the lieutenant-colonel, and the *Oberstwachtmeister* (future major), also referred to as 'staff officers'; then there was the 'Small Staff' with the Regimental Quartermaster, the Auditor, the Secretary, the Chaplain or *Regiments-Pater*, the *Wachtmeister-Lieutenant*, the Regimental Surgeon and the 'cum suis' Provosts, i.e. with their own bodyguards and assistants, which included the *Scharfrichter* and the *Steckenknechte* or punishment 'clubbers'. The 'Little Staff' had 9 people, also in peacetime, to which were added, in the event of war, the *Proviantmeister (Proviantmeister)* and the Transport Director (*Wagenmeister*).

Quartermaster and Auditor had an officer's rank. The Uditore also controlled the secretary service. The transport director was often represented by an NCO. If each company did not have an assistant surgeon, then the regimental staff kept 10-12 of them with it. The numbers of those personnel were never constant, nor were they ever included in the regimental strength calculation, according to the custom of the time. The same applied to regimental musicians who, if present, had to be paid by the owner.[38]

Ambosaten of the Landsknechts' companies, who had the task of passing on the soldiers' (Gemeine) wishes (and groans) to their Captains, via the Bishop (Fähnrich). The rank was more honorary than practical and not fixed, which is why he received no additional pay.

38 A decree of the *Hofkriegsrat of* 21 February 1750 threatened them with abolition if they '*were not paid for by the regimental owners, with their own means and without recourse to the* treasury'. Oboists and pipers were under the leadership and training of the regimental drums (common drums with additional compensation taken from the regimental funds). The Oboists were to play an hour before the changing of the guard, when it was noon, weather permitting. At prayer time, when in camp, a squad was led to the flag guard (main guard) and the chaplain recited the prayer, they were to play the appropriate song, with the squad praying and singing on their knees. During the funeral of the regimental owner, the oboists would follow the first half of the regiment, playing the 'Sterbelied' or funeral march, with muted instruments. On the march, if they were present, they had to play, alternating with drum rolls. The characteristic instruments (which still today give a cappella music the name 'Turkish music') Davul or Turkish drum, the çağana (*Schellenbaum*), the triangle, the zil (or finger cymbals - *Tschinellen*) will be introduced thanks to the example of the Trenck panduri.

The infantry regiments remained with a strength of 2000 men throughout the conflict until after the peace of Breslau; an exception was an impromptu resolution by Maria Theresa (*Hofkriegsrat* 30 September 1741) which, through Marshal Count von Khevenhüller, stipulated that the Seckendorff and Wenzel Wallis regiments were to be transferred to Prague and increased to 3000 men each, with Bohemian recruits. The exception stemmed from the necessity not to let young men, serving in the kingdom, fall into the hands of enemies, invaders of Bohemia. It was therefore not an organic rule and the two regiments, in December 1741, were increased 'pro tempore' to 3000 men with 17 companies. Also for emergency reasons, the five regiments stationed in Holland, (Arenberg, Heister, O'Nelly, Salm and Ludwig Wolfenbüttel), were increased to 2300 men by recruiting in the imperial territories and forming a fourth battalion; however, there were difficulties, so much so that in May of the following year it was still not possible to complete this expansion.

On the battlefields of southern Germany it was thought, until the end of 1743, that a force of 2,000 men per regiment could be maintained and in February of that year, the three German regiments (Neipperg, Sachsen-Hildburghausen, Jung-Königsegg), recalled from Italy at the end of 1741 (where, as is known, a nominal force of 2,300 men was standard) and transferred to Upper Austria and Bavaria, were brought up to that number. When the political situation began to become worrying, due to news from negotiations leading towards a Franco-Prussian alliance and the Union of Frankfurt, Maria Theresa ordered, on 18 December 1743, all German infantry regiments (up to that time still with the prescribed status of 2000 men) to immediately increase to 2300 men; with this resolution, in May 1744, permission was granted to the rifle companies to 're-appoint six corporals (instead of the previous five) and twelve Gefreite (instead of ten)'.

The two 'Italian' regiments Vasquez and Marulli had been ordered, first by a Supreme Resolution of 25 July 1742, to maintain the force at 2300 men, then, only a few months later (around the time of the Resolution for the Magyar regiments Vettes and Leopold Pálffy), an Instance of the Queen ordered the constitution of the fourth battalion to bring the force, now, to 3000 men. Also in 1742, similar increases in numbers affected the three national regiments of the Netherlands (de Ligne, Los Rios, Prie); from the court, moreover, came the order to form a 'Walloon' regiment with the territorial militia, which was assigned, in May 1742, to the Count of Arberg, as colonel commander. Those national regiments, now four, had reached their quota of 3,000 by mid-August and so easy was that completion that it was decided to form a fifth or 'second Walloon' regiment assigned, on 2 July 1743, to the colonel-commander Prince Arenberg. These regiments had from the beginning four battalions and the prescribed two grenadier companies. From August 1744, the battalions became five with a strength of 3560 men per regiment.

Shortly after the Peace of Dresden, when a number of regiments were available for the Netherlands from the Bohemian theatre of war, the fourth and fifth battalions of the Jung-Arenberg, the fourth battalion of the three old national battalions, were disbanded. Thus the regiments reached the formation of the rest of the German regiments (2300 men). Only the Walloon Arberg regiment maintained the prescribed strength of 3000 men until the end of the war.

The 'German' regiments, proper, remained, however, with their classical organisation, until the end of the war and the subsequent reform, with only one exception, in 1747, when the Sachsen-Hildburghausen regiment was endowed with a fourth battalion and increased to 3,000 men, thanks to the disbandment of the coastal garrisons (in Trieste, Rijeka, etc.) that acted as garrisons.[39]

According to a Capitolato by Marquis Clerici (23 January 1744) a „*wälsche National-Regiment*' (future IR 44) was formed in the Austro-Italian lands with the organisation of a German regiment of 2300 soldiers, two grenadier companies of 100 men and 15 *Ordinari-Compagnien* of 140 men, until the end of 1748. A similar extemporaneous regiment was created in the spring of 1744 with the troops of the Frei-Corps of the Trenck Panduri, which, by a decree of the *Hofkriegsrat of* 17 March 1745, was given the formal name of "Regiment Panduri Slavone" also with the strength and organisation of a German regiment.

The number of German infantry regiments varied during the war. Dissolved in 1741 were the regiment Schmettau, the Heister and Kheul regiments in 1747; in their place, the Sprecher regiment was formed in 1743 and, in 1745, the 'Tyroler *Land- und Feld-Regiment*', i.e. the Tyrol field and territory regiment. The constitution of the former was made possible on 12 March 1743 thanks to Colonel Salomon Sprecher von Bernegg, who

---

39   The permanent infantry assigned to the defence of fortresses or garrisons were usually volunteers or *Frei=Kompagnien*, usually composed of invalids or people with little income, who could seek part-time employment. There were no special hierarchies among them, no fixed number of troops, everything depended on the importance of the fortress being defended. At Brieg, for example, in 1740, there was a company of 300 men.

recruited Swiss, German and Ladin soldiers from Graubünden within four months to a total of 2300 personnel, based in Meran and Feldkirch. Before the year was out, it was decided to reinforce it to four battalions with a total of 2600 men, with two grenadier companies of 100 men and 20 'ordinary' companies of 120 men. It remained with this organisation in Italy until the end of 1749, when it was disbanded. The Graubünden regiment had a different pay from the German regiments and also had Swiss-style privileges, justice and discipline.

Much greater changes occurred in the number and structure of 'national regiments' such as the Hungarian ones. In 1745, the Tyrolean National Regiment was founded in the Tyrol. The two Silesian Wars demonstrated the need for a reorganisation of the Austrian army. This was attempted especially between the years 1748 and 1750, and some writings in the Kriegs-Archiv (KA) in Vienna testified to this: '*Opinions on the poor state of the k. k.Armee, in particular that of the infantry*'; from 1748 '*Expert opinions on military structures*', '*Conferenzprotocolle on the military system*' and then '*Project for a new organisation of the Hofkriegsrat and ideas of Duke Charles of Lorraine on the organisation of the army and the Hofkriegsrat*' and many others.

After peace, in 1749, an infantry regiment will have 2 companies of grenadiers and 16 companies of riflemen, a total of 2408 men. At the time of the Seven Years' War, an infantry battalion will have 6 companies, each divided into 4 platoons. In the field, the Austrians will maintain the four-rank deployment until 1757.

The Hungarian Infantry and the New Hungarian Regiments

The threat of war confronted Vienna with a forced choice. The almost total exhaustion of personnel from the countries of Austrian tradition and the empire, which could hardly provide a sufficient number of recruits to complete the 'German regiments', led only to hope for a large conscription in the countries of the Hungarian crown. These considerations were, quickly, followed by facts, and already on 24 October 1740, a voluntary conscription for military purposes was issued in the Hungarian crown countries, and an official request was made to convene the Hungarian parliament at short notice. The request was granted and it was subsequently decided that the Diet would be convened on 21 January 1741 in Bratislava (Pressburg), and officially opened on 18 May.

Maria Theresa travelled to Bratislava on 19 June for the coronation, which took place on 25 June. On 7 September she summoned the magnates to a court council at the royal castle. With vivid eloquence she presented her situation and that of the empire, a dangerous position due to the concentric attack by Prussia, Bavaria and France, calling on her Hungary to take up arms to protect the country and its queen. Apparently, the effect of the speech appealed to the adventurous spirits of the Hungarian magnates. The orders (the Magnates) gathered in Bratislava (Pozsony or Pressburg) at the so-called Coronation Diet voted their support (11 September 1741) and decreed *Insurrectio* in the Kingdom, as well as the establishment of 6 new infantry and 2 cavalry regiments. The conscription allowed by Act LXIII/1741, according to some Hungarian historians, resulted in an important novelty compared to the past: no difference was made between the call to arms of the orders and the conscription to the imperial army, resulting in the formation of a permanent imperial-royal army. In reality, only an emergency war recruitment took place; a national army was still far from being conceived. The result of the mobilisation was the 21,622 infantrymen of the portal insurrectional militia incorporated into the imperial army by filling the ranks of the six new and six three existing regiments.

Since the new regiments were being formed at the expense of the Hungarian counties, they could not be named by a real owner, according to the traditional institution. They thus bore the names of their commanding colonels, and only later were they appointed as true owners.

The hierarchical relations of the army of the time, in which all administrative powers were devolved to the nobility, and the clergy, jealous guardians of their rights, even when the haste of events necessitated important and quick decisions, particularly in Hungary still had a rather medieval aura. In a register of the staff officers of these new regiments, written in Latin during the year of their establishment, next to the name of the commanding colonel, the names of all staff officers were also marked - it read: '*Ad legionem primam : Colonellus Comes Ignatius Forgach* (the future IR32); *ad legionem secundam: Colonellus Baro Andrássy* (the future IR33); *ad legionem tertiam: Colonellus Baro Ujvary* (the future IR2); *ad legionem quartam: Colonellus Baro Samuel Haller* (the future IR31); *ad legionem quintam: Colonellus Thomas Szirmay* (*the* future IR37); *Vice Colonellus Baro Bossányi, Supremus vigilum Praefectus Albrecht* ; *ad legionem sextam : Colonellus comes Wolffgangus*

Bethlen (the future IR52)."

The newly formed units, authorised by the Resolution of the Pressburg Landstag (1741) were therefore six regiments, each of 3000 men, named after their commander and first colonel in their history (Forgách, Andrássy, Ujváry, Haller, Szirmay and Béthlen). They did not have grenadier companies, but had a staff similar to that of the German regiments, with 12 *Feldscherer-Gesellen*, counting 4 battalions of 5 companies with 150 men each. In addition to the normal complement of Prima Plana officers, the companies had: six corporals, three musicians, two stewards, 12 Gefreite and 121 soldiers.

The formation of the Forgács Regiment (future IR 32) gives us an example of how the Austrian army was expanded in view of the campaigns that awaited it throughout Europe. The Patente-colonnella (*Obristen-Patentes*) of 30 October 1741 was awarded to Lieutenant-Colonel of the Koháry Dragoons, Count Ignaz Forgács (Forgach) de Ghymes, who was appointed commander of the regiment in formation. The decree of appointment read: '*We Maria Theresa etc. ... who, during the present events, after several powerful enemies have attacked in various places, with foreign troops, brought from afar, and have infested, hostile, Our hereditary Lands, powerless, have decreed that Our beloved hereditary kingdom of Hungary organise a general Insurrectio, and also some regiments on foot, to edify the Hungarian nation, to bring troops to the kingdom and, consequently, to place themselves at Our service. Therefore We ask our Count Ignatius Forgach, in obedience, and in grace of his valiant, loyal and extraordinary military war services, rendered over the years, in addition to all the operations that have taken place and finally to the war experience he has acquired, in addition for the special trust granted to You to be kindly appointed Our infantry commander and to be elevated to the command of one of the new infantry regiments, of the Hungarian nation, as well as, at the same time, to be able to build and succeed in repairing everything that will be necessary "in militari et oeconomio", also everything that will be feasible, as requested by Our highest Service.*" Pressburg, 30 October 1741. Maria Theresa.

The regiment was thus named after its commander, who was only given the formal right of Ownership (*Inhaberrechte*) after his appointment as Major General in 1744. Until that date, the regiments had no numbering, and were mentioned in the hierarchy in order of seniority of their *Inhaber*.

The regimental staff was created by Her Majesty the Queen with a Patente of 1 November. It included Captain Nikolaus Mednyanszky de Megyer, of the de Vettes Infantry Regiment, promoted to lieutenant colonel, and Count Josef Draskovich (Draskovics) as *Obristwachtmeister*. The rest of the officer and non-commissioned officer corps came from other regiments, the troop from neighbouring counties; in addition, 50-year old serving officers from other infantry regiments such as the Pállfy, Vettes and Gyulai were brought into the cadre. The recruiting headquarters (*Werbetisch*) of the regiment was established in Turnau or Nagyszombat (today Trnava in Slovakia): 4 battalions were thus formed out of 5 companies of musketeers, each of 150 men.

The General *Insurrectio* and the formation of new troops had, therefore, been announced at the Diet of Bratislava, on 11 September 1741, in a lively speech by the Queen of Hungary[40], Maria Theresa, in '*dazzling youth*', a memorable moment in the history of the Austro-Hungarian Empire and its ancient dynasty. With unexpected eloquence, the queen had described the situation of an empire besieged on all fronts, by implacable enemies, to which the Hungarian deputies paid tribute with enthusiastic words, praising the queen. It was then that the queen pronounced the famous words '*Vitam nostram et sanguinem consecramus*', let us consecrate our lives and our blood. On the afternoon of that same day, a positive response from the parliament arrived, so that the threat of the Elector of Bavaria could be dealt with immediately. It was resolved to prepare 30,000 men for 13 regiments and to call an additional 100,000 Hungarians to the *Insurrectio Generalis*[41].

---

40   In fact, note how 'indigestible' the Prammatica Sanctio could be even in their own lands. Maria Theresa was crowned Rex Hungariae (i.e. king, not queen, since there was no functional female designation), although German-speaking chroniclers would refer to her as Königin (queen).

41   Péter Ujhely, *Az állandó hadsereg története. I.Lipót korától Mária Terézia haláláig 1657-1780* [History of the Standing Army. From the time of Leopold I to the death of Maria Theresa], A Magyar Tudományos Akadémia könyvkiadóhivatala Budapest 1914, V fejezet p. 247. The author expresses a theoretical assessment of the contingent that could have been enlisted in Hungary on the basis of the 'gates' system, itself taken from the History of the Hungarian Nation (S. Szilágyi, *A Magyar nemzet története*, VIII kötet/vol, p. 238): 30,000 infantrymen, 15,000 horsemen plus 6,000 from Transylvania, 14,000 ráci (as the Serbs of the Military Frontier were called), plus the Jászkuni and the militia of the Temesvár fortress district: in all, 100,000 insurgents, divided into different categories.

Hungarian Infantry Regiment Col. Ignaz Forgács (Forgach - future IR 32)

1741
UIR Forgács

Founded in 1741 by resolution of the *Landtag* (Diet) of Pressburg or Pozsony - today Bratislava - (in September - October) thanks to the Royal Patente of 21 October, which had appointed Colonel Forgach to the Pressburg assembly centre (for 20 companies in 4 battalions).

Recruitment was voluntary in the counties of Pressburg, Nyitra, Trencsén, Hont, Bars and other neighbouring counties. Later it was based in Kaschau (today Košice in Slovakia) in Upper Hungary.

The seat remained in Pressburg and moved to Lombardy in 1748.

Commanders and owners

From 1741 to 1744 it had no owner but was named after its commander, Colonel Forgach. From 1744 the owner became Count Ignaz Forgach de Ghyimes, promoted GFWM then FZM. In 1744 the command of the regiment was taken over by Colonel Baron János Mednyánsky de Medyer, who led it until 1753.

War of the Austrian Succession

1742 two battalions were assigned to the Bavarian campaign and then went on to garrison Linz. On 27 October, it was at the Battle of Obernberg against the Bavarians, where the first man was lost, whose name was later recorded by chroniclers: Alexander Soob, drummer of the Kerekes battalion.

1743 the regiment participated in the siege of Ingolstadt.

1744 to the Army of the Rhine, which with Forgách took part in the conquest of Lauterburg and Weissenburg: in the latter location the 2nd Battalion was left, which, after a fierce defence, was captured. The regiment took part in the assault against Zahern.

1746 the regiment took part in the campaign on the Main and then marched to Italy. Col. Mednyansky led it in the battle of Piacenza, and the battle of Rottofreno: it then marched on Provence. On the day of the battle of Piacenza, 16 June 1746, the chronicler recounted: "The *heroism of the regiment decided the fate of the battle, since, due to the pouring rain, it was not possible to use muskets, we beat the enemy with the sword.*"

1747 two of its battalions besieged Genoa, a battalion and a grenadier comp. (Obristlieutenant Count Draskovics) were at the defence of the entrenchments of the Assietta Pass (Exilles) together with the Piedmontese, which the Hungarian chronicles called the Col della Sieta where: "*...against the overwhelming power, ten times greater, the position was held so stubbornly that, after 4000 dead and wounded, the French had to retreat.*"; a battalion fought at Campofreddo against the Genoese.

To the "*Eljen!*" and the hurrahs, promises were not followed by deeds, and the aid in money, to create the troops, provided was not what was hoped for. In the end, only the *General Insurrectio* and 21622 men were left to build six new infantry regiments. The decision on the establishment of the regiments, translated verbatim from Latin, as to the reasons for it was as follows: "Since, *after the announcement of the general conscription, for the time being, twenty-one thousand six hundred twenty-two infantry soldiers have presented themselves to the contribution districts, to be divided into six regiments of equal strength, these are to receive their salaries, including that for the officers - among them the officers of the General Staff, who have been appointed by His Most Holy Majesty, and including the others, the captains, from the counties of the realm, in agreement with the colonel - using the tributary fund - and shall be clothed from the same sources, counties, towns, walled villages, and districts, and with all necessary requisites (except rifles, flags, drums, and tents to be sent by His Majesty).*"

Staff of a Hungarian Infantry Regiment (1741)				
Colonel Commander Owner				
lieutenant colonel	Obristwachtmeister or major	8 bishops (Fähnrich)		Regimental Quartermaster
Regimental surgeon		Proviantmeister (Rechnungsführer) for supplies		
Auditor and Secretary	Chaplain	1 Wachtmeister-Lieutenant (Regimentsadjutant) - Adjutant		
12 Feldscherergesellen - assistant surgeons		Provost cum suis (6 to 8 bodyguards)		
Ordinary or Fusilier Compagnie				
1 Captain	1 Lieutenant	1 Fähnrich or bishop	1 Feldwebel	1 Führer (sergeant)
1 Fourier	2 Fourierschützen	6 Corporals	2 drums	1 fife
12 Gefreite	121 Gemeine			

Hungarian Infantry Regiment Col. Ujváry
(- future IR 2)

1741

UIR Ujváry

Created after the Queen's speech at the Landstag in Bratislava with a Patente of 21 October and conferred on Col. de Ujváry, recruited from the counties on the right bank of the Danube (20 companies for 4 battalions). Like all Hungarian regiments, from 1748, the active force was equal to the 'German' regiments. It recruited in the county of Eisenburg (today Vasvár) and neighbouring counties (Vas, Sopron, Moson, Veszprém, Féjer) with the recruitment centre in Raab (Győr). The 1748 headquarters was moved to Prossnitz. The lieutenant colonel was Ernst von Sartori and the Obristwachtmeister was Count Ferencz Gyulai.

Commanders and owners

1741-1745 it had no owner but only the commander Colonel Ujváry, after whom it was named. In 1745 the owner was Commander-Colonel Ladislaus de Ujváry, later GFWM. In 1749 the regiment was taken over by the Habsburg Archduke Colonel Carl Joseph.

Commanding colonels: since 1741 Col. Baron de Ujváry, since 1745 Col. Ernst von Sartori.

War of the Austrian Succession

1742 two battalions sent to Upper Austria while the third was sent to Briinn (Brno).

1743 the regiment took part in the siege of Ingolstadt.

1744 Bohemian campaign; a battalion was at the defence of Prague; taken prisoner after surrender.

1745 campaign in Germany (on the Main).

1746 -1747 stayed in Holland (battles of Rocoux and Lauffeldt).

The first three battalions of a regiment followed the traditional nomenclature: *Leib-, Oberst-* and *Obristlieutenants-Bataillon*, i.e. owner's, colonel's and lieutenant colonel's battalion. The 4th battalion actually remained at the garrison or muster headquarters, and was called *Obristwachtmeisters-Bataillon,* (the future rank of major), had of course garrison duties and services, cadre training and recruiting - and in fact was never full. Each of the five first companies of each battalion had its own name, taken from the rank of the staff officers: the *Leib-Compagnie was the* first of the first, the first of the second was the *Obrist-Compagnie*, followed by the *Obristlieutenants-Compagnie* and the *Obristwachtmeisters-Compagnie.*

These so-called 'staff companies' were commanded by the most senior lieutenants or captain-lieutenants, a rank specially created for the commanders of such companies. The other companies of each battalion were called by the names of their captains, e.g. 'Captain Kerekes Company'. The order was completely identical to that in force among the 'German' type regiments.

Hungarian Infantry Regiment Col. Bethlen (- future IR 52)

Formed with a Patent of 21 October 1741 in Upper Hungary. Recruitment took place in the northern counties, the former Upper Hungary (Felső-Magyarország) of Kassa (Kaschau) with a muster centre in Ungarisch-Hradisch (today Uherské Hradiště in the Czech republic) where it was garrisoned before moving to Prague in 1749.

Commanders and owners until 1747 remained without an owner and was then entrusted to Colonel Count Wolfgang Bethlen (later GFWM and FML). In 1745 the command was taken over by Col. Count Jozsef Nádasdy and from 1749 by Col. Baron Gábor de Balassa.

War of the Austrian Succession

1742 the Leib-Bataillon was sent to the battlefields of Bohemia and the siege of Prague, as a defender, then to Bavaria; the 3rd Battalion was at the blockade of Eger in December.

1743 the Leib-Bataillon joined the 3rd Battalion in Eger.

1744 the same two battalions were sent to fight in Bavaria, then two battalions will be at the battle of Beraun.

1745 the entire regiment went to Bavaria, without fighting, then joined the Saxon army at the Battle of Kesselsdorf.

1746 the three battalions went to Holland and fought at Rocoux.

1747 were at the Battle of Lauffeldt.

1741

UIR Bethlen

The events of Colonel Ujváry's regiment make it clear today how difficult the departure of the new Magyar corps was. The commander denounced, repeatedly, the fact that people arrived without money, even almost naked, and that it was not possible to force the defaulting counties to do what they had promised. The delivery of arms, from the treasury, to the war commissioners was also lacking, so that the staff officers sent to form the regiment found themselves in very difficult circumstances. The troop could neither be dressed nor armed, and there was nothing to do but wait patiently and inertia for the arrival of the equipment. This, however, also gave rise to a new situation. The squads of soldiers, provided by the counties, remained at their charge, for provisions, until departure. As departure was increasingly delayed, the counties began to resist supplies, eventually sending only vegetables, in an advanced state of rotting, or even inedible for the young recruits. Faced with these 'stomach' problems, the most vigorous enthusiasm proved too weak and a certain discontent began to spread among the new recruits.

Amongst the troops sent from the counties there were also other disastrous problems; in some towns the penitentiaries had been emptied, opening their doors to more quickly cope with the need to reach the required number of suitable people, perhaps because, according to the conceptions of the time, 'being a soldier' was considered almost like being in a reformatory. The thinking of the time said: "*It is equally certain how war is a good school for uncouth and ill-tempered people, especially when they are under the command of intransigent officers; bad food, hardship, ill-treatment, labour and other such circumstances teach some people those virtues which would otherwise have remained unknown to them.*"

The surest means to rid the troops of bad thoughts was incessant training. "*Never leave soldiers idle,*" it was said, and Colonel Ujváry jumped at the chance, engaging those who arrived with constant drills, with corvées and with field exercises such as building fortifications.

Each company had one flag, the battalion two. The companies were arranged within the battalion according to the rank of their leaders, so that the oldest was on the wings and the youngest in the centre. Each battalion, once assembled, was to be divided into three equal tactical parts called 'divisions', independently of the companies (these were mainly administrative units). Each division formed two half-divisions and each half-division made two platoons (Pelotons or *Züge*). Thus, in tactical terms in the field, the battalion consisted of three divisions, six half-divisions or twelve platoons. When two grenadier companies were added, these would be deployed on both wings of the regiment.

Each regiment had special service regulations that depended on the colonel owner or the commander, if there was no owner. Only after 1848 did the regulations begin to be standardised. The *Feldwebel* trained the recruits and assigned the different shifts to the troop. The sergeant or *Führer was in charge of* guarding the sick and disabled and, in the absence of the company ensign, carried the flag. The Führer managed the company's accounts and was also in charge of finding quarters or having the camp removed during marches; during battle he had to stop at the company baggage. The medical deputy (*Feldscherergesell*) had to report daily to his captain on the state of the sick and acted as a barber for the troop, which he shaved at least once a week.

The three most senior corporals were in command of the three company corporals (*Corporalschaften*) and had an acting corporal (*Stellvertreter*), a younger corporal. The musicians, in addition to their service, had to serve the officers and carry the rifle on their shoulders during marches; for the same purpose, the captain used the two stewards (*Fourierschützen*). On closer inspection, there were not many differences with the historical Habsburg infantry, also known as 'German' infantry. The entire Hungarian infantry was to be reorganised in a similar way to the 'German' infantry from 1747-48 with the new regulations.

Hungarian Infantry Regiment Col. Szirmay (- future IR 37)

Entrusted on 21 October 1741 with a Royal Licence to Colonel Count Szirmay with an assembly centre in Leutschau (today Levoča in Slovakia) (20 companies for 4 battalions). It recruited in Upper Hungary in the counties of Zips (Szepes), Zemplén, and from the mountain towns (see below). In 1748 the headquarters were moved to Szeged and in 1749 to Olmütz.

Commanders and owners

From 1741 to 1744 it had no owner and was called by the name of Col. Szirmay, the same happened from 1744 to 1747 with Col. Esterházy, when he then became the owner: Colonel Count Jozsef Esterházy de Galantha then GFWM and FML.

The commanders were: 1741 the founding with Col. Tamas de Szirmay, in 1743 Baron Lt. Col. Caspar de Bossanyi, from 1744 Col. Count Jozsef Esterházy de Galantha, from 1747 the same but with the rank of GFWM and also propritorial, from 1748 Col. Count Josef Draskovich von Trakostyan, and in 1750 Col. Count Tamás Kálnoky.

War of the Austrian Succession

Like Szirmay. **1742** two battalions were sent to Bohemia at the siege of Prague while the 3rd battalion was stationed in Moravia.

1743 the regiment was at the blockade of Eger and the siege of Ingolstadt.

Like Joseph Esterházy. **1744** he was sent to the Rhine (before Lauterburg, and at the Battle of Zabern).

1745 the regiment moved to Silesia and fought at Jägerndorf; the 3rd battalion (Obristwachtmeister Szent-Iványi) together with the Trenck Panduri were on the assault at Kosel.

1746 sent to Italy participated in the Battle of Piacenza and operations in the Genoese.

1747 at the siege of Genoa.

1741

UIR Szirmay

According to a report by Field Marshal Harrach, Count of Bratislava, the following districts and recruiting places (with the number of troops to be supplied) had been assigned to the Szirmay Regiment in November 1741:

Distribution of recruitment for the new Szirmay - 1741 - regiment Northwest Hungary			
Officers	Obrist Szirmay	Obristlieutenant Br. Bossänyi	Obristwachtmeister Albrecht
Hungarian geographical locations			
Free Cities and Markets	men	Counties and districts	
City of Nagy-Banya	21 u.	Lesser Kumania district	66 u.
Felső-Bánya market	14 u.	Heves County	400 u.
episcopal town of Erlau	36 u.	Borsod County	330 u.
town of Kaschau	68 u.	Torna County	62 u.
town of Eperjes	38 u.	Abauj County	308 u.
town of Bartfeld	24 u.	county of Zemplen	720 u.
town of Szeben	6 u.	Sáros County	660 u.
town of Leutschau	34 u.	Zips County	404 u.
town of Késmárk	36 u.	Gömör county	466 u.
TOTAL			3673 men

It was not until the winter quarters of December 1743 that the new Hungarian regiments received their own regimental artillery. It consisted of two 3-pounder pieces with their carts. Musketeers, trained by an artillery gunner, who was salaried by the regiment - with infantry pay and 1.5 portions of bread - were employed as servants to the pieces, to move them and handle them.

Sooner or later the new Hungarian regiments also had grenadiers. It was GFWM Baron Andrássy, in April 1745, who was the first to order his own regiment of 20 *Ordinary-Compagnien* of 140 men and 2 *Grenadier-Compagnien* of 100 men. He took out 10 men per company to form the Grenadiers[42].

A Resolution of Maria Theresa of 22 October 1746 meant that the other five new regiments could also have the same strength as Andrássy; this was completed on 1 May 1747. The three 'old' Magyar regiments, Gyulai, Leopold Pálffy and Vettes, which had been sent to Bavaria from Italy at the end of 1741 with a force of 2300 men, increased their numbers to 3000 men more or less between 1742 and 1743. The central government had, in fact, convinced the Transylvanian authorities to set up a Siebenbürgen infantry unit instead of recruiting Insurrectio or forming a regiment of hussars. Of the 2000 Transylvanian infantrymen recruited, 1300 were sent to complete the Gyulai regiment in its then existing 17 companies. The remaining 700 men went to form a 4th battalion that was attached to the royal army in the imperial territories at the end of 1743.

In order to equalise all Hungarian regiments, around the beginning of 1743, a Royal Resolution was issued stating *"that all old Hungarian infantry regiments should be increased to 3000 men, like the new ones"*. The new battalions also to be formed at the Leopold Pálffy and Vettes regiments, were to be ready by the end of July 1744, but this may have been at the beginning of the following year's campaign.

The regiments got their flags in the summer. The Haller regiment got it in June and the colonel himself entrusted it to his ensigns. The flag of the *Leib-bataillon had a* new model toe, but the design was of the classic Hungarian model with the crown insignia, known as the 'krönel', which had the effigy of the queen on its back; in the other flags on the back was the coat of arms of Colonel Haller. The ranks of the officers of the Hungarian troops were as follows (according to a nomenclature corresponding to the time of the Napoleonic Wars):

Hungarian	German	Italian	Hungarian	German	Italian
Tábornagy	FM	Field Marshal	Táborszernagy	FZM	general of infantry
Lovassági tábornok	GdK	cavalry general	Táborhadnagy	FML	lieutenant field marshal
Vezérőrnagy	GFWM	major general	Ezredes	Obrist	colonel
Alezredes	lieutenant colonel	Obristlieutenant	Őrnagy	Obristwachtmeister	greater
Kapitány or Százados	Hauptmann	captain	Századoshadnagy	Kapitän-leutnant	captain-lieutenant
Főhadnagy	Oberleutnant	lieutenant	Alhadnagy	Leutnant or Wachtmeister	second lieutenant
Zászlós	Fähnrich	bishop	Őrmester	Feldwebel or Führer	sergeant
Szakaszvezető	future Zugsführer	platoon commander	Tizedes	Korporal	corporal
Őrvezető	Gefreite	soldier	gránátoshal	grenadier	grenadier
Hejduck o honvéd	Gemeine	soldier			

42 According to other Magyar sources, at the end of 1744, the first regiment to create (by itself) 2 grenadier companies taken from the 3 country battalions was Colonel Ujváry's, giving the regiment the same structure as the old Austrian regiments. Because of this 'selfish' approach, Ujváry was later expelled, but by this time the formation of the companies, already complete, was left intact.

Hungarian Infantry Regiment Col. Andrássy (- future IR 33)

The regiment's assembly location was Ödenburg (today Sopron). It recruited from the western counties (Sopron, Vas, Zala, Somogy etc.) and from the town of Ödenburg. At the end of the war, it was sent to garrison in Wiener-Neustadt.

Commanders and owners
From 1711 to 1744 he had no owner and was called Andrássy but from 1744 the owner was his colonel Baron Adam de Andrássy, future GFWM and FML. The Baron was always in command except from 1745 when the command was given to Colonel Alexander von Arnth.

War of the Austrian Succession
1742 two battalions were sent to Upper Austria but were not deployed except as garrisons in Passau and Braunau.
1743 all three battalions were transferred to Italy again without fighting or otherwise victorious outcomes.
1744 sent south, the regiment distinguished itself at the Battle of Velletri, attacking Mount Artemisio.
1745 now the regiment had formed two grenadier companies that, together with two battalions, were established in northern Italy, garrisoning Mirandola.
1746 the regiment was involved in the battle of Piacenza and at Rottofreno, and then went on to occupy the city of Genoa, of which it was, briefly, the garrison.
1747 he now went on to besiege Genoa, went to Piedmont and detached a battalion to the Riviera.
1748 the regiment took part in operations in the Riviera di Levante as in the clash of Monte Becco.

1741

UIR Andrássy

Hungarian Infantry Regiment Col. Haller (- future IR 31)

The regiment received 50-year veteran soldiers from the Hungarian Pálffy, Vettes and Gyulai regiments and had Szegedin as its assembly point. It recruited in the eastern parts of the crown along the Tisza River (see table). The Leib-bataillon was not ready until 1742 and was sent with Captain Anton Bakits to garrison duty in Kaschau, Eperjes and Leutschau. In 1748 he was at the garrison in Prague.

Commanders and owners
From 1741 to 1747 he had only the commander in the person of Colonel Baron Samuel Haller von Hallerstein, who also became the owner in 1747; he was later promoted to GFWM and FZM. The commanders were Haller until 1745, then Colonel Tamás Papp, and from 1750 Colonel Josef von Siskovics.

War of the Austrian Succession
1742 the first two battalions completed in June went to the Slavonian (Cordon) borders, remaining in the area between Banat and Slavonia until 1744.
1744 the regiment was sent to Bavaria, where, with the Bátthyányi corps, it fought in the Upper Palatinate and Bohemia; one of its detachments was deployed at the Elbe crossing at Teltschitz.
1745 participated in the Battle of Landshut, (at Hohenfriedberg and Soor he was not in the battle). The 3rd Battalion was sent to Silesia and involved in small actions.
1746 the 1st and 2nd battalions were in the Netherlands and gave a combined detachment of 200 soldiers to defend Antwerp, while the regiment was involved in the rearguard battle at Slins (on the Jaar); Rocoux did not participate in the battle. The 3rd battalion was in Luxembourg.
1747 the three battalions and the newly formed grenadier company were at the Battle of Lauffeldt, although only in a marginal role.
1748 the Leib-Bataillon was at the defence of Maastricht in the last act of the war.

1741

UIR Haller

The recruits of the regiment were distributed according to the following table:

Distribution of recruitment for the new Haller Regiment - 1741			
Officers	Obrist Haller	Obristlieutenant Tamás Papp	Obristwachtmeister Stefan Kerekes
Hungarian geographical locations			since 1742 Baron Jozsef Vécsenyi
Free Cities and Markets	men	Counties and districts	
town Hajducken	139	Szatmár	338
market town of Polgáry	6	Szabolcs	312
Royal Free City of Szegedin	44	Bereg	188
royal free city of Debreczen	184	Ungvár	166
Royal Free City of Szátmar	52	Jazygier and Kumanier District	204
Counties and districts	men	Bács	244
Zaránd	88	Csongrád	122
Arad	212	Csanád	48
Bihar	800	Békés	212
Máramaros	332	Ugocsa	84
TOTAL 3639 men			

INFANTRY IN 1749

At the end of 1748, the infantry regiments were given organic regulations thanks to the 'Khevenhüller'[43] regulation. Maria Theresa's *Allerhöchste Befehl (*Most Excellent Ordinance), which preceded that regulation, drew attention to the great differences from the previous regulations in the training requirements of the individual regiments and called for a future made by all the people in arms: "... *whether nation or Proprietor, all must adhere precisely to the new training and discipline regulations*. Each of the 53 infantry regiments was to have 2 companies of grenadiers, and 4 battalions of 4 ordinary companies (or riflemen). Each battalion carried two flags and was divided into two divisions (each of 2 companies). The grenadier companies were positioned on the wings of the regiment and each had 100 soldiers, the rifle companies had 136 men. In addition, the regiment had two light cannons (*Feldstück*) and a regimental 'music' or band of 36 men. The officer corps was increased with the creation of the post of *Oberlieutenant* (from then on it would be Lieutenant, while Lieutenant would become Second Lieutenant), which would be further regulated in peacetime.

The new rules radically changed the uniforms of the Hungarian infantry, who, although differentiated from their German counterparts, wore garments originating from their national costumes, had grenadiers wearing bear hair caps, infantrymen wearing tricorns and no longer columbos, moustaches that were now black and hair braided into a single plait. During parades, as well as in battle, the headgear was to be decorated with green field badges (leaves). Furthermore, the new regulations stipulated precisely

1748 Granatiere UIR Bethlen
1748 Granatiere UIR Haller
1748 Granatiere UIR Esterázy

[43] Ludwig Andreas von Khevenhüller-Frankenburg, not to be confused with the famous Prince Johann Joseph Khevenhüller-Metsch, High Marshal of the Hofkriegsrat in 1742 and High Chamberlain of the Imperial Peers (Oberstkämmerer des Kaiserpaares). However, it was the field marshal who freed Austria from the Bavarian Franks, earning him the Order of the Golden Fleece. From 1734 he tried to put the rules for the army in writing in his Observaktion Punkte. The 1748 edition came out in two volumes.

that: "*No company officer was to be seen wearing an overcoat (Mantel), winter cape (Winterhaube) or nightshirt (Schlafhauben).*"

The riflemen still deployed in four ranks to advance, but the grenadiers were in three ranks. The rifle was carried, bayonet cocked, on the left side, resting on the shoulder, perpendicular. The Hungarian grenadiers still had grenades, which they carried in the *Patronentasche* (bag) together with the fuses. The Hungarian infantry was equipped with iron stakes, like the German infantry, (*Schweinfeder*), actually for the Magyars the staves were made of wood, with the lower end fitted with iron points, again to form the 'Frisian horses' or 'Spanish horsemen', i.e. they were placed on the ground as obstacles to approaching enemy cavalry, around fields or along roads; they were carried by the troop on marches and in battle.

The tactical movements of a unit were always based on the then prevailing way of fighting, firing in close ranks. In all exercises and manoeuvres emphasis was now placed on the good orientation of the front, explicitly mentioning the regulations: '... *and as one goes against the enemy with rifles on the shoulder, flags in the wind and music, the whole front must advance slowly and resolutely. As a rule, all four ranks fire, the first two on their knees.*"

Due to the new service regulations, the responsibilities of non-commissioned officers and troops remained unchanged. The company camped, divided into three corporalschaften (*Corporalschaften*), each of which was divided into dormitories (*Kameradschaften*) to which a 'responsible person', the *Gefreite*, was assigned. The new rules 'were, *in general, more humanitarian than the customs of the past and aimed to raise the chivalrous spirit in the army. Harsh beatings, the main cause of numerous desertions, were limited.*" A non-commissioned officer could, "in the immediate aftermath of a well-deserved punishment", administer 2 or 3 beatings. Lieutenants and second lieutenants could, if they caught the offender '*in the act*', give the punished man six or seven strokes.

The maximum punishment a captain could inflict was 25 strokes; moreover, non-commissioned officers were advised to avoid vile, occasional beatings as much as possible, which should always be discouraged. If an extreme example was necessary, a *Feldwebel*, a sergeant (*Führer*), or a quartermaster should never be punished with the cane, lest he lose the respect of the troop. Officers or non-commissioned officers who confronted an offender with kicks, slaps or other insulting punishments, hitting him on the head, arms, face or feet with the cane, were to be censured in the clearest possible manner.

Beyond these details and without going into whether the new rules were fully implemented in all regiments, it must be said that the 1748 Regulations finally succeeded in producing identical regulations for all regiments, with new organic provisions that were paving the way for a true national army, leaving behind the agglomeration of private property that had characterised the beginning of the century.

Staff of an Austrian infantry regiment (1749)				
Inhaber or colonel owner				
Colonel Commander	lieutenant colonel	greater	8 bishops (Fähnrich)	Regimental Quartermaster
Auditor and Secretary	Chaplain	Adjutant of Reg.	Regimental surgeon and his 10 subordinates	
8 musicians		Provost cum suis (6 to 8 bodyguards)		8 Captains
Total regimental staff = 36 personnel				
Composition of an Austrian grenadier company (1749) - total of 100 personnel				
Captain (Hauptmann)	Lieutenant	Second Lieutenant	Sergeant (Feldwebel)	Furies
2 assistant furiors	4 corporals		2 drums	2 pipers
Zimmermann (carpenters) = 2 per company (in peace only one)			TOTAL soldiers = 84	
Composition of an Austrian rifle company (1749) - total of 136 personnel				
Captain (Hauptmann)	Lieutenant	Second Lieutenant	Sergeant	Furies
2 assistant furiors	5 corporals	3 drums	1 fife	10 elite soldiers (Gefreyte)
Zimmermann (carpenters) = 2 per company (in peace only one)			TOTAL company = 109 soldiers	
Composition of an Austrian Infantry Staff Company (1749) - 135 personnel in total				
2nd Captain or Lieutenant Captain	Lieutenant	Second Lieutenant	Sergeant	Furies
2 assistant furiors	5 corporals	3 drums	1 fife	10 elite soldiers (Gefreyte)
Zimmermann (carpenters) = 2 per company (in peace only one)			TOTAL company = 108 soldiers	
Headcount of an infantry regiment in 1749 = 1900 soldiers (2408 for the entire regiment)				

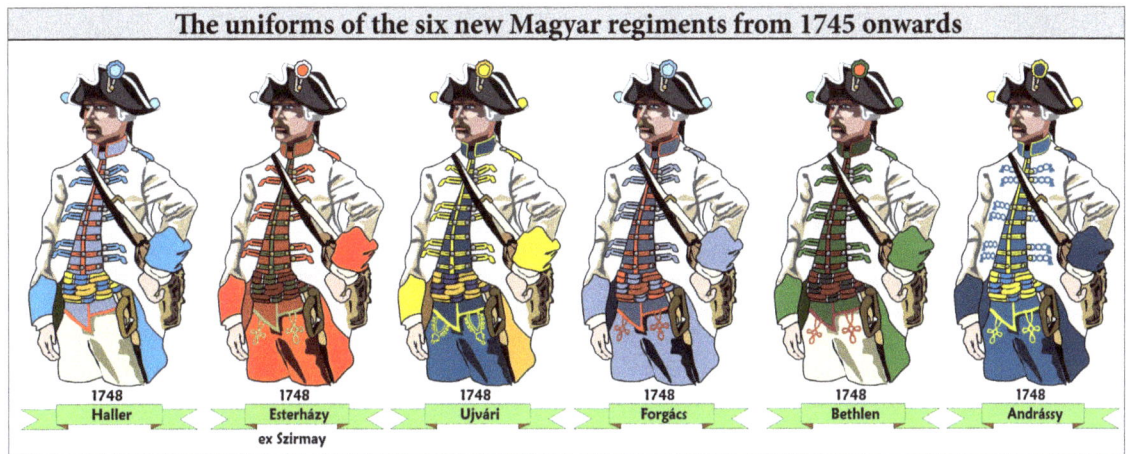

In the past, the House of Austria was considered more bound by marriage agreements than by the clash of arms: "*Bella gerant alii, tu, felix Austria, nube!*" But after the Silesian Wars, the whole system changed and, as finances improved, a complete reform of the army was gradually initiated, starting in the period of peace before the Seven Years' War. In the words of Baron von Fürst und Kupferberg, reaffirming the supremacy of the military high nobility: '*A prince who wants to keep the love of his subjects, must not interrupt the old traditions by force; the Queen Empress tried to gradually put an end to abuses, while maintaining the old formalities, with the great aim of creating a more numerous and more disciplined army than ever before ... In peacetime, the Austrian army was to grow to 200,000 men, including the Croats and, in general, all the irregular Hungarian infantry and cavalry ... As far as training is concerned, the regiments do it differently from one another. This is the most common reproach levelled at Marshal Daun and Count Lacy. If General Radicati directs the training of the entire cavalry, and General Anger that of the entire infantry, perfect uniformity cannot be achieved. There are reforms that only princes can think of.*

The Austrian artillery has been put in a respectable condition since Prince Joseph Wenzel Liechtenstein became its commander; it is said that he has brought millions from his private wealth. I have never been able to obtain an exact estimate of the expenditure of the army ... but I am very positive and believe that the Empress, in peacetime, will have allocated about 14 million guilders, a thousand plus, a thousand minus."

Garrison troops

The garrison of Vienna was always held, „*for the use of His Majesty the Emperor*" by a certain German cavalry regiment (in 1740: by the Althann Dragoons) together with the '*Wiener Stadt-Guard-Regiment*', an unusual troop corps, which had no field duty, made up of elderly veterans or wounded and invalids, both officers and troop; the troop could also perform other duties (today we would say part-time jobs). Due to the lack of military training, the monotony of guard duty, and also the often insufficient pay, the war value of the town guard was very low. Its strength was 1200 men, divided into 4 companies; in 1740, an effective force of 1134 men cost 34,336 florins annually. The salaries of the staff and senior officers were provided by the Lower Austrian authorities.

The *Stadtguard had been* dissolved by imperial decree by Charles VI on 2 November 1722, it was only truly abolished by a decree of Maria Theresia on 20 November 1741 (in 1773 the other capital guard, the *Rumorwache*[44], would also be dissolved, and in 1775 the two dissolved Guards would become the '*K. k.. Militär-Polizeiwache*', in practice the Police). From 1710 to 1741, its commander was Count Wirich Philipp Daun. At the time of the decommissioning, the 1,200 men, armed with halberds and muskets, were housed in *Basteihäu-*

44 The *Stadtguardia* was highly unpopular among the population, as relatives and relatives of the guards competed with the trade. To improve their meagre wages, the guards often also practised their original profession, but sold beer and wine on the ramparts, enjoying a large clientele. The wives of the city guards often ran the so-called '*Türkauf*' (the Turkish or black market, i.e. they bought food brought into the city from the farmers on the outskirts of Vienna and sold it at the markets at a premium). To deal with irregularities, as early as 1646 the Lower Austrian Lieutenancy had established the 'City Security Guard' or *Rumorwache* (Municipal Guard), which was to control areas not served by the City Guard, with the mandate to: "Avoid contact as far as possible."

schen (bastion huts). From that date, work began to equip the capital with barracks for its garrison.

The guards at the city gates were divided in different ways, with the strongest contingents guarding the main gates (Kärntnertor or Carinthian Gate, Rotenturmtor or Red Tower Gate, Schottentor and Stubentor). With the construction of the Linienwalls (1704), the outer line of fortifications, the *Stadtguardia* also inherited the garrison of the remaining nine gates and the extension of the service to the Glacis area, i.e. the rampart embankment (which, until then, had only occasionally been done by patrols). For an increase in personnel, however, the necessary funds were lacking.

In 1716, the *Hofkriegsrat* ruled against an increase in the duties of the *Stadtguard* by entrusting two companies of the Bayreuth Dragoons with the control of the Glacis, outside the city walls, in the outer city from 1720. The dragoons were to pass on to the *Wachtmeister-Leutnant* of the Stadtguard, information about the previous day's arrests.

As mentioned, in 1741, Maria Theresa had permanently disbanded the city guard regiment; it was to be disbanded when the court returned from Pressburg, but this did not actually happen until early 1743, mainly due to the salary demands of the disbanded troop. The totally disabled were transferred to the poorhouse (202 men); those who could support themselves by any profession were granted citizenship (385); those who had no trade and no livelihood were granted leave (34); a small part (34) went to field regiments, a large part (377) went to the volunteer companies of Raab (Győr), Komorn (Komárom fortress), Gran (Esztergom or Strigonius) and Graz. Some of the officers received pensions, while others were employed as fortress officers or in fortress construction work. The garrison in Vienna ended up with two regular infantry regiments.

Rumorwache

Polizia cittadina di Vienna

As for the 'Companies of Volunteers', which had been present since 1675 - not to be confused with similar irregular volunteer formations, which, although similarly named, had different tasks - they had been formed, in many fortresses, with the same composition and tasks as the Viennese *Stadtguard* and in 1740 still existed:
a) the *Frei-Compagnie* at Brieg (today Brzeg in Lower Silesia, near Mollwitz, site of the famous battle) with 302 men and an annual cost of 20,616 guilders. Also called the Finsch-Company, after the occupation of Silesia by the Prussians, it was moved to the Spielberg, with their troops sometimes employed as escorts of recruits or prisoners of war.
b) the *Frei-Compagnie* in Brünn (or the Spielberg fortress) with 153 men and an annual cost of 17274 guilders.
c) the *Frei-Compagnie* in Ungarisch-Hradisch (today Uherské Hradiště in the Czech republic) with 156 men and an annual cost of 14036 guilders. It was disbanded in 1742 and officers with troops were sent partly to Raab and partly to Komorn, as well as to the invalid company in Erlau.
d) the two *Frei-Compagnien* in Graz with 234 men, with an annual cost of 15928 guilders. One stood inside the city, the other garrisoned the Schlossberg. Both were disbanded in 1747.
e) five German *Frei-Compagnien* in Raab (Győr), with 795 men, with an annual cost of 32798 guilders, of which 12578 were an annual contribution guaranteed by the Lower Austrian authorities.
f) three German *Frei-Compagnien* in Komorn (Komárom) with 597 men, with an annual cost of 23626 guilders.
g) a German *Frei-Compagnie* in Gran (Esztergom) of 160 men, with an annual cost of 9390 guilders.
All these companies, apart from those in Graz, were dissolved in 1746.
The garrison in Erlau (today Eger in Hungary) organised an invalid company of 160 men, taken from the *Invalidenhause* in Pest, and had an annual maintenance cost of 11763 forints.
The Littoral (Adriatic) region had several garrison companies whose disbandment was announced by the FM Prince Sachsen-Hildburghausen and which were attached to the two Graz companies (the *Stadt* and the *Schloss-Compagnie*).
It was the Empress-Kingdom who decided the matter on 6 September 1746. Before their disbandment, the Littoral companies consisted (including officers) of 56 men in Gorizia (Görz), 87 men in Gradisca, 55 men in Trieste, the Commandant „and several troops" in Rijeka, paid for by the Carniolan authorities (Krain)

with another 25 men in Buccari; a garrison company also existed in Porto Re, but the number of men is not known. The Littoral garrisons cost a total of 17080 florins per year. After their dissolution, those garrisons were occupied by the fourth battalion of the Sachsen-Hildburghausen infantry regiment, which was formed expressly for that purpose.

The volunteer and garrison companies had ensigns among their officers, so they certainly had their own company flags. This, however, is only demonstrable today for the three German companies at Komorn. At Komorn, in addition to the three company flags, there was also, for a memorable time, a red '*Blutfahne*' flag, which was hoisted only at the most critical moments, 'as a signal of constant resistance', when the call for general *insurrectio* was evoked. It is, however, reasonable to assume that all *Frei-Compagnien* besides the Vienna *Stadtguard* had their own flags.

Among the garrison troops were the „*deutsche Fähnlein*" or German company in Carlstädt, disbanded by Prince Sachsen-Hildburghausen in 1747, whose 255 men cost the Carniolan and Carinthian exchequers 21192 florins per year, and, later, the four German garrison companies in Varazdin and Petrinja, 400 men used, from 1745 onwards, for the formation of the Varazdin regular regiments.

For the sake of completeness, it should be mentioned that the Royal Guard of the Hungarian[45] crown was located in Pressburg, disbanded in 1748, and many other town guards existed in various cities such as Innsbruck, Brünn, Olmütz, etc. Town guards were also to be found in numerous Hungarian towns (particularly on the outskirts of large cities), known as '*Hajduken-Compagnien*', which were organised on military bases but did not burden the military budget.

In Trentino, in Rovereto, there were two „*Frei-Compagnien*", one called „dell'arma bianca" and the other 'dei fucilieri', who in 1740 refused to take the military oath of allegiance to Maria Theresa if they were not allowed to carry rifles; they were therefore, only civil corps, civic guards or *Bürger-Corps*.

The Frei-Corps infantry

It was a common practice in the Habsburg lands for wealthy local magnates to organise 'legions' (a mixture of infantry and cavalry troops) financially autonomous from the treasury in the event of special emergencies, such as wars. Since these were irregular corps organised on a voluntary basis, they were called *Frei-Corps* (literally 'free corps' or 'Frankish corps') often with a mercenary character. It is therefore completely unfounded to attribute the creation of the first German *Freikorps* to Frederick II of Prussia, since Austria, as the leader of the Holy Roman Empire, was the highest expression of Germanism at the time.

The most famous of the Austrian volunteer *corps (Frei-Corps)*, that of von der Trenck's Panduri, will be discussed in the chapter on Military Border Troops. Other *Frei-Corps* that participated in the Silesian Wars were:
- from 1741, the *Frei-Compagnie* of Captain Anton Bischof, which provided great help to Colonel Roth during the siege of Neisse; it had 280 infantry soldiers and 50 hussars.
- In 1742, with a Patente of 23 March, the „*walachischen Frei-Compagnien*" (formed by Hannaken or Hanáci, rural Moravian people and Slovaks) of Lieutenant-Colonel Baron Franz von Sedlnitzky was formed in Moravia. Also called *Walachisches Frei-Corps* in the sense of southern (Moravian) corps, it had Charta and Marini as captains; according to Wrede, it would have reached as many as 4,000 men. They came to prominence in 1742 by holding out against the Prussians in Moravia and Silesia, in the fighting at Kokor and Fulnek, and at the taking of Freudenthal. In the same year they were disbanded.

Plans to organise some *Frei-Compagnien* between 1741 and 1742 with Major (*Obristwachtmeister*) Albert von Schlangen in eastern Moravia, Captain Alexander Chlebowsky (100 men), *Obristwachtmeister* Bukowsky (recruited in western Bohemia, in Landskron and Leitomischl, by order of the superior army command on 9 May), Count Celari, were blocked by the drastic development of war events in Bohemian lands. Count *Obristwachtmeister* Lambert Ludwig Celari's company had the strength of a battalion (1,000 men) and was recruited between the Oder river and the Galician border.

---

[45] The Holy Crown of St. Stephen (Szent Korona) had always been moved between Vienna and Bratislava (Pressburg) due to threats of invasion. In 1740 Maria Theresa was crowned Queen of Hungary in Pressburg with great pomp. For the first time since Mary of Anjou, a woman wore the crown of St. Stephen. Due to the dangers that the outbreak of the War of Austrian Succession threatened, the Holy Crown was taken to the fortress of Komorn for several months. In the course of time, St Stephen's Crown was one of the most 'adventurous' crowns in Europe. During Hungary's turbulent history, the crown was stolen, rescued, buried and even lost several times. It travelled from present-day Slovakia to the Czech Republic, Austria and Germany, and as far east as present-day Romania and the Ukraine. After 1945 it was taken to the United States for several decades, and then returned to Hungary.

The war against Bavaria was the cause for the creation of the 'Spanish Company' or „spanischenFrei-Compagnie" of Colonel Pedro de Carrasquet, consisting of 81 Spanish invalids, by order of the Queen in 1741. After defending the Klausen am Pyhrn pass (Klausen near Bozen), it was disbanded between 1 October 1741 and the end of May 1742. *The Frei-Compagnie Hasslingen,* on the other hand, was created in Silesia in 1743 with a force of 120 men. It was commanded by Captain Carl Friedrich von Hasslingen, who led it in battle, in Bavaria and then in 1744 in Italy. It then ended up on garrison duty in Mantua. In 1746, it was disbanded due to excessive desertions and those who remained were included in regiments stationed in Italy.

At the beginning of 1744, two larger *Frei-Corps were* created, which rendered excellent services: the *Dalmatiner-Corps* and the *Temesvarer Frei-Bataillon*. The former was formed by a Chapter of 11 January 1744, on the Littoral (Rijeka muster site) under the command of *Obristwachtmeister* Cognazzo, with a force of 800 men, divided into 5 companies of 160 soldiers; it was sent to the Bátthyányi Corps in Bavaria in June. At the beginning of 1745 it was under the command of Captain Josef Matthias Jaketić and reinforced by a sixth company, it was sent to Bohemia and Holland. The Dalmatian Corps was disbanded in 1746. In fact the *Frei-Bataillon* Cognazzo with 116 men had deserted in 1745 to go with the Prussians. In November of the same year, the Habsburg Major Cognazzo was 'mutated' into a Prussian colonel, in command of those 116 prisoners, at Olmütz; he was exchanged in 1748 for the Austrian Captain Damnitz[46].

The "Free Battalion of Temesvár" was commanded by *Obristwachtmeister* Simbschen with a force of five companies of 140 men and one company of hussars of 75 men; it was launched into battle in June. In March 1745 it was reinforced with two "foot" companies and a hussar company, returning again, after the Peace of Dresden, to the Banat, where it was later to form the local territorial battalion.

At the beginning of 1745, a number of *Frei-Compagnien were* established with recruiting offices in Trieste, Rijeka, Zengg, Pazin, Pedene, Buccari and Karlopago; they were dissolved immediately after the Peace of Dresden:
1. *Frei-Compagnie* Crusaz of about 130 men;
2. *Frei-Compagnie* Jovanović;
3. *Frei-Compagnie* Prinz Carl with about 160 men in April 1745;
4. *Frei-Compagnie* Podgorizani with 180 men at the end of the year;
5. French *Frei-Compagnie* Longueville.
6. *Frei-Compagnie* of Captain Pfeiler, mounted.

In 1746, there was also a '*Dalmatiner- und Jäger-Corps*' of about 200 men in Holland, which was disbanded in the same year.

In the Netherlands, in the year 1744, several *Free Companies* were created under the command of General de la Cerda de Villalonga. Each of these 'Frei-Compagnie' was supposed to have 150 men, but few succeeded in achieving the goal. They were named after their captains: Bethune, Lebrun, Jumeaux, Gauthoye (and from 1745 de Ligny), Humbert, Bouvier, Pertuisseaux, Jamar dit Libois, Poncelet and Dieudonné. At the beginning of 1746, all but two were disbanded and remained in the camp until 1748.

In Italy in 1742, a '*Frei-Compagnie*' was formed with Spanish and Italian deserters (many were Micheletti or „Miquelets", Catalans) whose command was entrusted to Colonel Count Johann Sebastian von Soro from FM Traun. The deserters grew to such an extent that the '*Frei-Corps* Soro' was organised into five companies the following year and even into two battalions, taking the name 'Partitanten-Corps' or Minchella Corps (Minquella) from its Lieutenant-Colonel commander. In 1744, he took part in the expedition against Naples, occupying Teramo and, in an attempt to defend Nocera, he lost many of his troops, who were taken prisoner. In 1746, he returned to the field in Provence and was then taken to Slavonia and disbanded there. Its members joined the 'Italian' Marulli and Clerici regiments (future IR 44). Of the Soro Corps, only a company of 200 men remained, which took part in the defence of Masone Castle after its capture with explosives; it then resisted until 1748, when it was disbanded.

Again in Italy, this time thanks to Prussian and Saxon deserters, under the patronage of Prince Wenzel Liechtenstein, in 1744 the *Frei-Compagnie* of Captain Friedrich Wilhelm von Campen was created, with 200 members, which was disbanded in the summer of 1745. In that year, there was also another *Frei-Compagnie* in Italy, that of Captain Rossi.

For the part of the Hungarian Frei-Corps, see the chapter on the *Insurrectio* corps.

---

46   „*Mittheilungen des k. und k. Kriegs-Archivs*", Neue Folge IX, Seidel & Sohn, Wien 1895, pag. 259.

THE CAVALRY

Dating back to the time of Charles VI, from 1711, the formation, in each cuirassier regiment, of a company of carbineers, and a company of mounted grenadiers, armed with sabres and not *Pallasch*, in each regiment of dragoons. The carabinieri also apparently had long curved sabres, while the cuirassiers and dragoons used long *Pallasch*. Carabinieri and grenadier companies had one standard, and the uniform was the same as that of the regiment. The grenadiers wore boots, the carabiniers wore gaiters. The former were also equipped with grenade bags and also had to train as infantry, while the carabinieri trained mainly in fighting and speed shooting.

From 1711, each cuirassier regiment had a commanding colonel, in addition to the owner, and in the war had 12 *Ordinary-Companies*, i.e. 6 squadrons (two companies made a squadron), plus the Carabinier Company; the first 6 Ordinary Companies (of 76 soldiers) had 456 men, the last 6 (of 75 soldiers) 450; the Carabinier Company had 94 men, the Regimental Staff had 9 men, giving a regiment of 1009 men. The Dragoon regiments also had 12 companies out of 6 squadrons from the time of Joseph I of Habsburg. The Dragoons, too, from 1711. had a colonel commander in addition to the owner.

As with the infantry, there was also a gradual expansion in the cavalry. Emperor Joseph I created two new regiments of dragoons bringing the cavalry, in 1711, to the strength of: 20 cuirassier regiments, 12 dragoon regiments and 5 hussars. Charles VI further increased the cavalry by establishing 4 new cuirassier regiments, 11 dragoon regiments and 6 hussar regiments (however, the army lost 6 cuirassier regiments, 9 dragoon regiments and 3 hussar regiments, demobilised after the war against the Turks).

The staff of a cavalry regiment included:

Staff of an Austrian cavalry regiment (1710)				
Colonel Commander	lieutenant colonel	greater	Regimental Quartermaster	Auditor
Chaplain	Adjutant of Reg.	Regimental surgeon and his 6 assistants		Provost and helpers

Composition of an Ordinary Company of Austrian cuirassiers (1710)				
Rittmeister (Captain)	Lieutenant	Cornet (bishop)	Wachtmeister	3 Corporals
1 timpanist				

Composition of an Austrian Carabineer Company (1710)				
Rittmeister (Captain)	Lieutenant	Second Lieutenant	Wachtmeister	4 Corporals
Trumpeter				

Each horse company also had 1 Furiere, 1 Compilatore or Musterschreiber, 1 Saddler and a farrier (Schmied).

The soldiers of the Carabinieri and Grenadier companies on horseback had to be very robust. *"They wielded long-bladed sabres, while cuirassiers and dragoons used Pallaschs."* The grenadiers could be recognised by their bearskin caps with a grenade embossed on the front plate. The companies always stood on the wings of the regiment, either to the right or left, depending on which wing was manned; during the march,

sella tedesca

Bock ungherese

however, they were always at the head of the regiment. Cuirassiers and dragoons used German-type leather saddles, while hussars used Hungarian saddles called *Böcke*.

Also in 1711, under Charles VI, the cuirassiers had a second colonel as commander, in addition to the owner (Inhaber) who gave the regiment its name.

In the 1930s, a cuirassier regiment, at the time called a 'horse regiment' (they would only officially become cuirassiers from 1736, instead of the old name of horse regiments - *Regimenter zu Pferd*) had 1094 men on the warpath, divided into 12 ordinary companies (*Ordinari-Compagnien*) of 83 horsemen and a company of Carabiniers of 98 men. The same organisation applied to the Dragoons, except that their 13th company was made up of mounted grenadiers.

The company was merely an administrative structure, which in training and campaigning lost all meaning; in that case, two companies formed the squadron. Similarly to the infantry, the mounted weapon was also regulated at the time of the war against the Ottomans. The Supreme Resolution of 23 February 1737 concerning 'mounted regiments' (cuirassiers and dragoons) increased them to 1054 men. The result of the ill-fated campaign of 1738 and the depletion of the state's financial reserves meant that, towards the end of that year, the regiments of cuirassiers and dragoons had only 1,000 men and the hussars only 800, both men and horses. Cavalry General Count Alexander Károlyi was also supposed to eliminate the 11th company of his hussar regiment, bringing it down to 800 men, but did not do so. The Károlyi regiment also maintained a higher strength than other hussars in the following years, although some regiments remained with about a thousand men.

During the war against the Turks only the Dragoons had a real increase in numbers, thanks to an imperial Concession for the House of Württemberg (Chapter of 5 October 1737), which was able to create the Dragoon Regiment Ludwig Württemberg (at its own expense). At the end of the war the cavalry had 18 regiments of cuirassiers, 15 of dragoons and 9 of hussars, a total of almost 40,962 cavalrymen. The cavalry had also been decimated by epidemics and losses in battle. Only the cuirassier regiments Miglio and Berlichingen, which were in Italy, escaped the decimations imposed by the unfortunate conflict, as did the Sachsen-Gotha dragoon regiment, which retained all 1094 of its regular strength; the same can be said for the Baranyay and Hávor hussar regiments, each with 1,000 men, and, finally, the Károlyi hussars, which remained with their 880 men; the aforementioned regiments maintained their strength until the emperor's death.

On the death of Charles VI (1740) the cuirassiers were left with 18 regiments, the dragoons with 14 and the hussars with 8. The force deemed official, with the advent of Maria Theresa in 1740, was therefore theoretically as follows: 18 regiments of cuirassiers of 1009 men for a total of 18.162 men on horseback; 14 regiments of dragoons of 1008 men for a total of 14,112 men on horseback; 8 hussar regiments of 809 men for a total of 6,472 men. Cuirassiers, Dragoons and Hussars formed the regular cavalry, while in the Hungarian and Military Border territories there were Hungarian and Transylvanian Mounted National Militia Units, Mounted *Grenzer*, some mounted *Frei-Companies* and *Insurrectio* Hussars. The Austrian army thus had a total of 38,746 horses. In this connection, it should be pointed out that, in the year 1740, 37 full-ranged infantry regiments (26,643 men) were deployed in Lombardy, Tuscany, the Netherlands, Siebenbürgen (Transylvania), the Banat of Temesvar and Slavonia and that, in the same regions, 19 cavalry regiments with approximately 3694 men and 5078 horses were stationed. It is from these numbers that the total strength of the army can be deduced, taking into account the regiments missing from the total count (15 infantry and 21 cavalry). This was what could be fielded at the outbreak of war.

Cuirassiers and Dragoons since 1740

Under the name 'German cavalry' or even just 'cavalry', in the first part of the 18th century it was understood to refer only to cuirassiers and dragoons, the regular imperial cavalry; from this also derived the common term 'cavalry and hussars'. Maria Theresa inherited 18 regiments of cuirassiers and 14 of dragoons in her reign. Considering that, in mid-1745, a Viñals Dragoon Regiment was formed, which was immediately disbanded in the spring of 1746, the number of cavalry regiments remained unchanged throughout the War of the Austrian Succession. The Dragoon Regiment Viñals y Verguez was formed thanks to the Royal Resolution of 23 August 1745, with Spanish deserters temporarily disbanded; however, as early as 8 March 1746 Maria Theresa ordered the new regiment to be sent to Slavonia and disbanded there (at the same time as Colonel Soro's *Partitanten-Corps*) . It was no longer desired to send unreliable elements against the enemy. The troops who wished to continue to serve were divided between the infantry of Clerici and Marulli (then stationed in southern Hungary). According to the *Geschichte der k. Regimenter*, (III, 229), there also existed a dragoon regiment de la Cerda de Villalonga, founded in 1744 and disbanded in 1748. If, however, it had really existed, as Gräffer says in his history of regiments, there would have been a trace of it in the Acts and Protocols of the *Hofkriegsrat* or *Hofkammer*, but no mention of it can be found; probably the author was confused with the *Frei-Compagnie* de la Cerda, of which no testimony ever refers to them as dragoons.

In the cavalry, the cuirassiers still had regiments of 6 squadrons, i.e. 12 *Ordinary* companies and 1 company of riflemen; a total of 13 companies (two Ordinary companies formed a squadron, as always). In fact, the 13^{e} companies were considered elite units. The Dragoons had 6 squadrons divided into 12 ordinary companies and one company of mounted grenadiers. more or less identical in numbers to the cuirassiers; the grenadier companies were often detached, dismounted and used for garrison duties. The carbine of the dragoons was longer than that of the cuirassiers and carried a bayonet. The carabineer and grenadier companies did not use *pallasch*, but curved sabres.

Khevenhüller, in fact, had declared that the true weapon of the knight was the sword, in the spirit of Charles XII of Sweden, and that firefighting should only be taken care of by dragoons, especially against the Turks. The majority of the cavalry, however, did not share that opinion. It was the Austrian custom to approach the enemy up to about 30 paces, shoot and then take up the white weapon. The attack on Mollwitz, without firing, was unintentional and disapproved of by superiors. In the dispositions of Prince Charles of Lorraine in Czaslau (or Chotusitz - 1742), it said: '... *when our cavalry attacks, they must advance to 50 paces, fire and then turn back. The hussars must attack frontally and at the shoulder at the same time. If the enemy cavalry anticipates you, you will advance up to 50 paces, then fire to send the enemy horses into disorder. Then you will open up, right and left, and drive the enemy through, and when he has gone over, you will close ranks and attack from behind.*"

At the beginning of hostilities, however, the actual strength of two cuirassier regiments (Miglio and Berlichingen in Italy) and three dragoon regiments (Styrum and de Ligne in Holland, and Sachsen-Gotha in Italy) was 1,000 men and as many horses, the rest of the regiments had 800 men and horses (consider that the hussars had only 5 squadrons of 80 men or regiments of 809 men, counting the 9 staff members).

The companies (administrative entities, which in two formed the squadron, a true tactical unit) in 1740 had the following constitution:

Carabinieri Grenadiers	Ordinary	Carabinieri Grenadiers	Ordinary	grade		breakdown	
strength 800 u. and cav.		strength 1000 u. and cav.		Armourers	Dragons		
1	1	1	1	Rittmeister (Capt.)	Hauptmann (Capt.)	officers	First Plana
1		1		Oberlieutenant	Oberlieutenant		
1		1		Second Lieutenant	Second Lieutenant		
	1		1	lieutenant	lieutenant		
	1		1	handset	bishop		
1	1	1	1	Wachtmeister	Wachtmeister	Small First Plana	
1	1	1	1	Furies	Furies		
1	1	1	1	Feldscherer	Feldscherer		
1	1	1	1	trumpet	drum	Troop	
1	1	1	1	saddler	saddler		
1	1	1	1	locksmith	locksmith		
4	3	4	3	corporals	corporals		
67	48	81 (87)	63 (64)	soldiers (Gemeine)	soldiers (Gemeine)		
80	60	94 (100)	75 (76)	TOTALS			

The ranks of subordinate officers were similar between ordinary companies and carabiniers or mounted grenadiers. The regimental staff comprised:

Col. Owner	colonel commander	lieutenant colonel	Oberstwachtmeister	Quartermaster
Auditor (secretary)	chaplain	Helper	Regg. surgeon	Provost cum suis
in war = director of commissions				

The force figures of the cavalry regiments usually did not include the General Staff or even mention a transport director. During the War of Austrian Succession, in practice, there was no substantial difference in employment between cuirassiers and dragoons, at least as far as their use in the countryside was concerned. The Dragoons still retained their character as mounted infantry, using many typical infantry ranks such as *Hauptmann* instead of *Rittmeister*, especially in the grenadier companies, same pay, armament and equipment as the infantrymen. They also did a lot of training on foot, hence the famous saying: "*As a dragoon falls from his horse, immediately a musket is raised.*"

At the beginning of 1743, Field Marshal von Khevenhüller, who held command in Bavaria, ordered the cavalry regiments from Italy, which, until then, had a strength of more than 800 men and horses, to conform to that lower number. At the end of the same year, however, the imminent and foreseeable outbreak of new Prussian hostilities prompted a new increase in cavalry numbers, together with an increase in infantry strength. On 18 December 1743, Maria Theresa issued an order *'to increase the strength of the royal regiments of cuirassiers and dragoons to 1094 men and horses'*. With this new strength figure, the grenadier and rifle companies rose to 94 men and horses, the ordinaries to 83-84 (in the former the number of soldiers rose to 81, in the latter to 71-72).

To achieve this, 6000 recruits were taken from the Bohemian crown lands and Germany. In March 1744, it was ordered that the cuirassier and dragoon regiments under the command of Bátthyány in Bavaria and the Upper Palatinate should recruit up to 1,000 men and horses, not more. The dragoon regiments Ballayra and Preysing and the cuirassier regiments Johann Pálffy, Portugal, Czernin, Carl Saint-Ignon, Birkenfeld, Lucchesi and Cordova conformed to that figure. Even for most of the other cavalry regiments, however, an effective force of 1,000 men and horses remained de facto.

Only the numbers of the de Ligne and Styrum dragoons, which were located in the Netherlands, were always given as 1094 men from 1744 onwards. It is not difficult to understand the reasons for these isolated deviations from the prescribed organisation, given the permanent monetary emergency of the state; this allowed Maria Theresa, only on 10 March 1745, to increase the strength of the dragoon regiments in Italy, the Savoy and Koháry, thanks to an exceptional investment of 30,870 florins.

There was no more change in the numbers of the cuirassier and dragoon regiments until the end of the war; only ten cavalry regiments were transferred to Hungary at the end of the Second Silesian War, not to receive replacements, but to be restored to the previously established horse force. Thus, in 1749, a cavalry regiment was still left with one mounted rifle or grenadier company and 12 *Ordinari-Compagnien*.

The Queen's Hussars

Jó legény! jó legény! jól megfogd a kantárt ...
(Good boy! Good boy! grasp the reins well).

The superiority of the Austrian cavalry over the Prussians during the Silesian Wars was not a feature attributed to their regular regiments, but was that of the light cavalry, especially the hussars. Already at the time of the War of Polish Succession, six new Hussar regiments had been created, which, together with the existing ones, had distinguished themselves so much that the Rhine campaign of 1735 was described as a *'Husaren-Krieg'*, Hussar war. In the war against the Turks they had gained experience, a marvellous schooling in the field, accompanied by the fact that they were born knights. In Frederick the Great's memoirs, it is stated that, in the autumn of 1744, the Austrian 'irregular' knights *'had almost dimmed the light of day, as six out of six orders failed to reach generals from outside the ranks. Three envelopes addressed to the king himself were intercepted, without even one being able to penetrate, so that, for four weeks, Frederick saw himself cut off from the rest of Europe."*

It was, trivially, obvious that the first imperial regulation of the hussars, printed in 1747, had, as its author, a Hungarian, Major General Nicolaus Esterházy de Gálántha, and that, curiously enough, its publication was almost contemporary to the first imperial regulation for the cavalry, i.e. *'Regulaments und Ordnung für die k.k. Kuirassiers und Dragoner'*, i.e. 'Regulaments und Ordnung für die k.k. *Kuirassiers und Dragoner'* (Vienna 1749-1751), drafted by a Walloon, Colonel Joseph Carl Count d'Ayasassa. At first sight it may seem strange that one regulation for hussars could have preceded the other (by 2-4 years), but the reason is not difficult to understand, because it did not take long to learn how to be a hussar; in fact one was born and raised as one. The heavy cavalry, on the other hand, had to learn a lot from clashes with opponents encountered in the field; for example, the Austrians stopped shooting and then charging, and learned to gallop, at full speed, brandishing their *Pallaschs*, as the Prussians did.

1740 - Pistola per ussari

Hussar or Huszár was a Magyar term. Some authors derive the word hussar from the Latin '*Cursarius*' *meaning* 'raider' or from the Serbian '*Husa*' meaning 'bandit'. Others, however, and especially the Hungarians, believe it derives from the Hungarian word '*húsz*' meaning a score (as Matthias Corvinus had stipulated, there were in fact 20 men that each village was obliged to offer as squires to the feudal lord in the event of a call to arms). The Hungarian motto '*one hussar is worth twenty*' seems to consolidate the relationship with the number twenty; 'húszar' being understood as one of the village's twenty recruits. The Huszár were skilled horsemen, soldiers dating back to the 15th century, armed with light weapons and originally from Hungary.

A Latin document from 1403 mentions a cavalry captain '*huszár kapitányt*' referring to a certain Imre Huszár, but more importantly, a letter written in Latin, in 1481, King Matthias defined his light cavalry: '*equites levis armaturae, quos hussarones appellamus*', knights in light armour we call 'hussarones'.

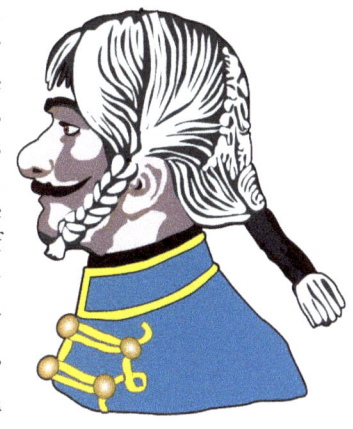

acconciatura da ussaro

After their experiences in the 15th and 16th centuries, the Hungarian knights were protagonists of the uprising of Ferenc Rákóczi or Francis II Rákóczi, Prince of Transylvania, conducted from 1703 to 1711, against the Habsburgs engaged in the War of the Spanish Succession (and fomented by Louis XIV's France). The insurrection led the Hungarian Parliament to proclaim that Francis II, Prince Regent of Hungary. In 1711, however, the rebellion was put down and Habsburg order was restored in Hungary. Rákóczi was sentenced to exile in Poland and became a symbol of Hungarian nationalism; he is still remembered as a national hero today. During the War of Independence, both Rákóczi and Emperor Joseph I made use of Hungarian troops; the emperor's troops were, for the most part, Croatian, which were disbanded at the end of the war. The captain of Rakoczi's bodyguard, however, Laszlo Bercsényi emigrated to France, where he created his regiment of hussars, inventing the tradition of the French hussars, made famous by the Napoleonic battles. It was Charles VI who welcomed the Hungarian cavalry into the official ranks, dividing the regiments into 10 companies (two of which formed a squadron). The hussars, who had regiments of 800 men under Charles VI, increased to 1000 men in 12 companies (6 squadrons) in 1726; in 1740 they went back to 800 men, until the final regulation of 1748, which brought them permanently to 5 squadrons (10 companies) each. When Maria Theresa enlisted the support of the Hungarian nobility and became queen, during the War of Succession, 11 Hungarian Hussar regiments fought for the Habsburg throne on the battlefields of Europe in 8 years. The Hungarian nobility pledged to increase their queen's army under the motto "*Vitam et sanguinem!*".

After a few increments, in 1743, there were 6 regiments of hussars in the field (to which were added the three new regiments formed during the Seven Years' War including the Transylvanian Hussars of the Siebenbürgen or *Székler-Grenz-Husaren* regiment). The regiments in the war all had 12 companies, i.e. 6 squadrons. In addition to the Hungarian hussars, Charles VI had also organised three *Grenzer* cavalry regiments on the southern border of the country: the Banat and Karlovac frontier regiments. Maria Theresa, on the other hand, established the *Grenzer* regiment of Székler hussars in 1762.

From 1702, the company of hussars consisted of:
1 captain (*kapitány*), 1 lieutenant (*hadnagy*), 1 cornet (*kornét*) (equivalent to standard-bearer), 1 sergeant (*őrmester*), 1 quartermaster (*szállásmester*), 1 scribe (*írnok*) 1 surgeon (*felcser*), 1-2 trumpeters (*trombitás*), 2-3 corporals (*káplár*), consisted of 80-90 hussars divided into three sections, 1 saddler (*nyerges*) and 1 blacksmith (*kovács*). To fight. To the regimental posts belonged (in addition to the colonel or *ezredes*), the lieutenant colonel (*alezredes*), the Obristwachtmeister (*főstrázsamester*) or major (*őrnagy*), the regimental quartermaster (*szállásmester*), the provost (*hadbíró*) or field judge, the regimental chaplain (*ezredkáplán*), the regimental archivist (*ezredtitkár*), the regimental car commander (*kocsimester*) and the regimental victualler (*élelmező mester*). The musicians were the regimental trumpets (*ezredtrombitás*) and the regimental drum (*ezred-üstdobos*). There were no 'official' flags, but each company had its own swallowtail banner. The hussar regiment traditionally emerged in the wars against the Turks, with its typical deployment of three lines in front and two behind.

Numerical progression of hussar regiments - years 1739-1748						
Years	1739	1741	1742	1746	1748
pre-existing regiments	9	8	9	11	15
new formations	-	1	2	4	-
dissolved regiments	1	-	-	-	1
rest	8	9	11	15	14

The FM Count von Khevenhüller, an experienced cavalry general, used to counter those who had recommended the reduction of hussars in 1740 that: "*by now they were disciplined and trained and capable, in the future, of taking on even heavier and more important tasks*". Regarding the hussars, it was also said: '*There had long been no troops more feared than the Hungarian horsemen. It was surprising that they had never claimed the first rank in the Austrian army."* The hussars came into their own in the wars against the Prussians. They filled their enemies with terror and were so superior to them that they soon gained a much more significant influence on warfare: "*more than was normally granted to light troops.*"

Not only that, they also influenced the evolution of the opposing armies: few national troops will, in all epochs, be as widely spread and imitated abroad as the hussars. Frederick II of Prussia himself, who, when he ascended the throne, possessed nine squadrons of hussars, had formed no less than eight regiments of hussars by the end of 1744 (a famous work in the Austrian *Kriegsarchiv* highlighted the participation of numerous Hungarian Protestants and Magyar boys serving in the Prussian army in the formation of their hussars)[47].

At the outbreak of war the following regiments were in service: György Csáky - István Dessewffy (Dessőwffy) - János Ghilányi - Gábor Splényi - Ferenc Károlyi - Miklós Hávor - János Baranyay - József Pestvármegyei.

The old regiments had, at the beginning of the Silesian War, a full strength of 800 men, instead of 600, divided over 10 companies, which, as was the case with the German cavalry, made up five squadrons. In contrast, the Károlyi hussars had a force of as many as 880 men and horses, and had eleven companies. The companies had the same ranks as the German cavalry (as an Ordinary-Corporal *Company*) with 4 corporals and 67 Gemeine. The General Staff of the Hussars was also like that of the cuirassiers. Grenadier companies did not exist among the hussars. In 1743, one was mentioned, belonging to the Nádasdy Hussars, but this was certainly a mistake. In 1741, the cavalry and hussar regiments assigned to Silesia formed, out of necessity and temporarily, squadrons of three companies (instead of two), however, maintaining a standard for each company.

Austria, too, planned the establishment of new regiments in 1740 for the next two years. There were three newly formed units: 1741 Beleznay, 1742 Pál Esterházy and the Transylvanian Hussar Regiment (*Kálnoky-Husaren* or *siebenbürgisclie Husaren*).[48]

The royal decree of 8 December 1741, concerning the constitution of the Beleznay regular regiment, described it as consisting of 800 men, but not of 10 companies, instead, of 8 companies of 100 men, including 87 Gemeine. The first 5 companies were formed and recruited directly by Colonel Beleznay, the other three were initially made up of mounted '*Portalisten*', i.e. insurrectionary troops, but would later be disbanded and recruited from scratch by the colonel as well.

The formation of the Esterházy hussar regiment was the result of a heartfelt appeal by Maria Theresa to the Magyar magnates to equip it with men and horses at their own expense. Prince Paul (Pál) Anton Esterházy managed to assemble 500 men in December 1741. The charter to make the regiment official arrived on 15 January 1742. It was to grow to 1,000 men for 10 companies of 100 men (87 Gemeine). To speed up and facilitate the formation of the regiment, the prince was allowed to subdivide the Portalists (about 400), which his vassals were to supply to his regiment, according to the *Insurrections-Articel,* and which were to be replaced by new troops at the end of the *Insurrectio*. The first six 'compulsory or regular' companies were already complete by the end of February 1742. The same negotiations that had led to the reinforcement of the Gyulai infantry regiment in 1742 also led to the formation of the Transylvanian Hussar regiment; the Royal Placet was given at the conference of ministers on 17 April 1742. The regiment was to have 1,000 personnel in 10 companies. Count Kálnoky, from whom the regiment took its name, was chosen as colonel and commander on 1 September, although he only became its owner with a Licence of 19 July 1749. In spring 1743 it was sent to Bavaria.

---

47   Kienhast, Ob.Lt. „König Friedrich II von Preussen und die Ungarn bis zum Hubertsburger Frieden 1763", in „Mittheilungen des k. und k. Kriegs-Archivs', Neue Folge IX, Seidel & Sohn, Wien 1895, p. 293.

48   The work of the Prussian General Staff '*Die Kriege Friedrich's des Grossen*', I, 56* mentions the new hussar regiments Beleznay, Halász and Esterházy as having been formed in 1741. This information must be corrected as the three regiments belonged to the recruitment of the first, partial *Insurrectio, and were, in* 1741 in Silesia only to be brought back in late autumn and disbanded there. (see Alexich, „Die freiwilligen Aufgebote aus Ungarn 1741 und 1742", in "*Mittheilungen des k. und k. Kriegs-Archivs*' Neue Folge, IV, 1890).

Hussar Regiment János Beleznay

It was created in 1741 with a Patente of 8 December by Colonel Beleznay (eight companies of which three were recovered from the return of the disbanded insurrectional hussar regiments), In 1748 it received a company from the disbanded Trips regiment. It was based in Debreczen from 1748.

Commanders and owners: Colonel Johann (János) Beleznay personally led the regiment until 1744, when Count András Hadik took command of the regiment (later a renowned cavalry general and then president of the Court War Council). From 1747 it was under the command of Colonel Count Samuel Teleky.

War of the Austrian Succession

1741: After the formation was completed, the regiment marched to Silesia, where about a hundred of its soldiers fought against the Prussians at Olbendolf.

1742: the regiment distinguished itself at Brünn, where it forced the Prussian encirclement line into the city; some units were deployed in the winter campaign in Moravia; it was also at the siege of Prague.

1743: the regiment was assigned to the *Pragmatischen Armee* in Germany without fighting.

Ussari Beleznay
1741

1744: the regiment marched to the Netherlands, a small part of which fought in Bruges. The regiment was taken over by Count Andras Hadik, later a famous cavalry general and later president of the *Hofkriegsrat*. Hadik's Hussars crossed the Rhine, roaming a vast area, creating terror everywhere and capturing a column of enemy supplies. In the Netherlands, in Maastricht, some Hussars recaptured cannon captured from the enemy. Hadik, with 300 horsemen, attacked 1,500 Frenchmen and captured 8 officers, 80 dragoons and 50 infantrymen.

1745: was in the Lower Rhine with FM Traun distinguishing himself with Hadik in the Battle of Nordheim.

1746: still in Holland he was at the Battle of Rocoux. **1747**: at the Battle of Lauffeldt.

1748: the war ended with a few troops engaged in the defence of Maastricht.

At the end of the campaign year (end of October) in 1742, Hungary's commitment to maintaining the *Insurrectio* was cancelled due to the cessation of hostilities against the Prussians. It was therefore thought that the Hussar regiments could be successfully reinforced by keeping all insurrectionary troops returning home. A Royal Resolution of 1 December 1742 thus increased the strength of all Hussar regiments (including also the two new ones, Beleznay and Esterházy, where Portalists were now stationed) to 1000 men and horses (and ten companies). It was easy to assume that the former insurrectionists could offer more motivated troops, perhaps by improving their rank and pay, but in fact lacked the funds to move on to further recruitment. Thus, the Ministerial Conference of 25 October 1742 recommended an optional reinforcement of the hussar regiments, without exceeding the 1,000-man threshold, by convincing the wealthier nobles and, in particular, the former insurrectional officers to submit additional companies of 100 mounted men to the regiments, '*ohne Entgelt des aerarii*', i.e. without the expense of the treasury, at their own expense. They were traditionally called „*Auctions-Compagnien*", this time without garrison or replacement duties and were assigned three per regiment. These companies, 'supernumerary' in peacetime, were not to be incorporated - i.e. paid from the state treasury - until the regiment reached the prescribed 1,000 personnel, i.e. in the event of a new war. Elder FM Páffy had strong doubts and salacious comments about those '*Auctions-Compagnien*', each of which, for a nobleman, would have cost at least 10-12,000 guilders, because, in his opinion, the insurrectional hussars, although already trained, could not be in sufficient numbers to be considered ready for action, which led to more prudent considerations.

Hussar Regiment Pál (Paul) Esterházy

At the beginning of the War of Succession, Maria Theresa appealed to the Hungarian lords for concrete help. In spring 1741, thanks to the direct intervention of the Hungarian Palatine Count Johann Pálffy, Prince Paul Anton Esterházy retrieved 100 hussars from the Ghilány regiment (where his brother Nikolaus served as colonel). By the end of December 1741, Paul Anton Esterházy had already recruited another 500 hussars before he even received his official licence; many of them came from his estates around Eisenstadt (or Kismarton) in Austria. On 15 January 1742, Esterházy was finally authorised to form a regiment of 1000 hussars out of 10 companies in Sopron (Ödenburg), completely at his own expense. The staff of the regiment came from the other regular regiments (Baranyay, Splényi, Károlyi and Ghilány). The headquarters were in Ödenburg (Sopron) from 1749.

Commanders and owners

1742: owner GM Prince Pál Antal (Paul Anton) Esterházy
1742: The commander was Lieutenant-Colonel Abraham von Handley.

War of the Austrian Succession

1742: Prince Paul Esterhazy trained him in Sopron, at his own expense. After training, he was sent to Bohemia, where he fought at Chotusitz and then at the siege of Prague.
1743: in Bavaria and participated in the Battle of Esslingen.
1744: fought at Nordheim; then, during the retreat, fought against the Prussians near Moldauthein.
1745: he had hard fights in the battles of Hohenfriedberg and Soor.
1746: sent to the Netherlands participated in the Battle of Rocour
1747: at the Battle of Lauffeld
1748: returned to Hungary.

Ussari Pál Esterházy
1742

In any case, the Hungarian Magnates undertook to provide the *Auctions-Compagnien*: Count Széchényi for the Nádasdy hussars, Count Kálnoky for his regiment, Count Adam Teleky and Count Nicolaus Esterházy for the Esterházy hussars, Count Szluha for the Károlyi hussars, Count Samuel Teleky for the Festetics hussars, etc. It is clear from the participation that the effort to create *Auctions-Compagnies* did not slow down, indeed, in some cases, during 1744, it was encouraged by the promise of special personal benefits.

Until 27 February 1745, *almost all the Hussar regiments were increased ... thanks to the number of those three Auctions-Compagnien*', but only on paper, because the completion of some of these companies lasted until the summer of that year. The Károlyi and Festetics regiments, thanks to the *Auctions-Compagnien, were increased* to 1400 personnel (out of 14 companies - 7 squadrons), thanks to the allocation of 3-4 of those particular companies.

The depletion of state coffers and material for recruits led, at the beginning of 1747, to the reduction of the *Auctions-Compagnien* in all hussar regiments as well. From then on, they again had a strength of 1000 men, only the Károlyi Hussars maintained a strength of 1100 men and horses. The troops that were eliminated were used to complete the remaining tenth (or eleventh) companies and therefore no more troops were recruited from that date onwards.

The volunteer hussars

During Maria Theresa's wars, in addition to the regular regiments, Hussar volunteer formations were also trained, all of which were linked to the Hungarian *Insurrectio* and only formed for the duration of the conflicts. The most important Hussar *Frei-Compagnien* (between the Military and Insurrectionary Borders) were:
a) **insurrectional volunteer regiment of Lieutenant Colonel Bertolotti or Bertholotti** (see *Insurrectio* section).

(b) Csernojevich's volunteer squadrons - three *Grenzer* companies of *Oberstwachtmeister* Johann Csernovich de Matsa (János Csernojevich), which were on the Rhine and Main with the army of Traun from June 1745 onwards and then went to Bavaria; in October they had 282 men and 201 horses in three squadrons. They were disbanded in 1746.

c) Franquini's volunteer hussars (Franchini) - these were 200 men (2 squadrons) recruited in Hungary and Slavonia in May 1745, commanded by *Obristwachtmeister* Pietro Franchini and sent to Silesia to Prince Charles' army. They were short-lived operating in Silesia and were disbanded the same year, remaining at 80 men. Smaller units were the *Frei-Compagnie* Pokitsch, which in February-April 1745, had just 30-40 hussars and was disbanded in September; the *Frei-Compagnie* Magyary, of about 100 hussars and Lieutenant Strozzi's *Frei-Compagnie* (or „Hungarian Volunteers'), created in February 1745 with 80 volunteers, which later became 130-140 men and horses.

Hussar Regiment Kálnoky

It was founded in 1742, by Supreme Resolution of 17 April, with the consent of the Transylvanian region (out of 1000 men) under the name '*Siebenbürgen Husaren Regiment*'. It was known, however, from the beginning by the name of the commander, the owner in 1749. According to the Supreme Resolution, this regiment was to be disbanded after 15 years. At the Transylvanian request and in view of the outbreak of the Seven Years' War, the regiment was kept in service. It was based in Torda at the end of the war. It became the 2nd Hussar Regiment from 1798.

Commanders and owners

1742: Colonel Count Anton (Antal) Kálnoky former officer of Reg. Pestvármegyei

1746: Colonel Wolfgang (Farkas) Makhászy (Macskassy)

War of the Austrian Succession

1743: In spring the regiment was complete and on 18 April it was reviewed at Hermannstadt (today Sibiu in Romania). It marched towards Bavaria following the Rhine retreat and fought at Breisach in August. At the end of the campaign the regiment was deployed between Laa and Heitersheim.

1744: He fought on the Rhine. On 17 May he was at Sondheim on the Rhine. Then he was in the vanguard in the retreat to Bohemia. At the end of October he was in the Nádasdy Corps.

1745: He was with the army in Silesia, with FM Esterházy, capturing a Prussian convoy at Mochbern and then was at the battle of Pretsch. On 11 November Kálnoky was promoted to major-general and the regiment changed command.

1746: sent to Holland to the FML Trips corps, fighting at Namur and the Battle of Rocoux. In that battle all 5 Austrian Hussar regiments were on the 2nd Line on the left wing alongside the Dutch. The cavalry was brought into battle in impassable terrain and suffered considerable losses.

Ussari Kálnoky
1742

1747: At the beginning of the campaign he was in GM Morocz's brigade (Trips' vanguard) together with the hussars Nádasdy and Esterházy. He fought at Roermonde and then advanced on Eindhoven. He attacked the French at Mechelen (present at the Battle of Lauffeldt with Prince Wolfenbüttel's Reserve covering the extreme right wing).

1748: move to Transylvania and Torda.

Other squadrons of volunteer hussars were formed in 1745 by Captain Jovanović, a squadron of 50 men, the second captain's squadron from Podgorica of 70 men, the Magyar Cornet of 90 hussars and 3 squadrons of citizens under the command of Lieutenant Colonel Ribitzey. In 1746, a group of 200 men was formed under Captain Springer. All these volunteer troops were disbanded in 1746.

The insurrectionary formations of Colonels Beleznay, Halász and Count István Esterházy date back to 1741. They were three regiments, two of which were provided by Pest county, of 800 men each (one under the command of Péter Hálasz and one under the command of János Beleznay). The two regiments returned to their homeland in October, where the troops were disbanded and a regular hussar regiment was organised, of which Beleznay became colonel in 1741 (and owner). Count Esterházy's hussar regiment, on the other hand, recruited men from the counties of Komarom, Gyor and Bratislava and had no different fate from the others. They fought alongside two insurgent squadrons from the counties of Kís and Kun, which took to the Silesian battlefields and then dispersed and returned home in October of the same year.

In 1746, Prince Johann Friedrich von Hildburghausen formed a *Grenzer* hussar regiment in the Carlstädt Generalate out of four squadrons, without giving it a colonel owner. From 1746 to 1748, he was employed on the German battlefields, while in peace he garrisoned the Croatian towns of Grahac and then Karlovać (Carlstädt).

In 1747, General Hildburghausen established the Varazdin Hussar Regiment with five squadrons, without any colonel owners. Its headquarters was Petrinja and in 1749 it was reduced to two squadrons. Also in 1747, the Sava and Danube (Szerém or Syrmia County) frontier hussar regiment was established by Lieutenant General Engelshofen with 6 squadrons, without an owner, which became the Slavonian Hussar Regiment in 1750.

In the Netherlands, the *Frei-Compagnie* Hussars Wiedebach (sister company of the *Frei-Compagnie* Dragoons Chappuy) were formed in 1744, which at the end of 1745 ended up with 56 men and later with only 15 Mann and a few horses. These companies were also all disbanded in 1746.

Light troops and the 'little war'

No nation could count more light troops than Austria[49] . The Hungarian counties (*Komitate*) had several thanks to the institution of *Insurrectio*, the national regiments or so-called 'irregular' units, formed by individual magnates at their own expense, including national hussars' and 'free companies of hussars'. To these were added the exiles from the borders of Slavonia and Croatia and the Panduri, i.e. the Croatian and Slavic national troops, also dependent on the wealthy nobility.

These hussars and *grenzers* were unrivalled in Europe at the outbreak of the Silesian Wars. The main task of the hussars was to support their cavalry, relieving enemy attacks and providing them with a favourable opportunity to counterattack. The irregulars, on foot or on horseback, fought in flanking units, controlled advanced positions, disrupted the enemy, covered the movements of their own army, intercepted enemy supplies, etc.

On the other hand, due to their ignorance, they often became inconvenient for their own armies, as their brutality and plundering also made their own supplies difficult; this is why many imperial generals opposed increasing the number of their regiments and the use of frontier troops. The 'little war or *guerrilla war*' (*Kleine Krieg* in the German or *Guerrilla* in the Castilian style) became, however, an important 'rear war'. Numerous testimonies proved this, such as this report: '*The Hussar Rittmeister Hallasch, with 20 hussars, captured 1733 barrels of salt at Austerlitz. At Olmütz they carried off 170, including Prussian horses and mules, and on the 16th they sabre-rattled down, at Lesch, 29 Prussians and captured a fine cannon, with 22 caissons and wagons loaded with sacks of precious objects ..."*

The irregular formations themselves brought to light valuable commanders, some extraordinarily gifted, such as Baron von Trenck and, later, Mensel, who were able to develop a very personal and effective way of guerrilla warfare. That experience, brutal in itself, would turn into a romantic literary movement in the years to come, which went from treatises on the art of Folard's '*Kleine Krieg*', or Bastas's '*Government of Light Cavalry*', to a century and a half of fictional and adventure fiction.

The definition of '*Kleine Krieg*' by the GFWM von Valentinis said: "*By 'Kleine Krieg' is meant all those actions that only favour the operations of an army or corps without having, per se, a direct relation to the conquest of territory of the country, but rather to the security and even to the cover of the main armed mass, whether in positional warfare, or in war of movement, and with those engagements that focus only on the destruction of the*

---

49   In France there were already, before 1740, 10 'Free' companies of riflemen and 8 of dragoons, in all about 40 officers and 620 men. To this meagre force was added, during the War of the Austrian Succession, Fischer's *Chasseurs* (a common soldier who had been at the siege of Prague and had formed a *Freicorps* counting 400 *Chasseurs* on foot and 200 on horseback, at the end of 1743) were created in 1743; then followed the *Arquebusiers de Grassin*, the *Volontaires royaux* and the *Fusiliers de Mortière*, all light troops.

adversary."

Von Decker added that: "The *first half of that definition corresponds to the fuller term; in the second half one could add that - with small warfare one wants to damage the enemy without decisive battles."*

Another German military theorist, Heinrich von Brandt, was more drastic in defining Maria Theresa's special war: *'The linguistic use of the definition has contributed in no small measure to leaving the terms and opinions on what we call the [small war] indeterminate. For our theorists it soon became the teaching of partial undertakings, encompassing the clashes of detachments or the warlike activity of outposts and patrols. Unfortunately, more often, it had become the alibi for all kinds of criminal activity, summed up in those examples of service. "*

Heinrich von Brandt's definition could be taken in its broadest sense; indeed, it could be extended a little further by indicating, for that 'small war', the necessity of always having to resort to 'light troops', because only in this way did it fully correspond to the 18th century conception. 'Light troops' and 'small war' were two inseparable entities. Finally, it had to be added that there were many relations connected to the so-called 'positional warfare', which linked the 'small war' of that time with the use of field fortifications.

The use of the Military Boundary Troops (*Grenzer*) as light troops on horseback and on foot, typical of the conflicts of the 18th century, led to a misunderstanding that they remained as such in the 19th century, which was only partially true for the hussars.

The Hungarian *Insurrectio* [50]

The protocol known as *Insurrectio* represents both a major problem to analyse, for Hungarian history of the 18th-19th centuries, and a fascinating topic. Insurrectio, of course, is reminiscent of the word insurrection, originally meaning '*der adelige Aufstrand*', the revolt of the nobility against foreign power (whether Turkish or Austrian), carried out by the feudal militia of the local nobility. If all kinds of organisation and subordination were clear in the 18th century, it would not be the same in the following century, when it was sometimes unclear who, how and where was to go to war (in the period of the Napoleonic wars, the *Insurrectio* would be summoned four times: 1797, 1800, 1805 and 1809; but only in 1809 did it actually go to battle). In 1740, it was still the ancient 'call to arms' for the homeland in danger, the *Aufgebot* of the landed gentry with their varied customs. A Royal Protocol of 25 October 1741 (*Rescript*) of Maria Theresa, issued in Pressburg (Bratislava) had brought order to the colourful uniforms of the Hungarian militia or *Insurrectio*, stipulating for the infantry:

Hungarian Insurgent Infantry uniforms from 1741			
1 Red Csakó	1 red tie	1 ivory cape	the blue Dolman
blue fabric trousers	2 shirts	2 'underpants' (Gattien)	Dolman colour belt
lace-up shoes (Tobanken) or Hungarian lace-up boots (Zischmen - Czismén)		bayonet	
cartridge bag with strap and with 24 cartridges		sabre with straps	
a leather cloth to protect trousers and Dolman			

The cavalry had the uniform of hussars and in the counties was organised into squadrons (and divisions) that had to train and equip themselves at their own expense.

The 'Magyars' or Hungarians were subjects of the Hungarian crown, a kingdom divided into two parts: the hereditary lands in the north-west and the Hungary taken from the Turks in the south-east. Croats, Serbs, Romanians living in Hungarian lands were still referred to as Magyars. Croats, Serbs and Romanians living in the Military Boundary, on the other hand, were only *Grenzer*, militarised citizens of those lands. With the aim of repelling the enemy at the border and obtaining the so-called 'Tregua *Domini*' (the Lord's truce), the high prelates, royal barons and barons of hereditary lands (latifundistas) had to recruit their own militia, which were to serve under their own flags (*Fähnlein* or *Banderia*). This was the core of the:

- **Insurrectio Banderialis**: where nobility and Orders of Chivalry formed regiments of hussars (*banderia*. Singular *Banderium*) according to their financial means. A '*Banderia*' was made up of at least 50 men (about 1/8 of the 400 men provided for a banderia unit) and had a noble (or chivalric Order) as its owner. One fought, therefore, under the banner of the financing owner. If a noble did not have enough resources to create the 50 hussars, some of the enlisted men 'went to the county chapter' and fought under that banner (county *banderium*). The King of Hungary, his Queen, the Lords curtensi, High Prelates and some Knightly Orders could all have their own *Banderium*.

[50] Nagy, István, Acerbi, Enrico, *A brief history of Hungarian Insurrectio*, www.napoleonseries.org.

The formation of units was not forbidden to the minor nobility, as long as they had the means to maintain it, they could, therefore, make their own small armies and join the *Insurrectio* (this variant was called **Insurrectio Particularis**). The insurrectional mode was reminiscent of voluntary enlistment, at least for commanders. There were, classically, at least two ways to invoke *Insurrectio*:

1) **Insurrectio Partialis**: when, out of three feudal curtial lords, only one or two were called to arms in all the lands or only in certain regions.

2) **Insurrectio Generalis**: when everyone was called to arms, nationwide. In this case, '*each and every*' prelate, hereditary or acquired baron, with their subordinate vassals, (in Croatia, called *Summalisten*), had to form and pay troops directly. The 'lesser' nobles personally enlisted '*pro bono rege*', under the king's banner in what was defined as:

2a) Insurrectio **Personalis**: where the entire Hungarian nobility (personalis = person, which also included organisations such as, for example, free towns) had to mobilise (albeit with many restrictions). Thus, the *insurrectio personalis* was an '*ad personam*' mobilisation of nobles and all their towns and villages, together with the guilds, run by the local nobleman, remembering that the nobility was, yes, exempt from taxation but, in return, was obliged to defend their counties. If they did not want to 'risk their skins' in war, they could send substitutes in their place; this, however, was never a widespread or popular custom, for obvious reasons of honour.

To calculate the wealth of the nobles, since they paid no taxes, there was a very simple system: the **Porta**. It was enough, therefore, to count the number of rural farms (Porte) owned to get a measure of the landowner's economic wealth. This value indicated how many troops could be recruited and paid.

3) **Insurrectio Portalis**: the less wealthy vassals (sometimes aided by the nobles to whom they were subordinate) enlisted hussars and militia up to the number stipulated by law. 'Porta' in Hungarian meant house, although the original meaning was not known. As mentioned, it was the standard unit of taxation, in case - medieval - money had to be taken from each farm owned by the landowner. In the Kingdom of Hungary (which was not the same as the Crown Lands, as mentioned above for Croatia, Romania and Serbia) there were 5405.5 gates (early 19th century figure). The 'peasant' soldiers were formally volunteer militias, although recruitment was not always free of coercion.

Portalis and *banderialis* insurrections were often associated and mixed and did not have different statutes. These statutes were often so complex that not all rules could be observed. At the time, with the exception of the *personalis* component, nobles and aristocrats enlisted as many troops as they wanted; almost always in greater numbers than dictated by the Statutes. In Hungary, laws used to change rapidly and the insurrections that were convened hardly maintained the same numbers of forces and the same organisations.

In 1741, insurrectional mounted regiments were formed, such as the Beleznay, Halász and Esterházy hussar regiments, two of which became regulars, and other small units of hussars that went to fight in Silesia. In 1742, 400 militiamen of the Croatian *Insurrectio* were sent to fight in Italy. Practically immediately after Count Palatine Pálffy's call to the *Insurrectio*, 50 hussars were gathered by the bishop of Neutra (Nyitra), 100 hussars from Prince Esterházy, the national militia from Raab (Győr) and Komorn (Komárom), the free hussars from the Banat of Temesvár, and three other hussar companies of aristocrats, as well as two others from high prelates. Not having large numbers, it was preferred to aggregate those formations as replacements for the Ghilányi and Dessőffy regular hussar regiments. Only the magnates of the «*Jazigi and Cumani*" counties[51] (Jasz, Pest, Pilis, Solt) managed to recruit 800 men, forming a regiment, which was also reinforced by troops (500) from the counties of Pressburg (Pozsony), Győr and Komárom, a total of five hussar squadrons. Prince Esterházy also managed to recruit 400 more hussars.

As many as three regiments of insurrectionary hussars were added to these initial units: Johann (János) Beleznay took command of the first or Pest, Peter Hálasz the second and Stephan Esterházy the third; each numbered about 800. To complete the panorama of hussars, one Colonel Csapó gathered more than a thousand *Grenzer* hussars, sent to Silesia, to form a regiment of provisional character.

As the insurrectional obligations in Hungary only existed for the period of the war, all regiments returned from Silesia in the autumn of 1741. On 1 November 1741, the commander of the First Pest Regiment, Johann

---

51   In reality, the Iazigi and Cumani occupied the central counties of modern Hungary (Jász-Nagykun-Szolnok) adjacent to the counties of Pest, Pilis and Solt. Very ancient ethnic groups, the former of Sarmatian origin, the latter from the Don area, had been included by the Roman Empire as barbarian allies against the threats to the east. By the 18th century, their culture and language had been lost, but the tradition of brilliant knights remained.

(János) Beleznay, was ordered, as the owner of the regiment, to transform the remains of the three regiments into a new, regular one.

In all the Teresian wars, the *Jazygo-Kumanen* played a leading role. A few weeks after Pálffy's call to *Insurrectio*, the hussars of the '*Jazygokumani*' districts assembled under the formal command of Colonel Johann Franz von Pratta - of the Pálffy armourers - but, in reality, under the command of Lieutenant-Colonel Michael Molnár, commander of the unit promptly sent to Silesia, which he reached on 28 May 1741. The ordeal to which they were subjected was quite difficult. This is how Molnár recounted those times, in a letter written to his family: '*On the third day the entire Prussian army came down on us with all its might ... we lost Lieutenant Aranyossy with his boys, Valentin Kovács, Andreas Csus from Fényszaru, Andreas Juhász from Arokszállás, Ferdinand Vienner from Mihalytelek, Martin Bali, Martin Kónya from Jakobhalom and Martin Bata from Felsőszentgyörgy. To this day it is still not known whether they ended up prisoners or fell... our people die every day, our weapons rot, our horses get sick and die, day and night our clothes tear...*" The '*Jazygokumano*' regiment was sent back in November, however, 300 new hussars from the same districts arrived in December and all were sent back to Silesia, still under Molnár's command, for the rest of the conflict.

The armistice closed in Breslau did not last long. The year 1744 brought new battles in Silesia. Throughout the duration of the Second Silesian War, Count Palatine again summoned the *Insurrectio*, but this time with smaller numbers than before.

The '*Jazygen and Kumanen*' sent another 400 hussars into the country, and from 1745 - for the duration of the *Insurrectio* - recruited another 1000 horsemen. The commander of the regiment became Colonel Gabriel Haller. The 'irregular Haller regiment', having done its duty - disbanded at the end of the year. Even in Transylvania, barely 600 hussars were recruited, three Transylvanian hussar companies of Baron Jósika were sent to the Netherlands. At the same time, another irregular hussar regiment was formed under the leadership of Colonel Andras Szentkereszty, but this one did not take part in military operations.

In the early years of the War of Austrian Succession, some 1500-2000 mounted militiamen were recruited from the Generalates of the Military Borders or from the Magyar lands, and were then deployed as extemporary units in the various theatres of war. These militias were only framed into regular regiments from 1746 (and were, for the most part, disbanded in 1780, with the exception of the *Grenzer* Szekler or Transylvanian hussar regiment).

In addition to the insurrectionary militia, there was also a historic Hungarian National Mounted Militia, historically known as the '*Magyar nemzeti lovasság*' or national cavalry. One has to be careful not to consider those 'national militias', stationary units, as part of the Hungarian *Insurrectio*, units recruited in times of emergency, a mistake too often noted historically. The 'nationals' were usually recognisable by their associated toponym.

In 1740, not all National Militia units were mounted and equipped, a custom also common to regular Hussar regiments in peacetime. The *Tschaikisten* (*Tzajkisten*), i.e. the Raab, Komorn and Gran National Militia, had the following forces at the beginning of hostilities (see table below):

Headquarters	men	horses	Headquarters	men	horses
Raab (Győr)	388	162	Komorn (Komárom)	212	66
Gran (Esztergom)	137	47	Szigetvár	131	0
Szolnok	59	0	Grosswardein (Oradea, Romania)	121	

Count Salaburg, the Supreme Commissioner of War, decided that the militia of Raab, Komorn, Gran etc. should be called "national hussars" in 1745, and that they should have eight companies (the *Tschaikisten*, those who remained on foot, instead only five), companies which, however, did not have the same strength as the regular ones. The 'national hussars' were partly employed in the countryside during the Silesian War. Their individual units were very weak and did not exceed 40-60 hussars. After the Peace of Dresden, they returned home and were completely disbanded in 1746. The officers, suitable troops and all those who had decided to continue their service were divided among the regiments, while the unsuitable ones were handed over to the civil jurisdiction according to Article 18 of the last Pressburg *Landtag* Convention.

The Komorn National Militia on foot and on horseback was commanded by an *Ober-Capitain*, in 1740 Zahler, then, from 1743, *Rittmeister* Alexander Nagy, of the Festetics Hussars. A supply report of 1746, however, established that there were three hussar companies in Raab, in the other five locations there was only one company left per town. The horns, officers of the 'National Hussars' remained in service, so flags could be preserved.

Insurgent Hussar Regiment *Jazygier und kumanen* then Haller

As early as 28 February 1741, Count Pálffy, on the basis of information received from Colonel Count Pratta, gave a favourable opinion on the formation of the 'national mounted militia' or, as it was commonly referred to, the 'Hungarian *insurrectio*'. They were called 'National Hussars' or also Hungarian '*Husaren-Frei-Compagnien*' or 'Horse Insurrectionists') and were independent companies, sometimes used to replace the losses of the regular regiments deployed in Silesia. The counties 'Jazygen and Kumanen' (Jasz, Pest, Pilis, Solt) managed to recruit 800 men, forming a regiment in 1741 that was entrusted to Lieutenant-Colonel Molnár.

Commanders and owners

1741: Oberts Johann Franz von Pratta - Obristlieutenant Michael Molnár

1745: Oberst Gabriel Haller von Hallerstein

War of the Austrian Succession

1741: In May he was sent to Silesia, joining Neipperg's army on 1 June. He took part in the first mass attack of the Hussars against the Prussian cavalry at Olbendorf, north of Grottkau together with units of the regular regiments (in total 1000 Hussars under the command of GFWM Festetics). It later returned to Hungary to reinforce itself.

Ussari Haller
1745

1745: new formation. 1500 insurgent hussars assembled in Ofen in May, were sent to Silesia via Turnau and Trencsen, reaching the countryside on 9 September, but many deserted to return to Hungary. However, the regiment stabilised at around 1,500 men and participated in the siege of the fortress of Cosel on the Oder.

A national militia also existed in Transylvania. Referred to as the Siebenbürgen National Militia, or, by their commander in 1740 as the '*Springers*', they were definitely better known by the nickname of „*raizisch*".[52] In October 1740 they had 633 men and 448 horses, in November just 460 men and 360 horses. They were divided into companies (248 men and 148 horses), which were positioned, at that time, in various posts (three to 39 men) on the mountain passes or at the main locations on the south-eastern mountain border, while the rest remained in Hermannstadt. Of the multiple militia of Archduke Eugene's time, only two foot companies remained, ten of hussars (including the three that were stationed in the Netherlands and were „*Auctions-Compagnien*"), which, in November 1745 amounted to a total of 782 men.

For the duration of the two wars they remained undisturbed. Only the three '*Auctions-Compagnien*', were taken into the country, with the force of regular Hussar companies, in October 1744 by Baron Mózes Jósika de Branička. The first two companies joined the main army at the end of August 1745, in Bohemia, while the third finished its training on 24 October and followed the previous ones. In 1746 all three marched with the Siebenbürgen (Kálnoky) hussar regiment to the Netherlands. With the reduction of the *Auctions-Compagnien* of the hussar regiments, any further recruitment or reenlistment for the Josika companies ceased.

---

52   *Raizen*, *Raitzen* or *Rascier* (a nickname also often given to the Panduri) was an idiom of the German-speaking population, which lasted until the early 19th century and referred to the Serbian Orthodox peoples inhabiting the lands of the Habsburg monarchy. The nickname was derived from the historical Rascien region, which today is called Okrug Raška in Serbia.

Insurgent Hussar Regiment Menzel then Bertolotti

Ussari Menzel 1743

Ussari Bertolotti 1744

Formed in Prague by Convention of 23 April 1743 as the Hussar Frei-Corps with 3 companies of 100 hussars, reinforced by 3 more in 1744. It was placed under the command of Colonel Menzel (who is said to have formed a unit of hussars with all-black uniforms). Menzel had been given command of the hussars by Khevenhüller during the First Silesian War, dividing his time between leading regular regiments and his Grenzer troops of the Maros. After Menzel's death, the command was handed over to Count Bertolotti, who supported him at his own expense. Colonel Johann Baptist Bartholotti von Partenfeld had an irregular regiment of volunteer hussars (a *Husaren-Frei-Corps*) sent into battle on 9 November 1742 against the Bavarians, where they suffered heavy losses. He later took his regiment to the Main and Rhine rivers. When the commander of the Panduri, Baron Johann Daniel von Menzel, fell in combat on 25 June 1744, Colonel Bartholotti took his place on 9 September, augmenting his troops with three more companies of hussars. The regiment was then called 'Husarenregiment Bartolotti'. From 1746 the corps was disbanded and divided between the regular regiments Dessőwffy (future HR4) and Splényi (disbanded in 1768).

Commanders and owners
1743 Obrist-GFWM Johann Daniel von Menzel,
1744 Obrist Count Bertolotti (Bertholotti) after his death in Mannheim the command was taken 'ad interim' by the
1745 Obristlieutenant Schwaben

War of the Austrian Succession
1742: Bertolotti in Bavaria at Ried, against the Bavarians led by General Claude-Louis de Saint-Germain.
1743: Menzel was first in Bavaria and then on the Rhine. He skilfully conducted his 'little war'.
1744: returned to the Rhine on the taking of Zabern. The commander GFWM von Menzel died of wounds suffered on the small Rhine island '*der Kühkopt*" near Stockstadt
1745: he was in the countryside with Traun on the Main and was then transferred.
1746: in Italy he was at the Battle of Piacenza and the taking of Madonna del Monte, where Colonel Bertolotti and Lieutenant Colonel Count Schulenburg-Oeynhausen distinguished themselves.

Military Border Troops or *Grenzer*[53]

In the history of the military border between Austria and the Ottoman Empire, the War of Austrian Succession initiated the so-called Second Period. During this period, the performance of the *Grenzers* in the various theatres of war began to gain in importance, as the number of their opponents increased (deployment outside the border territory) and the theatres in which to fight expanded. The indelible memory of the boldness of the border militia, which established itself in the battles of the War of Succession and in the dispute over Silesia, as well as its effectiveness in coping with certain *defaults of* the regular Austrian army, will remain. In the beginning, the primordial natural violence, still unbridled, and the greed for booty prevailed, which brought success and panic, in those who suffered raids, suppressing the courage of the enemy. As time went on, the bond to the regency was strengthened with renewed discipline, curbing the thirst for loot, and tactical

---

53   The term *Grenzer* derives from the Slavic word Granica (or Krajina), a word found in texts dating back to 1480 to signify the border.

training ensured more straightforward *governance*. After the Peace of Carlowitz (1699), the Generalates[54] of Carlstädt and Varazdin were joined by two others: that of the Sava-Danube and that of the Theiss (Tisza) and Maros rivers. At the time, all border territories had approximately 45,615 men on active military service, part of whom had to serve in the country, supporting its economy. Only the Generalate of Varazdin was exempt from service[55], as it had a more inland territory, not bordering the Turks, and could therefore offer a larger contingent. The rather unruly internal conditions of part of the border on the Sava did not favour the warlike deployment of their troops. The Danubian borders, of the river Theiss (Tisza) and Maros, did not belong to the territories of the Kingdom of Croatia and Slavonia, but were Hungarian lands. They were, however, part of the border defence system that began with the Sava River. The old borders on the Theiss and Maros were demilitarised in the years 1749-1750, causing a massive emigration of Serbs from those territories in the direction of Russia.

The most important reform, the one that determined the definitive military development of the frontier, was that of Duke Joseph Friedrich Wilhelm von Sachsen-Hildburghausen, who wanted to divide the Varazdin Generalate into two separate corps (called regiments), using the derived battalions as a new tactical unit, instead of the historical companies or Satnies (because they were commanded by captains or Satniks). The embryonic 'regiment' would be placed under the direct command of a staff officer, later establishing an autonomous command for the hussars through a lieutenant colonel. The differentiation between foot and mounted units helped to introduce specific training and the maintenance of discipline among the frontier troops. In time, the *Grenzer* regiments were equalised with the field regiments and had equal military rank. But before delving deeper into the subject, it is necessary to talk about a famous irregular corps of Croats, which will be made famous in fictional literature.

THE VON DER TRENCK PANDURI CORPS

The Panduri[56], wore a national livery and had two pistols and a *Handjar*, a long curved knife, of Turkish type. Baron Franz von der Trenck[57], was lord of the Slavonian localities of Pakrac, Velika, Platernica, Brestovac and Našic and maintained his Panduri as a feudal guard.

After the Prussian invasion of Silesia, Queen Maria Theresa had called 1000 of those Panduri to arms, armed, dressed and paid by von der Trenck. The baron appeared in Vienna with the rank of major (*Oberstwachtmeister*) on 27 May, where the queen gave her approval to these savage warriors;

---

54   The Generalate was a large region, subject to military jurisdiction, with the rank of territorial division (future possibility of forming brigades). It was divided into several 'Kapitanate' captaincies, smaller regions corresponding to recruitment areas for territorial battalions or regiments.

55   The term 'Kordun' comes from the border line of the sentinels during the wars against the Turks. Characteristic of the border region with the Ottoman Empire were the so-called Tschardaks (Croatian čardak) or Posten (Croatian pošte). These were small wooden huts built at regular intervals, which were accessed via a flight of steps up to an elevated observation post. If the enemy was signalled, the border guard would fire a shot. This was repeated by other border guards along the entire line, to allow for rapid warning. At the border posts, there were always 4-12 guards patrolling even at night. Until 1773, there were also hussars on horseback at Cordone to prevent robberies by the Turks. Most of the border posts were abolished in 1849.

56   The name panduri (*panduren* in German, *panduri* in Serbo-Croatian) comes from *pandúr*, a loan from the Serbo-Croatian *pudar* (from the verb *pudati/puditi*, = to chase, hunt); it designated a countryside or wine-growing area guard, later also a law enforcement officer. The original derivation seems to be the medieval Latin *banderius, bannerius*. The Panduri of the Teresian era were irregular light infantry soldiers, all Croatian and Serbian volunteers from Slavonia and the Croatian Military Frontier. In Maria Terézia hadserége.doc in https://air.uniud.it, p. 6.

57   Baron Franz von der Trenck, born in Reggio Calabria, (1711-1749), a Prussian but an Austrian citizen, was the son of an imperial army officer with landed property in Croatia. He joined the army in 1728, but was forced to leave the service after only three years due to his quarrelsome and undisciplined temperament. At the outbreak of the War of the Austrian Succession, he offered his services to the cause of Maria Theresa, who through a *Werbepatent* (February 1741) authorised him to enlist a thousand volunteers, soon to be known as Trenck's panduri. His men made the 'Kleine Krieg' a real guerrilla war, sparing no looting and brutality on civilians. Trenck would end up before a court martial and sentenced to death, later commuted to prison on the Spielberg, where he died in 1749.

In Maria Terézia hadserége.doc at https://air.uniud.it, p. 6.

they numbered 1022 men in 20 volunteer companies (*Freicompagnien*) of 50 men, with four Turkish drums and fifes, but no flags.

It was the first extemporaneous reinforcements that reached the newly appointed Field Marshal-Commander Count Neipperg. In fact, the queen had accepted Trenck's offer, 'with reservation', and the *Hofkriegsrat* had given its assent with the promise that acts of violence against soldiers and civilians would be prohibited. Trenck, in fact, had gathered his Panduri not only from his own possessions, but had added thieves and brigands (many overpowered and captured in Kobaš on the Sava River), pardoned them and enlisted them, along with many Sava borderers. In this way, he had fulfilled his promise to deliver the corps in three weeks. The basic core of the corps was made up of militiamen, however, not all of whom were subjects or expensed by Baron Trenck. Landowners and Slavic villagers had directly contributed to the recruitment, uniforms and armament. The assembly point was called Essek (today Osijek), where each man received six *kreuzers a* day in pay. As uniforms, the different national costumes were maintained, with only one garment in common: a long cloak, almost always with a red hood, a badge, which gave them their name (*Rotmäntler* or *Kaputziner*, in the French manner). Their armament consisted of two pistols, a sabre, a musket and a long Turkish knife. The royal treasury contributed by allocating 200 tents, powder barrels and ammunition.

On 1st April Trenck left Essek, commanding his corps with the rank of *Obristwachtmeister* (major) with 50 *Harambašen* (the *Serežaner - Harambašen* or 'Serezani Arrambasci' also known as *Hauptleute*, i.e. captains, in the future considered non-commissioned officers like the *Feldwebel*) as subordinates. Laudon himself, who would later become a famous general, started out as a captain at Trenck. Baron Franz von der Trenck joined the army in Silesia on 15 May 1741, one month after the defeat at Mollwitz (10 April). The task assigned to him was immediately to attack enemy supplies. Thus he immediately became a considerable nuisance for the Prussians and a bogeyman for the civilians, who feared and hated him.

Constitution. The corps became official in 1741 by the Patente of 27 February under the name *Panduren-Corps* of Baron von der Trenck, recruited in Slavonia; in 1745 (Patente of 17 March) it became a regular regiment (20 *ordinäre-compagnien*, 2 *grenadier-compagnien*). An impromptu regiment was created in the spring of 1744 with the troops of the *Frei-Corps of* the Panduri von der Trenck, which, by the Decree of the Hofkriegsrat of 17 March 1745, was given the formal name "Slavonian Panduri Regiment" with the strength and organisation of a German regiment; in 1748 it was reduced to a battalion (4 rifle companies and 1 grenadier company) with the name "*Slavonisches Panduren-Bataillon*".

Recruitment. Because of the bravery shown by this new troop, in 1744 Trenck was ordered to go to Slavonia again and strengthen his panduro corps by recruiting new soldiers. The *Hofkammer* paid him 80 guilders for each man, for which he had to procure weapons and clothing.

In short, he had 2500 infantrymen and 130 hussars in his service. The former had green uniforms with red or yellow hoods. Instead of flags Trenck gave them Turkish banners with crescent moons; their war cry was also Turkish: "*Allah ! Allah!*"

The *Panduren-Corps* (later regiment) von Trenck, organised, as mentioned, in Slavonia, later also had soldiers from Syrmia (region bordering Serbia). As a line regiment, in the future (Seven Years' War and beyond), it also recruited in the Hungarian lands of Bacs County and in Banat (it also had among its ranks 300 Triestines, although many of them were actually Dalmatians).

Freikorps von der Trenck 1748

1747 - Panduro Banalist Freikorps Trenck

From 1756, the Trenck Panduri became the future 53rd Infantry Regiment; but in Slavonia, they remained in the popular imagination and common memory, so much so that the local recruitment was, for years, known as the 'Baronowati' conscription, i.e. the people of Baron von der Trenck.

Garrisons: 1741 Esseg; 1749 Peterwardein.

Owner: 1741 Baron Franz vor der Trenck, *Obristwachtmeister* later *Obrist*. (from 1748 to 1756 became Slavonian battalion had no owner) - it was the forerunner of the future imperial regiment IR 53 (the Jellačić of the Napoleonic wars).

Commanders: Panduren-Corps (Regiment) 1741 *Obristwachtmeister* Baron Franz von del Trenck. 1747 ad interim Lieutenant-Colonel d'Olne. 1748 ad interim Major Count Madrenas. As battalion *Slavonisches Panduren*: 1748 Major Christian von Manstein. 1750 Colonel Adam von Buday. 1753 Colonel Baron Joseph Carl von Simbschen (note the curiosity of a battalion commanded by colonels).

Campaigns: **1741** he did the Silesian campaign after the Battle of Mollwitz (taking of Zöben), did several punitive actions and then organised a bridgehead in Vienna. He was then in Upper Austria and in the defence of Styria. **1742**: he continued his 'little war' and took part in the occupations of Claus, Windischgarsten, Linz and Deggendorf. He caused the destruction of enemy supplies in Brenz, later attacked Reichenhall, Munich and was at the Battle of Weissenstein. Baron Franz von der Trenck was promoted to lieutenant colonel for meritorious service. In the autumn he was at the taking of Cham and then transferred to Bohemia. **1743**: he took part in the pursuit of French troops towards the Rhine, fighting near Neckar-Sulm. Trenck was at the taking of the fortifications near Alt-Breisach finishing the year with promotion to colonel. **1744**: During the passage on the left bank of the Rhine, this corps was the first to cross, assaulting three cavalry regiments and covering the army's passage, later participating in the attack on Lauterburg and the capture of Kloster-Neuburg. During the retreat from the Rhine, the corps always formed the rearguard and Captain Prodanovich (Brodanović) distinguished himself in the defence of Donauwörth. In Bohemia, the corps fought successfully in a series of small feats such as at Budweis, Frauenberg, Kolin and others. **1745 : He was** in Silesia with the Nádasdy corps and at the capture of Kosel, then he was in the failed attack of Ziegenhals; it seems he also took part in the Battle of Soor (Trautenau), attacking in the vanguard and, when the battle was turning against the imperial arms, the Panduri sacked the Prussian camp, including King Frederick's tent. **1746 :** he was sent to the Dutch battlefields (in three battalions and two grenadier companies), his wards took an active part in the assault on Rousselaer and others in the attack on Viset on the river Ourthe, while at Rocoux he was not a protagonist. **1747 :** the grenadiers took Rosenthal Abbey while the regiment was at the Battle of Lauffeldt.

Uniform (according to Wrede at the time of the regiment): Ottoman-type costume: he wore a tall black shako (Czako), red cape with hood, red corset, trouser covers and wide blue breeches (*Pumphosen*), Turkish-style boots (from 1744 to 1746 the uniform would be green and red).

1748 - Battaglione von der Trenck (ricostruzione)

The Grenzer formations and uniforms

A Grenzer Generalate (according to the Hildburghausen reform and in Varazdin from 1747) provided for:

High Staff	
1 Generalobrist or general pukovnik - colonel general	substitute or Generalamtsverwalter
2 colonels - pukovnik - regimental commanders	2 Obristlieutenant (Lt. Col.) - potpukovnik
2 Obristwachtmeister (major) or Četnik	
Small staff	
1 War Commissioner or Kriegscommissär	1 Bau- und Construction Manager - 1 Bau- und Cassaverwalter
1 Ingenieurcapitän - 1 Captain Engineer	2 Quartermasters or Quartermasters
4 Auditors or Auditor	4 Dolmetscher - performers
1 Doctor (Medicus)	5 Staff Surgeons or Stabsfeldscher		4 Chaplains (Capläne)
1 Pharmacist (Apotheker)	2 Prevosti (Profosen)	2 Wachtmeister or Regimental Ordinances

At the Varazdin Generalate, each regiment was to have 4 battalions: 1 battalion had 5 companies of 200 men for a total of 1,000 men; the regiment was therefore to have about 4,000 men (the Generalate 8,000 men). In addition, there were to be 5 companies of 100 hussars for a total of 500 horsemen and 34 artillery men. This brought Varazdin's troops to a total of 8544 men.

Grenzer Hussar Company	
1 Obristlieutenant commander or Potpukovnik	1 Rittmeister or Captain - Kapetan
1 lngenieurcapitän - 1 Captain Engineer	2 Quartermasters or Quartermasters
1 Lieutenant or hadnak	1 Cornet or Barjaktar
1 Wachtmeister or stražmeštar	1 Fourier (furiere) or opskrbnik or končar
1 Pauker (timpanist or timbale player) or Tempani	1 Korporal (corporal) or Kaplar
100 Gemeiner or Hussars - Husar	
Infantry Company or Satnija	
1 captain or Satnik	1 lieutenant or vojvoda
1 bishop (Fähnrich) or Barjaktar	1 Feldwebel (serg. major) or stražmeštar
1 Fourier o opskrbnik (končar ?)	1 Korporal (corporal) or Kaplar
1 Drum or bubnjar	1 soldier with pay (Gefreite)
200 Hajduken or soldiers (Gemeiner)	

In the chapter on uniforms, the problems concerning the supply of uniforms and equipment to the Border troops have already been discussed. We describe here what was noted about the uniform of the Varazdin soldiers at the time of the War of Succession and beyond (three Silesian Wars[58]). The uniform of the Border troops was not constant, with the exception of a few distinctions, which were to differentiate the regiments in the future. During the Silesian War, and until 1760, the uniform of the Varazdin Generalate consisted of the following items:

For the infantry of the Varazdin regiments (known as *Warasdiners*):

1. a German-type corset (*Kamisol*) of green fabric with two pockets and 18 buttons. The sleeves had red hand guards. They were so long that they covered the trousers above the knee.
2. the trousers were of the Hungarian type made of red fabric with cords of varying colours to indicate the regiment. The flap had to measure a quarter of a Viennese cubit (about 20 cm).
3. the Colbacchi (*Klobuks*), which with the establishment of the *Grenzer* regiments had become the official headgear, had a helmet (*Casquet*) of black felt, with a brass plate on the front. The flap at the back of the head served as a shelter for the nape of the neck from the rain and cold. It was always rolled up. Inside the *casquet* was a three-finger wide lining of black leather. At the top, and precisely in the centre, was a brass cross the size of the curvature, with, in the centre, a hump with a cavity for attaching the companion bow. This covering was light and served to protect the nape of the neck from climatic influences.

The headgear of the grenadiers was a felt hat, *Filzhaube*.

4. the neck was protected by a band of crepe fabric with two narrow white collars and a brass tie buckle, which had to be covered with red fabric or linen cloth.
5. the jacket was a *Gunjac*[59] of green fabric, replacing the previous white one, with six pairs of red woollen cords, lined with red Boy (a type of downy fabric) and small hand guards of the same colour as those on the corset.

Varazdin Grenzer
1747 - 1749 (Vanicek)

---

58 „Die Montur zur Zeit der drei schlesischen Kriege und des Erbfolgekampfes" in Vanicek, Specialgeschichte ecc. vol. 2, pag. 62.
59 The Gunjac (in Hungarian Gunyácz) was a short caftan usually black when worn by Serbs. It was a jacket of clear Turkish origin.

The NCOs had long jackets (Kaputröcke), corsets and breeches of the same colours but of finer cloth. Their *Casquet had a* shinier and brighter plate, as did the buttons and buttonholes of the Gunjac, adorned with red camel hair. The other equipment of an infantry soldier were:

1 rifleman's cartridge box with strap; 1 cartridge box for 20 rounds with a white strap; 1 white leather musket strap; 1 pastern strap; 1 bayonet sleeve; 1 white leather bandolier with or without buckle; 1 grenadier's cartridge box with strap and rack; 1 sabre with brass handle;

Varazdin Hussar
1745 - 1748

Pukovnik di Carlstädt
(colonnello) 1746

As uniform for hussars or special equipment there were:

1 Csáko cape edged with a black band and with a black cord; 1 red cape with German collars and lined; 1 green Pelisse with yellow laces, four rows of buttons and edged with black lamb fur; 1 Dolman of green fabric with yellow laces, buttons and buttonholes; 1 pair of Czismén (Hungarian boots) with spurs; 1 yellow belt with 15 yellow and black buttons 1 Sabre covered in yellow; 1 Bandolier with yellow leather hooks; 1 Russian leather sabre strap; 1 *Sabretache* in red fabric with an eagle embroidered near three rings and a strap; 1 leather container for 20 cartridges with a leather lid; 1 *Mantelsack* or cavalry rucksack of green fabric; 1 carpet (*fleece*) 2 m 30 and 35 cm long and 35 cm wide (half-elle or cubit); 1 pistol holster; 1 crush (*Kotzen*) of Kazan? (*Kasansener*); 1 red cloth caparison with four eagles embroidered; 1 black saddle blanket lined and edged with yellow cloth.

The entire outfit cost 24 florins for a rifleman and 54 florins for a hussar. The cost of the complete uniform for hussar officers was 450 florins. According to Hans Bleckwenn, in 1743 the Grenzers were not yet mentioned for uniforms, in 1744 the three regiments were named, but without providing the distinctive colours; in 1745 there were already four regiments, all with red *Gunjac* and green hand guards; in 1746, Licca wanted to distinguish himself from the others by swapping colours (green jacket and red hand guards).

It was not until 1749 that regiments began to differentiate their uniforms, although not always completely. At best, all patterns would have to be considered with many doubts. It was not until the Seven Years' War that certain and decipherable figures became available (moreover, no one has ever clarified the differences between *Hausmontur* and *Feldmontur*, service uniforms in peace - at home - and in war, in the early days of the Border regiments).

Grenzer di Carlstädt
1744 (HGM)

THE BEGINNING OF THE WAR OF SUCCESSION AND THE NEW FORMATIONS

Maria Theresa also carefully observed the Grenzers of the Central and Lower Sava, who had occupied Esseg at the outbreak of war and intended to form their own corps. The Queen made use of the Patente of 1735, which had exempted the *Grenzer of* the Sava from taxation, provided that they were obliged to serve in the war even in foreign territories. Count Khevenhüller wrote to the Marquis de Guadagni, acting commander in Esseg, on 27 September 1741, that: *"the Queen would sign the patent and forward it to the Hofkriegsrat, adding only a few reservations in a handwritten note, namely that if the Slavic national militia did not field 2000 foot-soldiers and a few hundred hussars and if, as seen on the occasion of examples offered by those of Varazdin or other Grenzers, they did not do their duty and confirm their willingness to serve the kingdom, the patent would be withdrawn. If they then had no intention of even setting out, they would all have been declared completely undesirable."*

Khevenhüller avoided the dissemination of those royal remarks so as not to irritate the militia, spreading the request only to the higher captains (*Obercapitänen*) to prepare the troops for mobilisation. It should be pointed out that, after the last war against the Turks, the border on the Sava was still owed 6,000 guilders by the treasury, a debt that would never be settled after 1741.

From the borders, in early summer, four battalions of the Varazdin Generalate (according to Wrede only one[60]) arrived in Silesia . On the lower Sava there were 500 *Grenzer* and 200 hussars. Five hundred Danubian *Grenzers* guarded the territory and fortress of Peterwardein. After the Battle of Mollwitz, however, the war did not offer any critical events, apart from the siege of Gross-Glogau, so that the military border remained quiet.

In the report that Field Marshal Khevenhüller sent to Maria Theresa after the treaty of Klein-Schnellerdorf, the attitude of the Varazdin confinarians was openly praised, while the Slavonians (those from the lower Sava) were complained about. In the meantime, Croats from the upper Sava were sent to the Austrian littoral to occupy the most important coastal positions to avoid hostile landings. There were approximately 2,000 infantry and 900 mounted soldiers. In the war, the royal army received new contingents. In Hungary, where new regular regiments had sprung up, 2000 *Grenzer* from Varazdin, 2400 from the Sava, 500 from Theiss on foot and 500 on horseback, 4,000 from Carlstädt and Lika were called to arms. Only the Sava Grenzers caused problems, due to a bloody mutiny against their officers, in Požega. The inhabitants of the administrative districts of Pakrac and Požega offered to field 900 men on foot and 100 on horseback, who could be enlisted immediately.

The Austrian imperial commander, transferred to Austria before the conclusion of the Peace of Belgrade, Major of the Serbian National Militia Izaković took an oath of allegiance, with his 571 subordinate officers and non-commissioned officers, to sacrifice his life for the Queen and to increase his unit to 1475 men, all from Serbia.

As Austria's enemies were advancing through the Amberg towards the Eger Valley and through the Danube Valley towards Linz, Field Marshal Prince Lobković had to rally his troops in Bohemia and Count Pálffy had to put Upper Austria on the defensive, gathering all incoming troops to cover Vienna. Count Khevenhüller was in charge from Vienna, where he organised plans for the defence of the Danube valley. Pálffy, however, was forced to retreat to Sieghartskirchen, via Krems and St Pölten, ahead of the threatening enemy. Thanks to the support of 500 *Grenzer* of the Theiss and 400 of the Maros he was ordered to counter-attack at the Bilach stream, but was still forced to retreat, due to the lack of reliability and discipline of his irregular troops, to Maria-Brünn only 2 hours from Vienna. Varazdin's 2000 *Grenzer* troops, sent to guard and defend the passes leading into Styria, and sent through Tyrol, were still on the march. At the Spittal pass there were 250 men, at Schottwein 73 volunteers. Of the first 800 recruits from Varazdin, Field Marshal Moltke directed 200 at Aspang, 100 at Semmering, 200 at Mariazell and 300 at Spittal on the Phyrn, to repel the Franco-Bavarian patrols away from Styria.

Vienna and the throne of Maria Theresa were in the greatest danger when the French Marshal Belle-Isle advanced in the direction of Prague through the Eger Valley, while the Electoral Prince did not want to aim for Prague through the Vltava Valley according to the established campaign plan. When the French General Montagne threw himself on the outposts of Count Pálffy, to cover the Danube crossing, and drove them back as far as Sieghartskirchen, the *Grenzer* of the Maros, the Theiss, the insurgent hussars of Komarom and Raab (Győr) behaved so cowardly, that Field Marshal Count Khevenhüller openly complained to Pálffy, for allowing

---

60   Wrede, Alphons, *Geschichte der K. und K. Wehrmacht*, vol. V, pag. 212.

those troops to be sent into the line, asking to assign those hussars to manual field fortification work, after having requisitioned their horses, and to send the *Grenzers* to be farmers. The request was not granted for reasons of expediency. As the war years went by and the number of fronts to fight on increased, the *Grenzer*'s involvement became more and more important, until they were incorporated into quasi-regular units. They continued to be paid for their military service, but with one third of the common pay of an infantryman; the remaining two thirds of the pay, like a feudal jus, was paid to the family at home, in arable land. The Confinari performed infantry or cavalry service, with infantry outnumbering cavalry. The first regiments to be formed were two infantry regiments and one hussar regiment in Varazdin. The Varazdin hussar regiment, despite the fact that its name suggested it might be a regular troop, still functioned under the old militia systems. It had five companies, each with 100 hussars, who still received only a third of their pay, and had to buy their own weapons and clothing. It was not until 1755 that the treasury intervened by offering a bonus of 55 florins for equipment.

In 1746, a hussar regiment was formed in Carlstädt (Károlyváros or Carlovac), organised in 8 companies with a total of 800 horsemen. A year later, two large border regiments followed in Slavonia. Each regiment consisted of ten companies of 210 men; one was called Syrmic (of Szérem), the other Slavonian. The Syrmic regiment was disbanded in 1750, and later reconstituted.

The Carlstädt Generalate

It comprised the regions of Licca (Lika), Corbavia (Krbava) and Zwonigrad (Zanigrad and the non-Venetian littoral), the towns of Slunj (Szluin) Otočac (Otoschatz) and Ogulin: the so-called *Carlstädter Grenze*.

After the Peace of Carlowitz, the territories of Licca and Corbavia had returned under the Empire and, following numerous disputes with the *Hofkammer* of Inner Austria, which had acquired those territories, a border militia was created there as well, from families who had immigrated from the littoral, Herzegovina or Turkish Croatia. Only from 1712, however, after the handover of the lands. from the Hofkammer to the military administration (*Militär-Verwaltung*), everything was organised under the name '*Militär - Directorium*'. The *Grenzer*, thanks to the feudal system, the usual guarantees of 'militarised freedom' found themselves within a captaincy, under a superior captain, which was initially based in Carlopago (Carlstädt), and later in Ribnik.

The theoretical strength of the militia was 5000 infantry and 1800 horse soldiers. The new territory was then subject to the military code and united to the Carlstädt Generalate, subordinate to the military control of Inner Austria. Their *Hofkriegsrat was, in* fact, in Graz, itself subordinate to the one in Vienna since 1705, the one that directed all matters of the Frontier. Supplies for the new districts remained, however and always. the responsibility of Carinthia and Carniola (Krain).

A first attempt to reform the militia was made in the period 1729-1736 by Counts Rabatta and Stubenberg, colonels-general, but it was only an attempt to put an end to the *Grenzer*'s non-payment for Carinthian and Krajna supplies.

Chronology of Carlstädt:

1742: 3000 men from Licca and the littoral were sent to Bavaria with the Bärnklau corps, distinguishing themselves in the battle on the Rott; a group took part in the siege of Prague with the GFWM Helfreich; one of their units under the command of Colonel Herberstein went on the assault of Kaaden; 1000 men were de-

Grenzer di Carlstädt
1747 (Vanicek)

Grenzer Szluin (?)
1748

ployed in Moravia in the Festetics corps.

1743: 4000 men remained at the Bavarian campaign and the siege of Ingolstadt: a part of them (Licca) was employed in the Rhine crossing.

1744: they operated on the Rhine and in Bohemia; in the late autumn about 6,000 soldiers were sent to fight in Italy.

1745: 4,000 men under the command of GFWM Petazzi were in Bohemia, with detached regiments fighting in Landshut and Soor; there was no noteworthy operation in Italy. In 1745, the Military Director of the Borders, Duke FM von Hildburghausen, wanted to form regular regiments in this Generalate as well. Geographical boundaries were easily found to form four infantry regiments and one hussar regiment, boundaries that became official from 1746 (as a result, the German and *Leib-Compagnie* of Colonel General Carlstädt were abolished). Initially, they bore the name of their commander without the privileges of ownership, like the commanders of the six new Hungarian infantry regiments formed in 1741. Only from 1753 were they renamed according to the area they belonged to: *Liccaner, Otoschatzer, Oguliner and Szluiner*. In the beginning, the **Guicciardi regiment** (future *Liccaner*), the **Herberstein regiment** (*Otočaner*) and the **Petazzi regiment** (*Szluiner*) had 4 battalions and a strength of 5000 men. The Herberstein regiment recruited from the *Ober-Hauptmannschaften* (Upper Township) of Zengg with the towns of Bründl (1st and 2nd battalions) and Otočac (3rd and 4th battalions), the Petazzi from the Upper Township of Thurn, Barilović, Szluin and Sichelburg (each town, one battalion). Finally, the 4th **Dillis Regiment** (future *Oguliner*) had 4800 men and recruited from the High Captaincies of Trzić (1st batt.), Thurn (2nd batt.) and Ogulin (3rd and 4th batt.). In all, the Carlstädt Border was to provide 17,280 infantry and 800 mounted soldiers.

1746: many were in Italy and fought in Piacenza.

1747: part sent to the Genoese, part (two regiments) to Holland.

Their uniform was provided by the treasury, both in peace and war. At the time they had blue jackets with red laces and hand guards, red trousers. The uniform of the officers comprised a black polo neck with gaudy gold ornaments, a green dolman with round gold buttonholes, a red corset, trousers with borders, a carbine, a sabre with embroidered ornaments and a small cartridge box. The weapon was also a taxpayer's item, the Grenzer only had to buy the sabre, belt and *Bündel* (the rucksack); as a contribution to expenses a *Feldwebel* received 30 kreuzer per month, while a private, at the time known as a *Hejduck*, like the Hungarian infantry, 18 kreuzer. At every third military campaign, a new uniform was provided. The last act of the reform of the Duke of Sachsen-Hildburghausen was the adoption of an '*Exercierregoulament für die Grenzinfanterie und die Erhebung der Karlstädter und Warasdiner zum Range regulärer Regimenter*', i.e. a regulation to train the Border Infantry and to lead the soldiers of Carlstädt and Varazdin to become regular infantry regiments.

As early as 16 September 1746, he had already hinted at the need to take this step, but without reaching a real decision. However, when, in March 1747, General Petazzi, Major Mikašinović and Captain Rettel complained that, despite their joining the regular army, Carlstädt and Varazdin's militia could not be considered equal to the German and Hungarian regiments, but continued to behave like irregular troops, the duke decided to continue and renew his efforts, until he succeeded.

The Petazzi *Grenzer* Regiment of Carlstädt or Szluin

The Petazzi regiment took over the former captaincies of Thurn, Barilović, Szluin and Sichelburg, so that each captaincy provided a battalion. Thus he recruited from 64 villages, with 2276 houses, 5215 men fit for arms (aged between 16 and 60) and a total of 10444 men. Each battalion was to have four companies of 240 men. Its 12 satnije were: Slunj (Szluin) n.1, Vališ selo n.2, Krstinja n.3, Vojnić n.4, Veljun n.5, Krnjak n.6, Perjasica n.7, Barilović n.8, Vukmanić n.9, Švarča n.10, Kostanjevac n.11, Kalje n.12. The first owner and commander was Colonel, Count from Trieste, Benvenuto Petazzi, who was later promoted to GFWM and replaced by Colonel Benzoni in 1747. In 1747, units of the regiment fought in Holland, distinguishing themselves under the command of Major (Obristwachtmeister) Beck in the battle of Maastricht.

The 4th Dillis *Grenzer* Regiment of Carlstädt or Ogulin

The Ogulin border regiment was established in 1746 as the fourth of the Carlstädt border regiments. It had captains from Trsić, Thuin and Ogulin who formed the 1st and 2nd battalions, while the 3rd and 4th battalions came from Ogulin. The 12 satnije were: Krivi Put no.1, Brinje no.2, Jezerane no.3, Modruš no.4, Oštarije no.5, Ogulin no.6, Drežnik no.7, Plaški no.8, Rakovica no.9, Primišlje no.10, Tounj no.11, Dubrave no.12. The regiment initially recruited 9809 men of whom 4801 were fit for service. The first owner and commander was

Colonel Count Dillis. On 14 January 1747, von Dillis attacked the Bocchetta, near Genoa, with 200 *Grenzer* from Carlstädt and as many from Varazdin, but had to retreat on the second day. The battalion in Italy then advanced as far as Provence. "*On the 14th of January, having noted the tenacious resistance of the villagers, Botta ordered an attack in force: he divided his forces into two columns, General Andrassy, with the larger one, passed the Bocchetta and advanced two kilometres further, General Saint Andrè from the Giovi came down to Pontedecimo. Wherever they succeeded, the Balkans burned and looted houses and property and inflicted terror on civilians. On the 19th, the Austrian troops were pushed back towards the pass by the Genoese militia. For weeks, a guerrilla war of raids and reprisals was fought in the valleys, in which it was easy to drive the enemies away but impossible not to let them return. Border raids by Croats and Varasdinians posed a serious threat to the villagers.*"[61]

The Herberstein *Grenzer* Regiment of Carlstädt or Otočac

It had the captaincies of Zengg (1st batt.) and Bründl (2nd batt.) as well as that of Otočac (which provided the 3rd and 4th battalions). The number of those recruited was 9520, but that of those eligible was only 5014. Its 12 satnije were: Kosinj n.1, Klanac n.2, Perušić n.3, Bunić n.4, Zavalje n.5, Korenica n.6, Vrhovine n.7, Škare n.8, Sinac n.9, Otočac n.10, Brlog n.11, Sv.Juraj n.12. The first commander was Colonel Count Carl Joseph Herberstein. From 1747 he had a battalion in Holland and one in Italy, which was engaged in the defence of the Voltaggio outposts (two redoubts protecting the Bocchetta Pass).

The I Guicciardi *Grenzer* Regiment from Carlstädt in Lika

Formed in 1746 by Duke Hildburghausen. It was the first to be formed and the largest. It recruited from 137 villages (10523 houses) inhabited by 45586 people. There were 11569 recruits and 8980 fit for service. He succeeded in forming as many as 6 battalions and had a total strength of 9000. He took troops in the counties of Licca (Lika) and Corbavia (Krbava), the upper part of the littoral. The 12 satnije of the four battalions (which remained regular) were: Zrmanja No. 1, Srb No. 2, Donji Lapac No. 3, Bruvno No. 4, Udbina No. 5, Podlapac No. 6, Gračac No. 7, Lovinac No. 8, Medak No. 9, Kaniža No. 10, Smiljan No. 11, Osik No. 12. The first commander in 1746 was Colonel Count Giuseppe Filippo Guicciardi. In 1746 they fought at the Battle of Piacenza and in 1747 they were engaged in the defence of the Voltaggio outposts, an important position on the road to Genoa and the Bocchetta Pass.

Carlstädt *Grenzer* Hussar Regiment

It was formed in 1746 by the FZM Prince von Hildburghausen with four squadrons (it would be reduced to just two squadrons in 1756) without ever having an owner colonel. Apparently, the colour of their *Pelisse* was initially steel green. The Hussar Regiment had 4 squadrons (8 companies) and 800 horses. It was immediately based in Grahacz, then the capital Carlstädt. The first commander was Lieutenant-Colonel Baron Max Joseph von Mittrowski. In the period 1747-1748: he was always on duty in the Netherlands.
Bleckwenn suggests the following colours for the initial period.[62]

Regiment	Grade	Jacket	Handguards	buttons	Dolman *	Pants	Kolpak **
Licca	officers	red	yellow	golden	watergreen	red	red
Otočac	Sulak ***	red	light yellow	yellow	blue/red	red	(helmet)
Ogulin	fusiliers	blue	yellow	yellow	blue	red	red
Szluin	flutes	blue	yellow	yellow	red	red	red
* the Dolman here was worn under the Oberkleid (jacket) ** the red colour refers to the envelope not the coat							
*** Šulak was the Grenadier of the Grenzer regiments (1749-1751)							

What this table lists is to be taken with due reservation; it should be noted that, contrary to what has happened so far, the known sources gave the two last regiments (Ogulin and Szluin) the same jacket and handguard colours, thus differing only from the *Dolmans*. Below are three plates found in the collection of the Heeresgeschichtliche Museum in Vienna (HGM). The Lyca officer here wears a white jacket (*Feldmontur*?). Note the long *Oberkleid* with lapels also for non-commissioned officers.

The Varaždin Generalate (formerly *Windisches-Grenze*)

It included the towns of Kreuz (Križevci), Kopreiniz (Koprivnica), lvanić, Warasdin (Varaždin) . It was the

---

[61] Penchi Alessandro, *Assedio e fortificazioni di Genova 1746-1747*, tesi, Relatore: Prof. Emiliano Beri, Correlatore: Prof. Paolo Calcagno, Università degli Studi di Genova, 2022, pag. 34.
[62] Bleckwenn, Hans, *Uniformen und Ausrüstung der Österreichischen Grenztruppen 1740-1769*

Sottufficiale regg. Petazzi 1746 (HGM)

Grenzer regg. von Dillis 1746 (HGM)

ufficiale di St. Magg. regg. Guicciardi 1746

only Generalate that did not directly border the Turks, since the Peace of Carlowitz. For this absent border it had been planned to be removed in 1714, but the unrest that followed the order had caused the *status quo to be* restored as early as 1717. Emperor Charles VI himself had reconfirmed the privileges of the 'Warasdiners' by stating in his ordinance that they '*should not be turned into peasants, but kept as frontier soldiers, treated as such and with the possibility of war service abroad*'.

In the period from 1718-1737, i.e. from the Peace of Passarowitz until the death of Emperor Charles VI, further disturbances and riots occurred in the Generalate, partly due to organisational shortcomings, but often due to dissatisfaction caused by the officers' abuse. Fundamental credit for the pacification of tempers and the establishment of regular relations went to Prince FZM von Hildburghausen, who studied and had new statutes published in 1737. His main goal was the creation of a warrior-rich and economically viable state. Prince von Hildburghausen's main reform was to form the *Grenz-Truppen* into regiments replacing the militia of the Varazdin Generalate. The Generalate was until then divided into four High Captaincies (Creuz, Ivanić, Kopreinitz and St. Georgen) since the reform of the FML Cordova in 1732. The High Captaincies were, in turn, subdivided into a total of 30 Vojwodati (*Wojwodschaften*) with companies or *Harámien* of 143 men, in which only the officers and 12 Gefreite had pay. In addition, there were 500 hussars and 4 German companies (formed by the FML Cordova in 1732 and disbanded in 1745).

In 1736 the *Warasdiners* were divided into two corps (regiments) each of 4 battalions with 5 companies of 200 men. In addition, the Generalate was to form 5 companies of hussars. The war against the Turks, which broke out in 1737, partly blocked the completion of the reform.

1741: a battalion was sent to Silesia.

1742: 2,000 men took part in the occupation of Linz; other units under the command of Colonel Macquire distinguished themselves at Austup, Chotusitz and Moldauthein, later also at the siege of Prague; another 500 men, also under the command of Macquire, distinguished themselves at the assault on Kaaden.

1743: they were present at the taking of Dingolfing, at the siege of Ingolstadt (1,000 men under Lt. Colonel Benzoni).

1744: they operated on the Rhine and at the defeat of Lauterburg (with their hussars), were in the retreat to Bohemia and at the Battle of Beraun.

The formation of the Varazdin militia into regular regiments, initiated by Prince FZM von Hildburghausen and partially suspended, due to the Turkish War, was resumed by the Field Marshal in 1745, after he had been appointed '*Militär -Grenz - Director*', Director of the Military Frontier. The FMZ Hildburghausen had new statutes and articles renewed and officially formed 2 infantry regiments and 1 hussar regiment. Each infantry regiment, which at that time still had no territorial connotations, had 4 battalions, out of 5 companies of 200 men each and a total strength of 4000. The Militia of that Generalate grew to 8543 men, including 34 artillerymen; from 1751 they also had 2 grenadier companies.

1745: they partially took part in secondary battles in Bavaria and, later, in the Battle of Kesselsdorf; about 800 men were sent to Italy, to cover Lombardy, under the command of FML Pertusati staying in Milan Castle.

1746: they were at the Battle of Piacenza, at the taking of the Bocchetta with Macquire, now General, marching as far as Provence.

1747: took part in operations against the Genoese and in the defence of Voltaggio.

Empress Maria Theresa made it clear in her Supreme Resolution of 23 April 1747 that: "*the Varazdin and Carlstädt regiments were never again to be regarded as irregulars, but as entirely regular troops, like other German and non-German troops, and that from then on they would have their own rank or position within the army, like the common infantry troops.*" On 16 October 1750 an Ordinance stated that the rank of the newly formed Grenzer regiments would be: "*the Warasdiner and Carlstädter first, the Banalisten second the Slavonians third.*"

The Leylersberg *Grenzer* Regiment of Varaždin

Although since 1745 the FML Hildburghausen had divided the territory of the Generalate into two large sections to provide the Varazdin militia, the two regiments were not ready until 1749. At the beginning, the regiment had Colonel Baron von Leylersberg as its owner and commander (from 1756 it took the name *Warasdiner Creuzer Regiment*). Actually, in the years 1746-1749, von Minkwitz (later GFWM) and Macquire alternated as owner colonels, both of whom were sent to Italy to command divisions of that militia in that theatre of battle. It is not certain whether they acted as owners, as the regimental staff was not yet formed. Macquire, however, commanded the Generalate at the time. His first regimental seat was probably in Križevac, but from 1758 it was moved to Bjelovar, and his 12 satnije: Vukovje no.1, Garešnica no.2, Hercegovec No. 3, Berek No. 4, Ivanska No. 5, Čazma No. 6, Farkaševac No. 7, Gudovec No. 8, Križ No. 9, Kloštar No. 10, Mali Ivanić No. 11, Vojakovec No. 12. Its name, Kreuzer or Kürüz in Hungarian, indicated its recruiting territory and referred to the anti-Islamic crusader flags. Its troops, as militia, were in Italy between 1746-1747 to fight in the Genoese and at the Bocchetta. In 1746, Colonel Count Macquire led 500 *Creuzers* over the Apennines and at Pontremoli against Spanish outposts. The sequel is described below in the section on the other regiment. In 1747 they attacked the Bocchetta in January with General St.Andrée.

The Kengyel *Grenzer* Regiment of Varaždin

It appears that as early as 1745 the colonel-owner was Baron Nicolaus von Kengyel, but he did not officially take over the regimental command until 1749. From 1756 it took the official name *Warasdiner Sankt Georger Regiment*. Its recruitment territory was the eastern part of the Generalate (Captaincies of Ivanić and St. Georgen) with its headquarters in Sankt Georgen (Đurđevac) and 12 satnije in: Grubišno Polje #1, Kovačica #2, Severin #3, Rača #4, Đurđevac #5, Pitomača #6, Trojstvo #7, Virje #8, Novigrad #9, Peteranec #10, Sokolovec #11, Kapela #12. Soldiers of the 2nd Varazdin Regiment also fought on the Italian front as militia.

1746: Browne assigned *the* 1,200 *Warasdiner* militiamen from the German battlefields under the command of Bärnklau to the Italian front. They crossed the Po, while Nádasdy threatened Parma. On 26 March, Browne surrounded Guastalla and the next day, two battalions of Đurđevac were ordered to attack. The Spanish General Castilla was repulsed at Gualtieri (west of Guastalla) and surrendered. Von Kengyel himself led his troops to attack Piacenza. On 1 September, the Bocchetta pass was attacked: General Meligny's right column had 200 militiamen, in the centre was the FML Novati with cavalry, on the left General Macquire's (newly promoted) column with 400 *Creuzers*. Varazdin's battalions (two *Creuzer* and two St. George's) in total about 4,000 men reached the Bordighera - Ventimiglia - Menton - Monaco line on 17 October, pressing the Franco-Spanish retreat on the Var. In 1747, they fought in France.

Grenzer Hussar Regiment of Varazdin

Founded in 1747 by Prince FZM Hildburghausen. Its headquarters was Petrinja and its first commander was Obristwachtmeister Mannhardt followed in 1749 by Obristwachtmeister Anton von Kukez. The Hussar regiment had five companies with a total strength of 500 horsemen; in 1749 it was reduced to two companies. In the period 1748-1749, it did not actually take part in any military operations.

The Sava and Danube Generalate

In practice, it was the region of Slavonia with the districts of Djakovar, Požega, Little Wallachia and the Seignory of Sirac, the towns of Verőcze (Verovitica), Vučin, Vukovar (Petrovaradin and Syrmia), Brod, Gradiška, Vinkovce, Petrinja and Esseg. They were to be the future soldiers of the Banan of Croatia, known as *Banalisten*. After the Peace of Belgrade, by which Austria had lost the territories of Serbia, Wallachia and Bosnia, the Slavonian border increased significantly, as a result of the migration of Serbs (*Servianem*) from the former Austrian territories, and of the 'Clementini' (Bosnians, called, from Latin, "*Clementiner*" or Albanian peoples from Kelmendi, who were Catholics) and Albanians (Kosovars) of the patriarch Arsen Jovanović, from European Turkey, who were assigned settlements on the lower reaches of the Sava, as far as Sémlin (Zemlin). These settlements formed the so-called '*syrmischen Militär -Grenze*', which became the future Peterwardein regiment.

Grenzer Slavone 1747 (Vanicek)

Following a Royal Ordinance (*Rescript* of 6 October 1713), FM Khevenhüller began his announced reforms, separating exactly the border of the Slavonian province from the new border known as the 'Sava and Danube' border. The separate provincial territory now consisted of the counties of Verovitica (Verőcze), Požega and Syrmia, which were to remain under the Hungarian crown. The Slavonian military border was now to comprise the course of the Sava and Danube rivers and the borders of Syrmia. The former was divided into Upper, Middle and Lower Borders, with the Upper reinforced by the Subocka district; however, the number of captaincies remained unchanged. When the Danube Boundary, of which part of the captaincies of Sid, Perkoszova, Öerevic and Palanka now became provincial, the boundaries were transferred from the hilly areas of Fruska Gora to the Peterwardein-Semlin Danube line.

The border was manned by a Militia of four foot companies of 200 men each (Carlowitz, Szlankamen, Belegis and Krcedin), and that of the Sirmic border by four foot and 10 horse companies.

Before making radical changes, Maria Theresa convened the *Landtag* in Bratislava in 1741 and through Articles 18 and 50 ordered the k.k. *Hofkammer* to incorporate part of Slavonia and Sirmia directly into the Hungarian crown. With this Act it was decided to abandon the division of the south-eastern border into three parts (Sava, Danube and Syrmia) and to turn parts of the military border into provinces. Count Bátthyiány, Bano of Croatia, FML Baron von Engelshofen, Count Patačić, representing the Bano, and Baron Ladislaus Vávay were entrusted with the implementation of the provisions reaffirmed by the imperial decree of 30 October 1743.

At the end of 1744, the military border was reordered by creating three new counties: Verovitica (Verőcze) County had the settlements of Vučin, Orahovica, Našic, Valpo, Diakovar, Ridfalu, the free town of Esseg with its district, Almas, Dalja and Erdöd; Požega County had the settlements of Podvorje, Sirac, Pakrac, Cernek, Požega, Stažiman, Velika, Prestovac, Plačko, Kaptol, Pleternica; Syrmia County had the villages of Nuitar, Vukovar, Ilok, Neradin, Karlović, Ruma and Semlin.

The contingents of these *Grenzers* always played a secondary role during operations.

1742: a division of about 1,000 men was at Mirandola, which they had occupied while fighting in northern Italy.

1744: a Hussar unit was in Bohemia, at the Battle of Moldauthein.

1745: They, under the command of Lieutenant Colonel Patačić, fought at Vilshofen.

The *Grenzer* of the Sava (Sau river in German, Száva in Magyar)

1741: 500 men from the Inner Border (Captaincy of Raca) were sent to Silesia, while another 2400 from the

Upper and Lower Borders garrisoned the coast under the command of Colonel Hohenau; part of them were then sent to Upper Austria.

1742: they were in Bavaria, at the battle on the Hott and then at the siege of Prague. About 1,500 infantrymen (almost all from the Upper Brod Border) and 300 hussars were sent to Italy, again with Obrist Hohenau, to fight.

1743: they were at the Battle of Camposanto; more of their units were in Bavaria, at the Battle of Simbach and the taking of Dingolfing.

1744: they collaborated in operations on the Rhine; those in Italy defended the lines of Mount Artemisio (Velletri); they also participated in the Battle of Velletri, where Obrist Buday distinguished himself.

1745: Colonel Hohenau was sent to Germany and fought at Yilshofen and later at Soor; those in Italy, like the rest of the troops, were never engaged.

1746: 1,600 men from the Central Border (Brod) fought in Piacenza, were then at the taking of the Bocchetta and continued their march towards Provence; finally, another 3,000 Serbian *Grenzer* (the future *Peterwardeiner*) were mobilised under the command of Colonel Monasterly.

1747: Some 1,600 men stopped in Italy to take part in the operations against Genoa.

The Generalate of Slavonia, in 1747, abandoned the border division of the Sava, Danube and Syrmia and divided the whole territory into three large districts headed by the towns of Brod, on the Sava, Gradiska and Peterwardein. The new border territory was organised by Count Bátthyiány, who envisaged the recruitment of 16800 riflemen and 4200 hussars; a total of 21,000 men from the new three counties. At the same time, Baron FML von Engelshofen began the formation of the new *Grenzer* regiments. Each district was to give rise to a regiment of 5600 men, out of 2 battalions of 5 companies: each company was to have about 140 men in 4 divisions (the first three company divisions were made up of the "suitable" or *Dienstbar* for active military service in the territory and abroad, calling up the three marching ranks, the 4th division was made up of *Undienstbaren* to be used for maintenance service in the territory).

Two 10-company hussar regiments of 210 men were also to be formed. The militia of the Generalate amounted to 16800 infantry and 4200 horse soldiers. The Gradiska regiment district took the entire Upper Sava Boundary and part of the centre, while the Brod regiment took the Lower Sava. Initially, the staffs of the two regiments, which were fully prepared only in 1750, were assigned to Bogosevce and Podvin.

Peterwardein's 'Serbian' regiment was based in Mitrowitz, gathering the levers of the Danubian-Syrmic Border. Among the Hussar regiments there was one Syrmic and the other was obviously Slavonic. The former was based in Banovce and recruited along the Danube between Szurdok and Peterwardein; the latter, Slavonian, had its headquarters in Vinkovce and recruited in the same territories as the two infantry regiments. Apparently, the first uniforms of the Slavonian regiments were blue, with the details left to the commanders. Later they would have a brown jacket instead of blue.

Gaisrugg or Brod's *Grenzer* Regiment

The regiment was established in 1747 (1748) thanks to the FML Baron Engelshofen with the permanent militia of the Sava Border as a 'regular Slavonian regiment'. According to Wrede, it remained without an owner until 1750 and the commander was Colonel Adam von Buday. In reality, the owner of the regiment was the general commander of Slavonia, Feldzeugmeister Count Gaisrugg[63]. At the time of its establishment, it was never deployed outside Slavonian territory. It was based in Brod on the Sava.

Recruitment took place on the territory of the Middle and Lower Sava, the former Slavonian border, with the Captaincies of Brčka and Illok and the 12 companies (Satnije) of: Podvinj No. 1, Trnjani No. 2, Garčin No. 3, Andrijevci No. 4, Sikirevci No. 5, Babina Greda No. 6, Ivankovo No. 7, Cerna No. 8, Vinkovci No. 9, Nijemci No. 10, Županja No. 11 and Drenovci No. 12. Each company had its own villages in which to recruit. For example, the Vinkovci company had the villages of Laze, Mirkovce, Nove i Stare Jankovce, Orolik, Privlaku, Slakovce and Vinkovce under its command. The administrative system was based on house numbers (portal system) to which soldiers were associated in order to control military taxation (male population aged 20 to 60). In addition to the military command, the administrative offices of the regiment (e.g. forestry and territory) were located at the company headquarters. The basic units in the villages were domestic-agricultural cooperatives.

---

[63] Ex Regulament of June 29, 1747 in Vanicek, Special Geschichte ... vol. 1, p. 521.

Gradiška Slavonian *Regiment*

The regiment was established in 1747 (1748) thanks to the FML Baron Engelshofen with the permanent militia of the Sava Border as a 'regular Slavonian regiment', although it was not operational until 1750, when it had a colonel commander and an owner.

Actually, from 1748 the owner was Colonel St. Andrée . His recruiting district, Central Sava, practically coincided with the Kobaš Captaincy and had 12 Satnije: Lipovljani No. 1, Novska No. 2, Rajić No. 3, Čaglić No. 4, Okučani No. 5, Masić No. 6, Rešetari No. 7, Petrovo Selo No. 8, Nova Kapela No. 9, Oriovac No. 10, Stupnik No. 11, Sibinj No. 12. It was based in Nova Gradiška. It was not operational in the country, abroad, until 1757.

Helfreich Regiment or Syrmic *Grenzer* of Peterwardein (Petrovaradin)

The regiment was established in 1747 (1748) by the FML Baron Engelshofen with the permanent militia of the Lower Sava and Syrmia Borders as a 'Syrmic regular regiment'. It recruited on the Sava and Danube Borders, and on the Syrmic Borders. From 1748 it was under the command of Colonel Monasterly, while the title was held by FML Baron Helfreich. Its headquarters were initially in Mitrowitz while its Satnije were at: 1st Morović, 2nd Adaševec, 3rd Lačarak, 4th Mitrovica, 5th Hrtkovče, 6th Kupinova, 7th Surčin, 8th Simanova, 9th Golubinče, 10th Alt-Pazua or Staroj-Pazov, 11th Alt-Banovče or Starim Banovče, 12th Beška. It had no wartime employment.

***Grenzer* Syrmico Hussar Regiment**

Founded in 1747 by the Engelshofen FML with 6 squadrons and based in Banovce, as mentioned. It actually failed to complete the formation (in 1750 it was merged with the Slavonian Hussar Regiment). Its first commander was Lieutenant Colonel Athanasius Ratkovics. It had GFWM Helfreich as its inspector and as its owner apparently Baron von Engelshofen himself.

***Grenzer* Hussar Regiment Slavone Petardi**

Like its twin it was founded in 1747 by FML Engelshofen with 6 squadrons and based in Vinkovce. It had Colonel Petardi as its first owner (from 1750 it became FML Baron Engelshofen), but it seems that the command was held by its Inspector, FML Guadagni.

The Generalate of Theiss (Tisza) and Maros

It comprised the Hungarian counties of Bacs, Bodrog, Csongrad, Csanad, Arad, Zarand (Bihar), Bekes and Torontal. In the '*Grenz-Generalate an der Theiss und Maros*' known as the '*Grenz-Generalate of the Csarda peoples*' were the captaincies of Arad and Szegedin. The regular militia had 18 horse and 10 infantry companies, a total of 2000 men. In addition to these, in the districts of Halmagy and Deés, there were 3 companies of Bulgarian mounted militia and 3 Bulgarian foot companies with strengths varying between 70-100 men, totalling 525 men.

By 1715 the militia of Maros and Theiss had increased to 17 horse and 19 foot companies, in all 2740 men (Company headquarters were: Szabadka, Mártonyos, Klein-Kanizsa, Zenta, Osztrovo, Moholy, Petrovosze lló, Földvár, Csurog and Szent-Tamás with one company on foot and one on horseback, Zombor with one company on horseback, 2 on foot, Zsablya with one on horseback and one on foot, Óbecse (the Serbian Bečej) with one on horseback, 8 on foot and finally Szegedin with 3 companies on horseback and 2 on foot. Small contingents were deployed from these populations, in most cases half infantry and half hussars.

1741-1742: 500 infantry soldiers were with Khevenhüller's army in Upper Austria and Bavaria; those on horseback served with Major Menzel, who commanded all the mounted *Grenzers* and not just the Hungarian hussars. All distinguished themselves in 'small war' actions; some units served in Moravia with the Festetics corps.

1743: 2000 men were in Bavaria; later, a division of 250 hussars from the Maros border was sent to Italy, where they fought at the Battle of Camposanto.

1744: participated in the Rhine campaign.

1745: 800 Maros and 500 Theiss were on the Bohemian campaign.

Theisser Grenzer 1747 (Vanicek)

The Irregular Border Wards

In addition to the aforementioned contingents, many irregular formations from the Border participated in the various campaigns, such as:

1741: the best soldiers of the old Austro-Serbian Militia, about 580 men under the command of Obristwachtmeister Izaković.

1742: the so-called **Grenz Frei-Corps** commanded by Bakić and Hasslingen.

1744: the **Carlstädter Freischaren** (Irregulars) of Prodanović and Vuk, in Bavaria; also with a section of Clementines (Kosovars).

1745: Popović's **Serbian Militia.**

1744-1745: the **Banat Militia** of Obristwachtmeister Simbschen, with 1,300 men and 400 hussars, which came to the fore at the battles of Beraun, Vrchovin (1744) and Landshut (1745).

The Banat militia

In 1744, Baron Ferdinand Engelshofen, acting commander of the Banat, was commissioned to recruit a corps there as well, specifically using the militia formed by General Mercy. The Serbian dignitaries of the Banat (Ober-Knezen) had formed a volunteer corps (*Freikorps*) of 700 men on foot and 106 hussars, mostly Serbs, during the war, and marched it under the command of Captain Simbschen. In the course of the campaign, this corps received several reinforcements of different nationalities who, after entering Habsburg territory, had settled in the uninhabited grasslands of Banat.

As their numbers continued to grow, more and more, to the detriment of taxpayers, causing new taxes, Engelshofen tried, between 1746 and 1747, to contain this influx by recruiting only the already existing militia. He originally intended to form:

4 infantry companies of 400 men each for 1600 men.

2 hussar companies of 210 soldiers for a total of 420 hussars.

A total of 2020 personnel.

These had the name 'Banat Militia', and guarded all the village guard posts, the border cordon, the border towers (*Tschardaken*) and the contumacial areas, where the quarantine of those crossing the border took place, in times of epidemics. The service required 720 men a day and, despite this battalion's obedience to its officers, it was not possible to control all that vast territory, as if it were a real military border. In fact, the country was subordinate to civil authority. The name *Landesmiliz* was later changed to 'Territorial Battalion' and, in 1751, it was separated from the civil authority and subordinated to the military administration.

TRAINING AND MILITARY TACTICS

Official Western European military doctrines evolved little at the beginning of the new 18th century, considering the traumatic transition from the *Tercios* to the battle lines. It was not until the 1920s that theoretical observations began to appear, thanks to military writers such as the Knight of Folard or Marshal Maurice of Saxony, writings that were influenced, above all, by the Great Northern War (1700-1721) between Swedes and Russians. These authors intended to analyse manoeuvres in an attempt to make them more dynamic by bringing troops into hand-to-hand combat and seeking mutual support between infantry and cavalry. In 1740, at the beginning of the War of the Austrian Succession, almost all European armies used the same tactics, dating back to the War of the Spanish Succession thirty years earlier. With the exception of the British, the infantry advanced at a cadenced pace without firing, the cavalry attacked at a trot stopping a few metres from the enemy to unload rifles and guns. Clearly the difference would be made by Frederick II's Prussians, the only army to show the first, timid innovations on the battlefield.

Since the 16th century, war had been a 'game' for sovereigns and armies were mainly made up of mercenaries. Each army reflected the social status of its nation, with the nobility at the command and the petty nobility very active in occupying the middle ranks of officers, in order to maintain their monopoly. The rule stating that the petty nobility was completely ignorant of the art of war was an exception in Austria, thanks to its imperial size and the presence of wealthy nobility (princes, electors and grand dukes) who were able to provide even a minimum of instruction to the regiments, which they paid directly. Obviously, the benefits were reflected in a few units of the *Reichsarmee,* while the deep territory of the Habsburg crown was plagued by quite different problems: very different languages and cultures, a lot of militia, few and poorly educated officers. Moreover, officers in general and throughout Europe tended to have a high mortality rate; they stood in front of the lines issuing orders and setting an example. In doing so, however, they could not bring order to their troops and were too often wounded or killed in battle. The generals were not at all trained to manoeuvre large masses of units, apart from a few trials attempted during peacetime exercises; in war they were in the position of senior officers, with no help other than their own initiative or sagacity. There were no staffs in large units; in fact they began to appear and function more or less in the middle of the century.

In sometimes multinational armies, one cannot deny that there were diatribes of internal hierarchy and deployment in battle, disputes that would make one smile today, but which, at the time, could provoke very harsh reactions for alleged 'attacks on honour'. Duffy[64] recounts that at the Battle of Camposanto (Italy 1743) the Spanish right wing suffered a surprise attack by the Austrian front line. The Spanish line was reconstituted thanks to the intervention of Lieutenant General Macdonnell with the clearly Irish regiments Ireland and Hibernia. When the two regiments were in line, lined up to the right of the Spanish Guard, they raised the question of honour, forcing the Irish not to stand too close to the Guard, but to stand a few metres further back, so as not to appear 'more important' than the Spanish. A more defiladed position better guaranteed Iberian honour at the time, however, in doing so, they left a gap in the line, into which the Austrians infiltrated.

In all armies there was a huge cultural gap between officers, all more or less belonging to the aristocratic classes (and because of this there was a mutual and chivalrous respect even between enemies) and the troops. In many armies it was preferred to recruit volunteers, even from different countries (the so-called 'foreigners'), rather than resort to one's own civilian population, in others, as in Russia and Austria, a large part of the troop was made up of feudal serfs, some even '*ad personam*'; thus, from a chronicle of the siege of Belgrade, one could read that an Austrian officer had lost three horses and four familiars (the serfs).

It took iron discipline to keep together men without common motives or goals, who served only to be fed, housed and clothed. Soldiers, if deprived of the benefit of plunder, had nothing more to look forward to from combat, so values such as courage, loyalty and sacrifice were scarcely popular, let alone the honour of the regiment. Desertion in the armies remained endemic, despite punitive discipline, and, like a snake biting its own tail; the more punitive it was, the more soldiers fled, perhaps in search of another nation where conditions in the army seemed better. There was no soldier's loyalty to a homeland, except for those who fought on or for their own land, as sometimes happened to the Hungarians. For the sake of benefits and pay, the exaltation of loyalty to one's master regiment was emphasised, but not to the point of risking one's life for the colonel.

The staggering increase in the number of soldiers had also led to severe logistical and supply problems. Marshal de Saxe (French for "marshal"), as well as Frederick II himself, estimated the maximum war effectiveness of an army at 50,000 soldiers - if there were more, it was difficult to feed them. Continuous conflicts, even if not always on a large scale, had reduced the number of veterans everywhere, who were destined to die or remain invalids, creating an unbalanced ratio between experienced soldiers and new recruits, preventing education by direct experience in the countryside and thus creating units of poor military efficiency. In logistics, there was the system of storehouses, created by the Marquis de Louvois, Louis XIV's Minister of War, established in strategically important cities or fortresses, where food, ammunition and armaments were stored. This had to be able to prevent the plundering of the territories crossed. The dependence of armies on a chain of depots, however, made the lines of operation shallow, hampered by the distance from the mother country and poorly served by roads and the crude transport of the time.

The war campaigns themselves had evolved to create new types of military operations, ordered to cut off enemy supply lines and protect their own. Battles, though less frequent than sieges, had become very bloody, thanks to technical advances in firearms. There were more casualties than a century earlier. Calculating, then, the cost of a soldier in the country (pay, bread, weapons and clothing), not all national treasuries could afford endless wars (Maria Theresa herself was paying the price of war debts left by her father). For this practical reason, sieges were preferred to pitched battles rather than pitched battles. Sieges allowed slower progress, but less risk of economic loss and loss of life, opening up the possibility of seizing enemy supplies. For about half the year, armies rested at winter quarters, continuing only with sieges. The battles themselves were conducted in order to occupy important strongholds. In the event of defeat, with part of the army fleeing (routed), the troops could be recovered and reorganised at a later time.

---

64 Duffy, Christopher, *The Military Experience in the Age of Reason* pag. 141.

The Austrian army entered the Silesian War using a 1734 regulation by FM Khevenhüller, which was more instructions from a commander than common rules, so much so that they were called '*Observations Puncte*'. The old tradition was still so strong that regimental owners sometimes still issued their own personal instructions even on conduct in battle. The particular instructions mentioned, the '*Observations puncte*', had been revised by Baron GFWM von Thüngen on 10 July 1741. Thüngen emphasised the need to start firing as late as possible and, in particular, to prevent chaotic and irregular firing in the absence of command. In point VI of the remarks he said: "the *best thing would be never to fire, while advancing against the enemy; but as this, unsuitable, might prove necessary, the discharge should be made in position, by the soldiers themselves, instead of advancing, avoiding stopping not earlier than 50 or 60 paces from the enemy on the level (plain); I want to bring a very recent example, not much described, of the massed clash at Mollwitz, which very evidently shows how harmful it is to start firing too early and that, by acting in this way, the troop is no longer able to advance in an orderly manner against the enemy. He should pay with his life who fires his weapon, leaving the ranks, as unfortunately often happened at Mollwitz, to our detriment.*"

The Austrians gladly sent forward the grenadier companies, musket in hand, leading the advancing battalion a few paces. Thüngen, on the other hand, wanted to bring out ordered platoons of 20 to 25 men, under the command of a second lieutenant, who was to march them on the wings of the battalion divisions, this alone in medium or sheltered terrain, pressed him forward. On the plan, in fact, the same manoeuvre would have been more harmful, than useful, "*for if one of those platoons had straggled it could have dragged the battalion or even the regiment into disorder.*"

Infantry fights often became a kind of duel of nerves, where the most restless would start firing first, getting into disorder and losing the advantage of close-range fire (more or less 50 metres away). However, it was also not necessary to fire too late, because the attacker, caught up in his momentum, had no time to realise his possible serious losses. Bayonet fights were not very popular, except in the attack on trenches; usually, one of the two protagonists would retreat before impact with the other.

There were many officers in the Austrian army who underestimated the value of fire tactics and, like Folard, placed all hope in the white weapon. Prince Charles of Lorraine. before Časlau (May 1742), ordered that as soon as the enemy moved, '*If he comes too close, you must attack him with sword in fist*'. After all, the provisions of the 1734 regulations were already outdated in battle, although at Kolin, during the Seven Years' War, the Austrians still advanced on four ranks.

Imperial infantry exercises had become more complicated with the adoption of the bayonet than they had been before. The bayonet, already in the early 18th century and later in Austria, had an external attachment to the barrel of the weapon. This meant having to resort to new and different commands such as '*grasp your bayonet*' - '*bayonet up*' etc. The very substitution, in the musket, of the fuse for the flintlock had generated additional commands such as '*raise your hammer*', '*rest your hammer*' etc. Manoeuvres with the musket required at least 56 command phrases to be executed three times faster than in the past.

One of the new commands was: '*Hair under the hat*', which, although it was a gesture dictated more by necessity than by ceremony, was not spontaneously allowed to the soldier; the man could not remove his hat and raise it, but had to push the hair back with his hands until it disappeared. By this time, cartridges were already in use, although the old loading system was not infrequently used. In the latter case, one acted as a hundred years earlier; the shooter put the balls, which he intended to shoot, in his mouth at the old command '*Ball in mouth*'. The shooter's mouth was not idle with the new system, even though he had no bullets to 'bite'; in fact, it was necessary to tear the cartridge out with his teeth. If, then, before inserting the cartridge he had to put in more powder from the horn (*Pulverhorn*), he had to hold the cap in his mouth or place it on the cap.

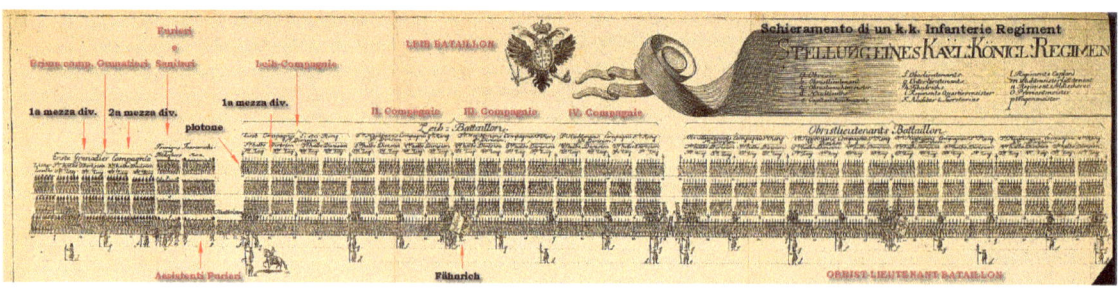

At that time, some regiments had organised themselves in the same way as the Dutch, at the beginning of the 17th century, by equipping their powder horns with pin closures, which allowed for a quicker time in the barrel. Now it was customary to put a pad on the ball, which was not done before, and the soldier carried the paper of these pads in the brim of the tricorn; then there was also the command "*pad out of the hat!*" which instructed the soldier to put it in the barrel and push it onto the ball with the baton.

Different types of musket fire were being studied and developed. There was a platoon fire ('*platoon-Feuer*' or '*peloton- Feuer*' in French, while the German term was *Zug* and the fire *Zugweise*), sometimes even executed by marching forward, bringing the first rank back, after firing, and bringing the second rank forward, to the left of those ahead; this was done by marching with the 'old imperial step', but soon, the marching fire was abandoned altogether.

The grenadiers' drills were similar to those of the infantry, except that, in addition to handling the musket, they had to deal with lighting and throwing the dangerous hand grenades. Some special drills were done with the pickets used to assemble Frisian horses (then called Spanish riders or *Spanische Reiter*). These '*Schweinsfeder*', spikes of the Friesian horses, gave rise to purely formal exercises, assuming that, in battle, the infantry was engaged more in shooting than in entrenchment. In times when each regiment had its own regulations, the one given by the colonel who owned it, the drills were often sketchy and improvised.

In the end, however, the Austrian army managed to make very significant progress. This was due, above all, to the application and efforts of the diligently military-minded FM Leopold Josef, Count Daun. In practice, his hidden aim was to transfer Prussian institutions into the imperial army. Under his supervision, the so-called '*Daunsche Reglement*' was drafted with the co-operation of General von Winkelmann and Count Radicati. It was two quarto volumes, richly illustrated with figures, with the title '*Regulament und Ordnung ...*', in full 'Regulations and Order ..., to which all imperial infantry (*k.k. Fuß=Volck*) shall adhere in the handling of arms and in all war exercises, which shall be practised uniformly by the troops, for all customs of war'; published in Vienna in 1749. The first volume explained the training of the infantry and the new strength of the regiments: 36 men for the General Staff, two grenadier companies of 100 men, 16 rifle companies of 136 men; total strength 2408 men. In deployment (and on Parade) the grenadier companies were on the wings of the first battalion (*Leib-bataillon*), which was followed by the 2nd or *Obrist=Lieutenants*, the 3rd or *Obrist=Wachtmeister* and the 4th or *Obrist-Bataillon*. The grenadiers, including the officers, had bear hair headgear, the riflemen the tricorn. The four battalions each had four companies.

The order of battle remained in four ranks, spaced 3 paces apart, each row (*Reihe* or *Rotte*) having the distance of one step. In battle, since each platoon had 7 Rotte, the front of an Austrian battalion measured 96 steps (about 72 m). The officers no longer stood at the front, but in the ranks; between two battalions stood an artillery piece, in the middle of the 6-step interval. The distances between rows and ranks were important for 'countermarchs', i.e. to turn the front behind and double the ranks. In the country at the wings of the regiment stood 3 grenadiers taken from each company. The rifle companies were divided into 4 platoons, although in training the companies were formed into two divisions (two platoons formed a half division). Of their 136 personnel, there were 109 soldiers.

The training of the senior officers, described in the regulations, included exercises of the *Obristwachtmeister with the* sword, exercises of the senior officers with the partisan, of the bannermen with the '*Springstock*', and of the grenadier officers with the rifle. This was followed by exercises of the non-commissioned officers, the drummers, the carpenters (*Zimmerleute*) with the axe and, finally, the grenadiers and riflemen. Then there was the opening and closing, ranks and services, of the so-called battalion square (*Bataillons=Quarrée*). The squares known as *Carrés* were made up of 1, 2, 3 and 4 battalions. In the battalion *Carré* each company could deploy to form a side; the internal space depended on the width of the company ranks, with a maximum limit of four. The formation was made by bringing forward the left or fourth wing division (company), the second division formed the rear, the first division the left side and the third division the right side of the square. When the Austrian battalion increased to six companies in later years, the composition of the square was a little more extemporaneous.

Fire training or *Chargirungen* comprised as many as nine types, ranging from the fire of smaller units to the discharge of entire battalions, while the most commonly used fire was platoon fire. C'erano, inoltre, particolari tipi di fuoco speciale (*Extra=Feuer*) come il *Lauff=Feuer* o fuoco da parata (*feu roulant* in francese), fuoco a salve o celebrativo che partiva da destra ed andava a sinistra del primo rango, invertendosi al secondo rango

ecc.; the *Höckenfeuer*, similar to the Prussian square fire, but which the Austrian Regulations apparently referred only to a force standing in column or on the march, where the Routes[65] had to go out to the side and front on the flank; the *Retranchementfeuer* or trench fire; the *doppeltes Weegfeuer* or doubling of fire on the road, where the enemy appeared unexpectedly, in front or behind (as in woods or other areas of complex terrain), the attacked platoon could quickly deploy to defend itself commanded by the Obrist-Wachtmeister; the *Brückenfeuer* when a bridge had to be crossed; the *Hohlenweeg und Gassenfeuer* when attacking on a sunken road and had to fire in a narrow space. The apprenticeship then described manoeuvres called *Douplirungen* or doubling of rows and ranks when, marching through bottlenecks, half platoons had to be used to cover the march of the battalion or regiment on the sides. With these, 2-3 rank units were formed, starting with 4. To make a three-rank unit, starting with the fourth, the men were taken 3 by 3 and brought forward into the front three ranks, so that every three Rotte a new one was formed with the soldiers of the fourth rank.

Column formations were formed with departments of different types, from platoons to divisions. Formation in Line or *Aufmärsch was* done by sending the various divisions into an established flank or at the head of the column, but not with a generic *deployment* (*Deployirung*), but by forming successive lines by platoons, in half divisions, these half divisions into whole divisions, the whole divisions into wings and the wings into the whole battalion.

On the march, the assigned direction was never reversed, so a column formed on the right had to line up on its left, so as not to get in the way of other flanking columns. Lines with front reversals were never necessary, because the entire army had to be a single body and, the route of the columns had to be planned in advance, allowing them to reach the established line (first or second in general, called in German *Treffen* or ranks) on the prescribed army wing, without moving the columns in disarray. The Regulations, however, also prescribed certain manoeuvres on the march. The *Creis=Schlüßungen*, the *Contre=Marches by ranks* or rows, the *Schwenkungen* or deviations, the *Marche=Observationes* and the *Lager=Einrucken* were other manoeuvres addressed by the manual, especially for moving. Exercises for riflemen with the musket and the construction of the 'Spanish knights' ended the volume together with the 'Honours to be performed on Guard duty'. Volume 2, on the other hand, dealt with how to behave in the countryside.

It cannot be said that this regulation in itself constituted a striking advance over the 1737 regulation. Substantial improvements were barely hinted at, but some manoeuvres seemed even more pedantic than the old regulation. Daun, however, was able to animate these formal rules with vitality, teaching the troops, through the influence of his personality, the secret of effectiveness. Thus it seems that, at the Battle of Lobositz seven years later, a few Prussian veterans shouted: "*There are no more Austrians than there used to be!*". They were right because much had improved, raising the training standard of the imperial army.

The biggest criticism of the Rules, made by military analysts, was that the four-rank line had been maintained; since the Battle of Kolin, the Austrian infantry would also be deployed on three ranks. The change took place precisely because that battle highlighted what happened if a wing was attacked from behind. The Austrian wing at Kolin was thus attacked by the Prussian cavalry and forced to turn back; with the lines on four ranks the confusion was really difficult to manage. The main points of that regulation, given to the line troops, also agreed with two other writings from 1749: '*Exercitien und Handgriffe nach welchen die kgl. mährische Landmiliz sich zu reguliren und die Mannschaft zu exerciren haben wird*' for the Moravian rural militia and '*Belehrung, wie der Feind durch das Fußvolk anzugreifen ist*', rules on how to attack the enemy. A new and comprehensive regulation was issued on 12 March 1759, at the height of the Seven Years' War: *Militär=Feld=Regulament* (Wien 1759).

As already mentioned, the Regulations were now no longer issued by the regimental owners, but directly by the military government. In 1749, Maria Theresa had written instructions published for both infantry and cavalry (in 1759 there would be a single General Field Regulation).

Due to its central geographic location and the various peripheral enemies, compared to an irregular Turkish cavalry or disciplined European cavalry, the Austrian cavalry had to train in two different tactics. Against

---

65   In an Austrian four-row formation there were four soldiers in a line, one behind the other, an aspect of the formation called in German Rotte (rout). If there were four soldiers it was called a full Rotta; if there were fewer, a "blind" Rotta.

the Turks, the cavalry was arranged in three ranks, in close order and with no spaces between squadrons. It approached the enemy at pace and fired, avoiding getting involved in melees, where the Turks excelled with their scimitars. To protect themselves from the galloping charges of the Ottomans, the Austrians protected themselves with Friesian horses tied together by chains.

Against the European cavalry, the Austrians would preferably form in two ranks, advance at a trot and fire their guns 10 m from the enemy and then gallop. They often tried to stop enemy charges by firing, as they did against the Turks, hoping to disorganise the enemy. The tactic had little success with the Prussians, after some partial successes at Mollwitz and Časlau. At Soor in 1745, Prussian cuirassiers repulsed 50 Austrian squadrons waiting for them with carbines on the top of a hill. In 1748, a military commission was created, chaired by Charles of Lorraine, to update cavalry tactics and eliminate the defects found during the war. That work was completed with the Regulations of 1751, which proved firing while charging and introduced a few other changes, insisting on training in the art of horsemanship.

The cavalry, in particular, had to be trained in the use of *Pallasch, and* the first two ranks had to practise firing with carbines, so that the squadron learned to shoot on horseback and the horses got used to the sound of fire. The rest of the cavalry was also trained on foot, just as they were infantry soldiers, doing the same rifle exercises and manoeuvres. In cavalry exercises, command signals given, sometimes simultaneously, with the kettledrum and drum were important, although marching signals were given with the bugle. When the entire regiment advanced at a trot, the command signals were given with the drum and bugle.

Against the enemy infantry, the Austrian cavalry would gallop very early, in the last 100 m, to avoid too many casualties from musketry fire, but in this way they were in complete disorder. The cavalry, formed, preferred to attack at a trot, because galloping put the unit in disorder, and preferred to keep the best horses and riders in front. Charging the infantry was not a pleasant undertaking[66]. From the front, the risk was high due to musketry discharges or because of the soldiers, who defended themselves with muskets plus bayonets, as if they were 17th century pikes. For these reasons, the Austrian cavalry preferred to hit the enemy lines on the flanks, as did the other European armies. The frontal attack was also detrimental because of the problem of losing too many horses in battle, as the replacements were not always plentiful and, above all, not trained.

The regiment deployed in 3 ranks, with a distance of 5 paces between them. The interval between the squadrons was short (12 paces) only on parade; in the field it was as long as the squadron itself. The following types of units were formed in the squadron:

1) the designated centre, 2) three-platoon divisions, four-platoon divisions for riflemen and mounted grenadiers, 3) four-man divisions, 4) divisions with the third rank divided into four or eight parts, to reinforce the first three ranks, 5) divisions with alternating cavalry (even or odd). In front of each line stood the officers, with the rump of their horses at the height of the head of the soldier behind.

The manoeuvres of the regiment were: reverses with different ranks; side march with four, called *Contremarsch*; formation of 2 ranks starting with 3, where the third rank was already divided into parts of 4-8, so that their halves (2-4 men on the right, as many on the left) could move forward on both wings of the squadron (right - left - rotate and line up) forming only 2 ranks. Forward marching could only be performed at a trot.

The cavalry column had to line up by platoons or squadrons, either to the flank or to the front; the front of the line formation was achieved by compact rotation of the units or by deployment of each of them. Firearms were never to be used in action, but the Pallasch was always to be in hand. The trot advance before the attack was initiated by the bugle signal, which was followed by the "*Marsch!*".

The two inner ranks would close in on the first and the entire regiment would shorten and, after 15-20 paces, a brisk trot would begin, with the men brandishing the Pallasch above their heads. After about 100 paces in the drill there would be a halt. It should be noted that the horses of the cuirassiers of the time weighed almost 100 pounds more (just over half a quintal) than those of the 19th century and stopping them was not easy.

---

66   Because trotting charges often ended in a melee where fencing qualities prevailed over tactical discipline, after Mollwitz, Frederick II of Prussia replaced them with galloping charges, which gave more confidence to the attacker and could send those who suffered the impact into disarray. The distance at which the gallop started varied from 20 meters before the impact in 1741, to 900 meters in 1755, including 500 meters at full speed.

Weight allowed for war horses according to 1749 regulations					
soldier in vest, shirt and stockings of medium build	84 kg	150 Pf	cloak bag	4,5 kg	8 Pf
boots	4,7 kg	8 ½	Armor	7,8 kg	14
Hutkreuz (canopy)	0,5 kg	1	Carbine scabbard	0,8 kg	1 ½
Cartridge box	2,25 kg	4	Carbine	5 kg	9
Forage rope	2,25 kg	4	oat sack	1,1 kg	2
Forage blanket	1,1 kg	2	blanket strap	0,5 kg	1
1 pair of shoes	1,1 kg	2	Sleeping bag for provisions	0,5 kg	1
Tallow or boot grease	0,5 kg	1	cream for leather	0,2 kg	½
Guns	4 kg	7	Pallasch and pommel	2,25 kg	4
Saddle with own harness	14 kg	25	red caparison	4 kg	7
Stake for horse	3,4 kg	6	reins and harness	2,25 kg	4
TOTAL				139,7 kg	249

Cavalry materials					
SUITCASE (*Mantelsack*)			SUPPLIES (*Verpflegung*)		
suitcase	1,1 kg	2 Pf.	Bread (for 4 days)	4,5 kg	8 Pf.
1 pair leather breeches	1,1 kg	2	Oats (for 4 days)	15,7 kg	28
6 shirts	3,4 kg	6	Hay (for 4 days)	22,4 kg	40
2 pairs of socks	1,1 kg	2	SHOULDER SACK (*Zwerchsack*)		
1 red vest (*Leibel*) with fatigue hat (*Fouragemützen*)	1,6 kg	3	Zwerchsack	0,5 kg	1
1 work coat (*Fouragekittel*)	1,1 kg	2	2 irons and 100 nailsString (*Striegl*),	2,25 kg	4
2 pairs of Gattien* and 3 pairs of boot bands (*Stiefelmanchetten*)	0,2 kg	1 ½	brushes (*Kardatschen*) cleaning implements (*Wischfetzen*)	1,1 kg	2
* underpants			Comb, cutlery, scissors (*Scheere*) and razor	0,5 kg	1
TOTAL clothing and tools = 21 ½ pounds (12 kg)					

Campaign materials (distributed among 5 soldiers of the squad or *Kameradschaft*)					
Tent	11,2 kg	20 Pf.	ropes	2,8 kg	5 Pf
Tent poles	6,7 kg	12	8 wooden water flasks (*Wasserlägel*)	3,4 kg	6
1 Tent hook	1,6 kg	3	casserole	3,4 kg	6
tent stakes	1,6 kg	3			
TOTAL field materials = 55 Pf (30.8 kg) or 11 Pf (6.1 kg) per soldier					
for each team member			vegetables	2,25 kg	4
meat for 2 days	3,4 kg	6	scythe with sharpening stone	1,6 kg	3
TOTALS per man in the team = 24 Pf. (13.5 kg)					

The Austrian order of battle

The Austrian army generally deployed on two lines (*Treffen*), on several lines only if fortified positions were to be attacked. As with all European armies, deployment in battle lines was complex, requiring advance orders on marching and precise instructions on column formation. In Austria, the rigidity of the regiments did not allow the lines to be flexible. The second line did not have to be very far from the first, so that it could be supported, but neither did it have to be too close, because of the risk of disorder if the first line straggled.

Co-ordinating the advance was an art, but Austria did not ask its troops to march forward, as the Prussians did. Battalion officers aligned their men, while senior officers attempted to align battalions with each other. Battalions had a natural tendency to close in on the centre, where the number of ranks sometimes doubled, due to soldiers deployed on the flanks, who tended to fall back to protect themselves. The role of the superior generals in the field was limited to rushing reinforcements to the threatened points or, if it happened, to rally the fugitives.

On the eve of the Seven Years' War, the custom remained that of gathering the smaller tactical units into groups and so on, until the whole army was included, under the command of a supreme general, trying to form stronger and stronger groups.

After the abolition of the pikemen and the arming of the 'people on foot' with musket and bayonet, the battalions were forced to form thinner lines. Usually 2 regiments formed a brigade, under the command of a GFWM or Generalmajor, 2-3 brigades formed a divisional group (which later would be placed under the orders of a Lieutenant Field Marshal or FML), several brigades (or 2 or 3 divisions) formed a wing, commanded by a *Feldzeugmeister* (FZM, higher rank derived from artillery) or a General of Cavalry (GdK), often when cavalry troops were present.

The brigades formed a single line of the order of battle. Battalions were deployed according to regimental order and these flanked each other in the established brigade. A line, as mentioned, could be divided (divisions) into wings, right, left (sometimes centre), which formed the same line (*Treffen*); after the first, in front, the others were placed one behind the other, usually a 1st Line and a 2nd Line, plus possible Reserve. The *Feldzeugmeister* or wing commander (*Flügelcommandant*) gave commands by standing between the troops of the 2nd Line.

The infantry of an army generally compacted in the centre, as an army mass (*Corps de Bataille* or *Hauptkorps*), but in some cases could only be divided into the two wings, left and right, without an obvious centre. In the future, planning armies of 6 divisions would make it possible to structure two wings and a centre, each with 2 divisions, as a third wing (or as a reserve). The division into wings was thus essentially the precursor of the future division of armies into corps. Like the infantry, cavalry was also divided into brigades, but, from the moment the tents were arranged in the camps, its order of battle was destined to end up outside the infantry wings, in the 1st or 2nd Line. Therefore the cavalry held one wing, right or left, and the General of Cavalry commanded it on both lines. Sometimes a *Vorhut* or vanguard was formed, made up of a single line, or a reserve corps was created; very often the cavalry was deployed on both wings of the infantry and was subordinate directly to the wing commanders, for convenience of command. Of course, not everything will always be so schematic, depending also on the types of terrain of the battlefields.

Each regiment had its own light guns, 3 or 6-pounder, usually two per battalion. Since brigades generally had 4 battalions and 4 grenadier companies (two regiments), each brigade had 8 light pieces. If the brigades were not side by side but, as was often the case, deployed in two lines, one behind the other, the battalion guns of the front line could fire, while those behind were forced to wait; for this reason, some commanders thought it better to assemble the pieces in autonomous batteries, deployed separately, removing them from the limiting possession of individual battalions.

It was also said that, for example, if an army had 20 brigades in its *Corps de Bataille*, this meant that 10 brigades could be placed in the front line and 10 in the second, making it impossible to use artillery completely. In reality, however, the arrangement of the two front lines was not so formal and often brigades and divisions alternated, depending on the needs of the battle.

Artillery, at the time, had no autonomy, being considered a part of the infantry or fortress armament. It did not require manoeuvring, nor did it have tactical regulations, for its use on the battlefield. The equipment included heavy, hard-to-move pieces and light pieces. The heavy guns were positioned in front of the front or on the wings in fixed batteries, their only role being to widen the area beaten by infantry fire. The large-calibre batteries placed on a wing, in a dominant position, had the task of sneaking up on the enemy lines; as at Dettingen, sheltered behind a stream. They were not effective weapons in terms of accuracy and lethality,

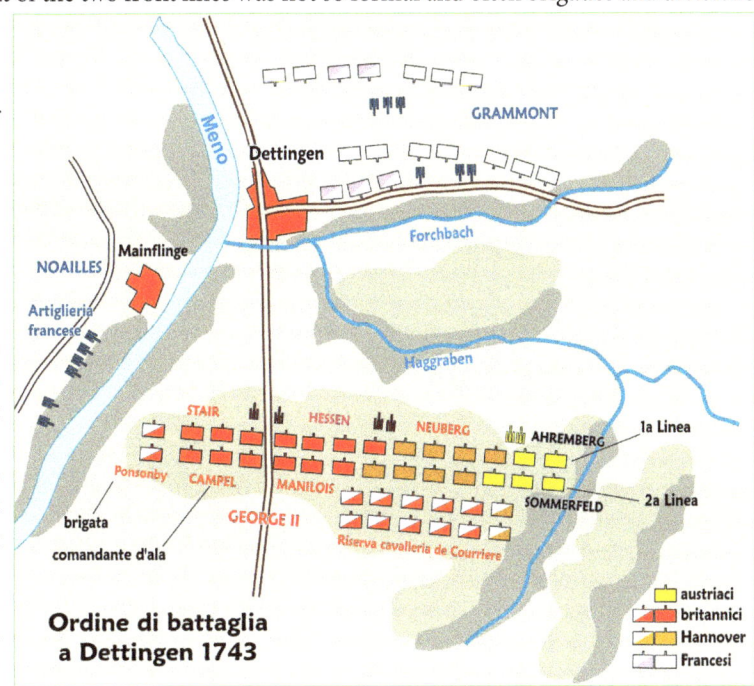

Ordine di battaglia a Dettingen 1743

compared to the effort required to place them in firing positions. The effect on enemy morale, however, was important: it reassured friendly troops and demoralised the adversary, who suffered a long-distance bombardment without being able to counterattack, dazed by the smoke and noise and terrified by the severity of the wounds the balls caused.In addition to battles, there were sieges, made by all European armies according to the art of 17th century polytheistic warfare. When a city or fortress surrendered, the fate of the garrisons was different. If their defence had been militarily valiant, they could be left free to leave, with military honours from the victors, or they were freed 'on parole', i.e. they undertook not to fight the victors of the moment for longer or shorter periods. (Of course, if they failed to keep their promises and were recognised by the appropriate registers, they would certainly come to a bad end. For obvious economic reasons, in the early 18th century, prisoners were a complication. The exchequer had to pay to keep them in captivity (it was neither 'courteous' nor simple to dispose of them on the spot). For this reason, prisoners were often traded or given away for payment.

In 1742, a treaty was made (*Tractat über die Auswechslung ind Ranzionierung der Kriegsgefangenen*) regulating these exchanges. There were fixed rates for ransoming a prisoner: an imperial field marshal was worth 25,000 florins, a lieutenant general 5000, a GFWM or major general or field marshal was worth 1500, a brigadier general between 700 and 900 florins.

A war commissioner or supply officer was exchanged for only 150 florins, a colonel for 670 (perhaps he was an owner), a lieutenant colonel for 300, an Obristwachtmeister or major 150, a captain 100, a lieutenant 40, a second lieutenant, Wachtmeister or second lieutenant 30, a cavalry soldier 7 florins, an infantry soldier 4 florins. Exchanges 'in kind' could also be made, releasing a captain for 6 men, a lieutenant for 4, a second lieutenant or ensign for 3, a Wachtmeister or Feldwebel for 2 soldiers. Article 47 prohibited 'freeing' prisoners altogether. Not everyone adhered to the practice and, in particular, King Frederick II of Prussia did not, as demonstrated by the fate of the Austrian prisoners in Prague in 1744, despite the fact that the clauses were expressly laid down in a treaty, signed with Maria Theresa on 9 July 1741 in Grottkau, which was to last six years.

Similar agreements were concluded between Austria and France in the years 1742, 1743 and 1745; such agreements were also to be concluded with Bavaria and Spain. They were all very similar to each other; in each of them is found the provision that, on certain dates, prisoners would be exchanged reciprocally, man for man, respecting the equality of the groups. Where it was preferred to ransom prisoners with money or where there was not enough money, officers could be exchanged for a certain number of soldiers. Tables were also created to help calculate exchanges, like this one below. Priests and field chaplains, medical personnel of all ranks, field post officers, pharmacists, wives and children of soldiers were given free passes.

The provisions of the Treaties, however, denied any state reimbursement for the prisoners' living expenses (wood, candles, straw, clothing, bed cleaning, etc.). In 1743, the *Hofkammer was* even forced to threaten to suspend supplies for the opposing prisoners in Austria and to refuse any responsibility for the inevitable harsher development of their captivity.

Grade	change for men (Gemeine)	money	
		PRUSSIA	FRANCE
Field Marshal	3000	15000 fiorini	15000 fiorini
Feldzeugmeister	2000	10000	6000
General of cavalry	2000	10000	10000
Lieutenant Field Marshal	1000	5000	5000
General Feldwachtmeister	300	1500	1500
colonel of cavalry or artillery	130	650	700
infantry colonel	130	650	600
Rittmeister	16	80	100
infantry or artillery captain	16	80	70
infantry lieutenant	6	30	24
cavalry lieutenant	6	30	40
private knight	1	5	4
private	1	5	4

In any case, the imperial treasury had always had a total lack of means in this matter. In order to finance the coffers, thanks to the ransoms of prisoners of war, since the end of the War of the Spanish Succession, an Observance had been made compulsory, forcing regiments to pay the treasury 30 florins for each ransomed cuirassier, 25 florins for each dragoon, 20 for each hussar, 10 for each non-commissioned officer or common soldier. These taxes ended up in the war chest, at least one third of the contents of which was to go directly to the troops.

The new *Reglement of* 1748 of the FM Daun now stipulated that in peacetime the infantry regiment was to be increased to 2408 men (2600 in case of war) with: 2 grenadier companies, four battalions made up of 4 ordinary rifle companies (in this way Austria would face the Seven Years' War). The so-called *Stab-Compagnien* named after the battalion (Leib-, Obrist-, etc.) were always at the battalion wing; the remaining 12 ordinary companies numbered according to the rank of their captain had a strength of 136 men in peace (as opposed to 135 for the *Stabs-Compagnien* and 100 for the grenadiers).

The grenadiers were equipped with two cartridge bags (*Patronentaschen*), one was larger than the rifleman's bag and, like this one, supported by a wide shoulder strap and intended for the storage of grenades and a metal storage compartment; the smaller one, with the leather strap, contained the musket cartridges. The grenadier's armament consisted of the flintlock and bayonet musket and hand grenades. They were hollow spheres, usually made of cast iron, with a diameter of about 8 centimetres and a weight of 1.5 to 2 kg. They possessed an internal explosive charge and an incendiary tube that caused them to ignite. To throw the grenade by hand, the grenadier had to put the musket on his shoulder, on his back, with the strap, pick up a fuse and insert it, then ignite it to quickly throw the grenade at the enemy. Despite many exercises and manuals, the throw was always more dangerous; very often the grenade would explode first, damaging one's own ranks. The last imperial regulation, which expressly provided for the use of hand-thrown grenades, was Reglement 1748, but the use of such weapons ceased around 1760, well before the new provisions of FM Lacy in 1769.

In times of war, however, it had been the practice since the War of the Spanish Succession for grenadier companies to be separated from their regiments, forming an autonomous tactical corps under a specially appointed commander. The formation or rather the naming of actual grenadier battalions in Austria took place during the Seven Years' War.

Military Border Troops or *Grenzer*[67]

In the history of the Military Boundary between Austria and the Ottoman Empire, the War of Austrian Succession began the so-called Second Period. During this period, the performance of the *Grenzers*, in the various theaters of war, began to grow in importance, as the number of their opponents increased (employment outside the border territory) and the theaters in which to fight expanded. It will remain, indelibly, the memory of the boldness of the border militia, established in the battles of the War of Succession and in the contest for Silesia, as well as its effectiveness, which was able to cope with some of the defaults of the regular Austrian army. In the beginning, the primal natural violence, still unbridled, and the yearning for the greed of booty prevailed, which brought success and panic, in those who suffered raids, suppressing the courage of the enemies. As time went on, ties to the regency were strengthened with renewed discipline, curbing the thirst for loot, and tactical training ensured more straightforward governance. After the Peace of Carlowitz (1699) the Carlstädt[68] di Carlstädt and Varazdin generalates had been joined by two others: the Sava-Danube and the Theiss (Tisza) and Maros rivers. At the time, all border territories had about 45,615 men on active military service, part of whom had to serve in the country, supporting its economy. Only the Varazdin Generalate was exempt from Cordon service[69], having a more inland territory, not bordering the Turks, and thus could offer a larger contingent. The rather unruly internal conditions of part of the border on the Sava did not favor the warlike employment of their troops.

---

67   The term *Grenzer* is derived from the Slavic word Granica (or Krajina), words found in texts dating back to 1480 to mean the border.
68   The Generalate was a large region, subject to military jurisdiction, with rank of territorial division (future possibility of forming brigades). It was subdivided into several "Kapitanate" captaincies, smaller regions corresponding to recruitment areas for territorial battalions or regiments.
69   The term Cordon "Kordun" comes from the border line of the sentinels during the wars against the Turks. Characteristic of the border region with the Ottoman Empire were the so-called Tschardaks (Croatian čardak) or Posten (Croatian pošte). These were small wooden huts built at regular intervals, which were accessed by a flight of steps up to an elevated observatory. If the enemy was reported, the border guard would fire a shot. This was repeated by other border guards all along the line, to allow for early warning. At border posts there were always 4-12 guards patrolling even at night. Until 1773 at the Cordon there were also hussars on horseback to prevent robbery by the Turks. Most border posts were abolished in 1849.

The Danubian borders, of the River Theiss (Tisza) and Maros, did not belong to the territories of the Kingdom of Croatia and Slavonia, but were Hungarian lands. They were, however, part of the border defense system that began with the Sava River. The old borders on the Theiss and Maros would be demilitarized in the years 1749-1750, causing a massive emigration of Serbs from those territories, in the direction of Russia. The most important reform, the one that determined the final military development of the frontier, was that of Duke Joseph Friedrich Wilhelm von Sachsen-Hildburghausen, who wanted to divide the Varazdin Generalate into two separate corps (called regiments), using the derived battalions as a new tactical unit, instead of the historical companies or Satnie (because they were commanded by captains or Satnik). The embryonic "regiment" would be placed under the direct command of a staff officer, establishing, later, an autonomous command for hussars through a lieutenant colonel. The differentiation between foot and mounted units helped introduce specific training and the maintenance of discipline among frontier troops. In time, Grenzer regiments would be equated with field regiments and had equal military rank. But before delving into this topic, it is necessary to talk about a famous irregular corps of Croats, which will be made famous in fictional literature.

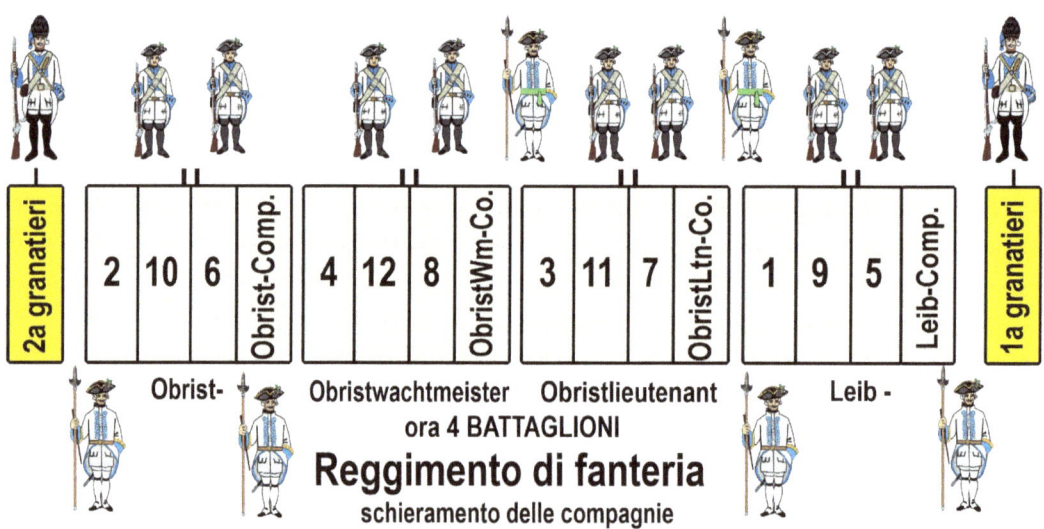

▲ The Empress Maria Theresa d'Austria. Martin van Meytens, courtesy Accademia di belle arti di Vienna.

CONTENTS OF 1ST VOLUME:

Introduction	Pag. 3
The recruitment in Austria	Pag. 7
The Imperial uniform	Pag. 21
Imperial commands	Pag. 36
Maria Theresa's first Infantry	Pag. 51
Infantry in 1749	Pag. 67
The cavalry	Pag. 73
The Von der Trenck Panduri Corps	Pag. 88
The beginning of the War of Succession and the new formations	Pag. 93
Training and military tactics	Pag. 102

TITOLI PUBBLICATI - ALREADY PUBLISHING

WWW.SOLDIERSHOP.COM   WWW.BOOKMOON.COM

SOLDIERS&WEAPONS 047 EN

www.ingramcontent.com/pod-product-compliance
Lightning Source LLC
LaVergne TN
LVHW072124060526
838201LV00069B/4967